T0339879

ORGANIZATIONAL REACTION TO
SOCIAL DEVIANCE:
THE MILITARY CASE

ORGANIZATIONAL REACTION TO SOCIAL DEVIANCE: THE MILITARY CASE

Robert J. Stevenson

Algora Publishing
New York

Library of Congress Cataloging-in-Publication Data —

Stevenson, Robert Joseph.
  Organizational reaction to social deviance: the military case / Robert J. Stevenson.
    p. cm.
  Includes bibliographical references and index.
    ISBN 978-0-87586-789-2 (soft cover: alk. paper) — ISBN 978-0-87586-790-8 (case
laminate: alk. paper) 1. Sociology, Military—United States. 2. Military discipline—
United States. 3. Social control—United States. I. Title.
  UA23.S697 2010
  306.2'70973—dc22
                          2009054253

Front Cover: US Marines at the start of a major US-led offensive against a key Taliban
stronghold in southern Afghanistan. February 14, 2010. (AFP/Patrick Baz)

Printed in the United States

TABLE OF CONTENTS

TABLES, FIGURES AND CHARTS

TABLES

FIGURES

CHARTS

CHAPTER I. SOCIAL DEVIANCE AND MILITARY SOCIOLOGY: INTRODUCTION

Military institutions require that varying degrees of coercion be used against their members as well as against enemies. On one level, the military is an agent of the state; on another, it imposes demands on citizens who must serve therein. The military also exposes soldiers to the authority of its officers, and to certain physical risks. There is also the possibility that time spent in the soldier role may result in formal sanctions being applied to soldiers if they are identified as having failed to meet the expectations of their superiors.

In this book I address the problem of social order *within* the American military. It is an examination of how and when commanders used various sanctions over four decades. As such, it identifies the changing patterns of organizational reaction to deviance and offers an interpretation that these represent the changing *social control requirements* of a complex organization.

The role officers play in controlling their troops gives meaning to an important part of the institution of soldiering. It also forms the social basis upon which "command" is predicated: that order takers in the ranks must comply with the demands and expectations of order givers. An internally coercive structure—the hierarchy of command—thus attempts to produce predictable behavior on the part of soldiers. This is a study of how such order is imposed.

The data used in this study show the different rates at which commanders sought to punish soldiers for shortcomings: through the courts (courts-martial); by discharge under less than honorable conditions (bad paper discharges) and through the use of non-judicial sanctioning (Article 15). That is, rates of organizational reaction to deviance are examined.

The study is guided by five postulates:

1. The use of deviance categories, i.e., unfitness, rule breaking, and inappropriateness, is a management decision involving the mobilization of social control resources by commanders.

2. The social outcomes that are the result of formal social controls, i.e., punishments meted out, create two distinctive deviant populations: those kept inside the military for remediation and those discharged with varying degrees of stigma.

3. To instill order in a changing environment, commanders rely on the formal control apparatus to different degrees. This results in a variable distribution of offender types.

4. The need for social control in the military may lie in the external environment, for example wars, or the quality of the soldiers with which the military must work. It may also be embedded within the context of the service branches (Army, Navy, Air Force, and Marines). For example, troops sent to the field, aboard ships, or in airplanes present their commanders different problems in exercising command.

5. The differential use of deviance categories, a variable distribution of offender types, and the managerial decision to contain or expel wayward soldiers may be broadly conceived as ways in which commanders attempt to adjust the need for order to a changing environment. This attempt to manage the flow of deviants in the system is the product of an *ethos of control*: a willingness on the part of commanders to use a range of social controls to instill order and discipline in light of changing contingencies.

While it is axiomatic that all social institutions are likely to identify certain of their members as candidates for sanctioning, the degree to which they do so is an empirical question. My interpretation of the data has come from personal experience, and two substantive areas in sociology: social deviance and military sociology.

PERSONAL EXPERIENCE

My personal experience in the military trained me to view the armed forces from a somewhat restricted but rather systematic angle of vision during the middle and end of the Vietnam War (1969–1973). I was involved in numerous aspects of the operation of the formal Air Force personnel system.

From Wing Headquarters, I processed the personnel records of thousands of Airmen and Officers who were permanently assigned to, or in some stage of training at, an Air Force Base located in the southwestern United States. My many changes in occupational specialty within the personnel division invariably altered the focus of my interaction with military personnel.

I would, for example, process personnel "in" upon arrival to the base and "out" upon separation. I was called to write up the paperwork when awards and honors were given; when an airman had to attend a parade or a ceremony; when he was assigned to special temporary duties away from post; when he was applying for, or completed, mandatory or voluntary occupational training; when he, or his dependents, sought medical care or wished to borrow utensils or housewares upon their recent arrival to family quarters; when his legitimate or illegitimate offspring were brought into the world; when an airman was put in jail; became a casualty, or had an official organizational representative and/or administrative document sent to his next of kin.

I have spent hundreds of hours attending to some small part in the generation and updating of files which represent a vast administrative effort to keep documents on all members of the military. A good part of this time was spent at the paperwork necessary for formal social control.

When "trouble" enters the official docket of an Airman or Officer via court-martial, Article 15, unauthorized drug use, marital or medical problems, or via conscientious objector petition, "hardship", or a work-related accident, documents are generated and some commander's signature becomes part of the official record.

Anyone who has spent time in a military records section will have noticed that negative information is common enough in the dockets of enlisted personnel to be handled routinely. Such material is so rare among the records of officers as to attract considerable attention—at least among records clerks. Discrediting information is an item of concern to commanders and is duly reported on the appropriate forms (see Little, 1969b).

At the higher levels of the organization—in staff meetings—commanders assemble a working picture of their organizations with this and other information. Data on the social climate wherein they practice their trade is interpreted, acted upon, and integrated with data on the physical environment. In this manner problems are identified and kept within manageable proportions to meet the defined mission of the organization.

The format of staff meetings is usually informational but sometimes results in changes in the required *level of work*, i.e., extra duties—for certain sectors of the organization. Also, as the briefing sequence moves down the chain of command, the informality and collegiality of the meetings declines. In this way a General officer's concern over, say, an outbreak of illness is transformed at the bottom level of the organization into concrete demands for additional efforts on the part of varying numbers of affected troops—which carry "force of law" sanctions for non-compliance.

If there is bias in some of the perspectives from which I view military reality—that may frame the background from which I address larger issues—it is this: I am convinced that social organizations create meanings for the actors bound up in them and that much of the procedure involved in day-to-day activities takes on a life of its own.

What amazes me about the operation of the armed forces—and I should note this as a central and lasting impression that originally piqued my interest in the formal study of "things military"—is the sheer volume of time and energy spent on decision making of the most diverse kind.

In the social world of those who wear uniforms the pervasiveness of *order, authority,* and *control* is compelling. It is exaggerated in the extreme by military ceremony with its rigid and formal style and, more often than not, rendered less ominous (sometimes comical) by the comforts of familiarity and routine. It is the underlying theme of military life that someone is ultimately responsible for the demeanor and performance of subordinates in ways which are more precise than in non-military settings.

This concern would likely be understood by soldiers who, doubtlessly, could provide many anecdotes from their experience of the world that they know. Officers would likely recognize my conceptualizations as constraints with which they must deal on a regular basis. These concerns, for them, make command a demanding profession as this is experienced with an admixture of both change and routine.

MILITARY SOCIOLOGY AS A POINT OF VIEW

Some of the best writing on the military system concerns its dominant or subservient relationship to civil political order. I have had to reformulate some of this work as the major line of argument is tangential to my prime research concern with *internal order* and social control. Thus, throughout this research, many key concepts are implicitly borrowed, modified and directed at a subject matter different from that which encouraged their original conceptualization.

Lasswell's concept of the "garrison state" (1941), for example, was formulated to account for the dominance of military elites over the civilian centers of power. I have implicitly borrowed the notion to suggest that the officer corps vis-à-vis the troops will act to preserve its position of privilege. One of the ways it is able to do this is to exert its authority to proscribe certain behaviors, postures, attitudes and styles on the part of its enlisted charges.

Janowitz's (1971) and Nisbet's (1976) concepts of modernity in military institutions—in that the social composition of the forces in the recent past is significantly different than that which has been historically the case—were also used. Not to specify the distinctiveness, or similarity, of the military system to some aspect of the civil order (as they have done) but rather with an eye to show how such tendencies may have influenced the kind of social controls which have been used by commanders.

In like manner, Maury D. Feld's concept of "military discipline as a social force"—which frames much of my analysis concerning the "ethos of control"—is not directed, as was Feld's concern (1977a), with assessing a consequence of a military innovation on the civil society, but rather, gain, on the maintenance of internal order. Feld, for example noted that:

> The discipline of controlled firepower thus played the role of being the basic form of productivity for those whom neither crafts, agriculture, nor commerce could absorb (1977a, 12).

For my purposes, "controlled firepower" subjects soldiers to differing degrees of physical risk, and I am concerned with the impact this has on the use of social controls by officers.

In like manner, Finer's suggestion that "political culture" (1966) is the central determinant of civilian control over the military, contains a powerful idea that I have tried to operationalize: that the "officer–enlisted" distinction forms much of the *basis* of social control in the military: it grants officers the right to command, and discipline, their enlisted charges.

From Kurt Lang's definition of "military" (1968) I have extracted distinctive determinants of military control: namely that physical violence influences the shape and types of social controls used by the officer corps. It forms the substructure of controls used on the troops themselves. The officer–enlisted distinction grants legitimacy to officers as agents of control, and the use of physical violence against enemies helps shape the pattern of responses used against soldiers. In short, the level of risk and violence associated with wars may be expected to influence the decisions of commanders to use *alternative* forms of social control.

A note on usage is appropriate here. Since I am concerned with the caste-like distinctions (Cox, 1970; Murdock, 1951, 1954; Holbrook, 1971) between officers and those in the enlisted force, I refer to this as the officer–enlisted distinction. Those with commissions in the military service are not called "officer-men" but "officers." Those who serve without commissions are called "enlisted men" while, in the early 1970s as many as 10% of their ranks contained women (SAUS, 1976). Furthermore, an "enlistee" denotes, technically, mode of entry into the military, while it also has a voluntaristic connotation, i.e., a non-draftee—or regular (Mullan, 1948)—in the Army. I thus refer to the officer–enlisted distinction without regard to gender, while I defer to the more traditional military usage for reasons of style, as well as recognition of the fact that combat and its images reflects a largely male world.

This book has also been heavily influenced by the work of those concerned in some way with the role of the officer corps and the technology of war with an eye to how this influences social control in, or of, the military. Huntington's notions of "objective" and "subjective" control (1956) which are theoretical statements of *idealized* civil-military relations (and which were modified by Abrahamsson (1973) and Janowitz (1972) to include, more properly legislative and normative constraints *on* the military's role in *civil* affairs) appear in my work as conceptualizations more appropriate to the study of social deviance: namely the operation of punitive and normative controls used *on* the troops, *by* the officer cadres, *within the military itself.*

Lastly, John Keegan's conceptualization of the "killing zones" (1974) is used in this research to sketch the patterns of branch specific risks, as these are faced by officers and men, and the degree to which this may influence the shape and types of controls used against soldiers. I am using many of the ideas of these thinkers in ways which perhaps violate the letter but not the spirit of their formulations: all of which attempt to increase our understanding of military reality.

THE PERSPECTIVE OF DEVIANCE THEORY

Few students of social deviance have attempted to apply the concepts from that discipline to the operation of the military system. Following the lead of Daniels on combat psychiatry (1973); Williams (1970, 1970a, 1970b), on homosexuality; Radine's work on social control (1977), and the work of Bryant (1974a, 1974b) and Hodges (1974) in the occupational-organizational tradition, I see this as one of my central tasks.

This study is intended to be a start in bringing together military sociology and the study of social deviance. It uses data from military settings which are conceptualized along lines drawn from that perspective and then reformulated in terms of my central concern of social control and imposed internal order.

The degree to which theories of deviance "work" in military settings is a fruitful question in its own right. In the process of raising this question we hope to simultaneously refine our theories and also gain an understanding of the operation of the military system.

I seek to apply and expand an assertion by Durkheim (1960) that the nature of society can be known by the manner in which it treats its deviants. That is, if crime and social order are intimately linked, so a military and its deviants are ineluctably bound together. The character of military institutions is likewise known, in part, by the kinds of reactions its officers take against their charges.

PART ONE: DESCRIPTION

The body of this work contains two main parts. The first part (Chapters II, III and IV) describes the kinds of sanctions available to commanders, the frequency, duration and severity of sanctioning, and the different types of deviant populations that have emerged as a result of such activity over four decades.

Chapter II begins by examining the rates of internal punishment in military settings. Legal sanctions (court-martial rates) are one type of control used by commanders to insure order.

Did commanders' preferences for harsh over mild forms of court-martial bear any relation to movements in the *general level* of court-martial activity? If so, were commanders becoming more selective in their use of harsh sanctions during certain periods? If not, was there a general pattern of indiscriminate harshness? If there is a relationship between severity and frequency of sanctions, does it hold for the entire military system or only for specific branches of the service?

Chapter III examines the *banishment* of wayward soldiers from the organization via the "Bad Paper" Discharge. This chapter explores the discharge process, the kinds of bad paper sanctions available, and the overall movement in bad paper rates—as well as movements within the components of bad paper, i.e., administrative and punitive dispositions. The structure of bad paper is discussed and the changes over four decades noted.

Here, the second component of formal control is described. Together with the data on court usage (Chapter II) these controls constitute the bulk of commanders' decisions to *punish* and/or *remove* wayward troops from the system.

Chapter IV concludes the first half of the book by examining the relation between commanders' decisions to contain or expel deviants over time. Here I focus primarily on the rates at which soldiers are punished inside the military and the degree to which they are expelled. The decisions of commanders to "keep in" vs. "throw out" certain *kinds* of offenders suggests the possibility that these deviant populations serve differing functions for the organization as well as pose differing kinds of threats to its social order.

PART TWO: INTERPRETATION

The last half of this work is interpretive. Chapters V, VI and VII seek to explain the meaning of organizational reaction to deviance in military settings by conceptually isolating relevant aspects of the military form and juxtaposing these against the changing patterns of organizational reaction noted in the first three chapters. The operation of social forces in the military system, at certain times, given certain contingencies, is examined so as to provide a tentative explanation for the emergent patterns of organizational reaction.

The application of violence for social ends (Lang, 1968) has, in the last analysis, social as well as structural determinants. The former are influenced by the willingness of commanders to apply controls. The latter are greatly influenced by the degree to which the technology of war results in the distribution of physical risks which, in turn, influences the need for coercion. There is some overlap of the two determinants, and, as I shall show, under certain circumstances some priority as to the salience of each as well.

Armies with bare fists—and no technology to speak of—face the problem of social control. Robot armies do not. Barring a final evolution to the latter, the social determinants of the control of armies will remain important as long as armies continue to be social forms.

This theme is expanded by focusing on five possible sources of stress in the military system that may influence the identification of deviants therein:

1. The distribution of risk.
2. The social qualifications of manpower.
3. Changes in the size of the force.
4. Changes in selection criteria for military service.
5. The volume of deviance in the system.

Chapter V examines the relationship between physical and social risk in military settings. Physical risk is measured by the combined rates of battle deaths and wounds for the last three wars (WWII, Korea and Vietnam). Social risk is conceptualized as the likelihood that a typical soldier will run afoul of military rules and be the recipient of a bad paper discharge. This chapter answers the question: Over the three wars under discussion, is there any relation between physical and social risk in the American military?

Chapter VI is an attempt to qualify theories of deviance using the military as a test case. Organizational reaction rates are postulated to be influenced by the social makeup of the officer cadres. I then locate a *critical period*, i.e., a period of years when social control patterns were decidedly atypical, and suggest that styles of control used by officers in the various branches of military service are explainable, in part, by the social characteristics of the controllers and the degree to which soldiers share these characteristics. That is, the hypothesis of "social similarity" between officers and troops is examined as a possible explanation for differing organizational reaction rates across branches. It is suggested that the *ethos of control* is influenced by the distribution of social qualifications of officers and their charges.

I hope to specify exactly *when* the social distinctiveness of the officer cadres from their subordinates was most notable, and to see if this corresponds with periods when control patterns were most atypical.

Chapter VII raises a counter hypothesis: that rates of organizational reaction on the part of the officer cadres are more influenced by the volume of deviance in the system, than by factors thus far discussed. My analysis focuses on the Vietnam Era and the U.S. Army.

I examine rates of soldier initiated deviant *acts* (AWOLS and desertions) along with officer initiated organizational *reaction* (Courts-martial and Article 15s). This chapter reviews how social scientists have viewed "the problem of AWOL"; explores the incidence, and meaning, of absenteeism; and explains the two tiers of legal and quasi-legal control which operate in the military.

Chapter VIII provides a summary of my major findings and suggests the limitations of this exploratory research and where future research may prove useful. As part of a discussion on social change in the military, I also explore the possible relevance of my findings for deviance theory and speculate concerning the changing functions of punitive and normative controls in military systems, given the changing nature of the officer–enlisted distinction.

Lastly, my major findings are examined in light of the labeling perspective, sub-cultural theory, the socio-legal perspective and insights from the functionalists. I provide a concluding linkage between complex organizations and the functions of technology on patterns of social control.

CHAPTER II. INTERNAL CONTROLS: COURTS-MARTIAL

The military is a social institution that is dominated by martial goals. These goals may prove more important during war when commanders must carefully coordinate actions, resources and efforts in directing and attempting to control the behavior of soldiers. This possibility is suggested by Black:

> So-called 'military law' increases during a war, with more kinds of deviant behavior, more trials, and more severe punishments. (1976, 101)

An alternative view is that the military, while retaining special purposes, is similar to other social institutions in the same manner as are churches, schools, corporations and families. In this perspective, organizational imperatives, i.e., winning and preparing for wars, are subordinate to larger societal influences.

While it is likely that the press of events in military settings will leave traces (Webb, et. al., 1966) of the degree to which the organization has mobilized social control resources, the overall patterns of social control will be likely to be more similar to those in other complex organizations than they will be distinctive.

This emphasis on the operation of larger societal forces is suggested by Barber:

> The essential point is that the military services are not something different and apart from American society, but are an integral part of the fabric of that society. (1973, 310)

In addition, some military branches are more martial than others, i.e., a larger fraction-of-force may see combat. Some are more technological, i.e., few men may actually face battle. Those who do are highly trained and employ sophisticated machines and machine-systems which the remainder of the force is charged with maintaining, servicing, etc.

There is a tension in the military between institutional goals and organizational imperatives, both of which may be influenced by the structure of battle and more routine concerns. It is my thesis that rates of social control activity—specifically court-martial rates—are telling indicators of how commanders sought to resolve the problem of order in a changing complex institution. I believe that there are fewer more telling measures of the character of an institution than how its managers react and attempt to control the numbers of deviants seen to exist therein.

Moreover, one of the ways an institution may become "modern" is for it to rely less on coercive sanctions and more on the internalization of corporate goals. Robotics is an example of such an extreme accommodative possibility: social control is reduced to programming, maintenance and repair. Coercion lies at the other extreme: rules are enforced—and values reaffirmed—by selecting a population to whom sanctions can be applied.

The degree of official reaction to deviance in the military can be ideal-typically suggested by examining extreme possibilities. First, a military dominated by exclusively martial (organizational) concerns would be expected to exhibit extreme sanctioning patterns during war. Such patterns would be noticeably distinct from peace-time reaction patterns. Second, a military more under the influence of larger, societal (institutional) pressures would be expected to exhibit a long-term secular trend in its patterns of social control which would transcend the temporary disruptions of war.

THE USE OF LEGAL SANCTIONS

> Division of command responsibility and the responsibility for the adjudication of offenses and accused offenders cannot be as separate (in the military) as it is in our own democratic government. — General Dwight D. Eisenhower, 1949 (cited in Sherman, 1973).

This chapter describes the application of one type of organizational reaction in military settings: the punishment of soldiers through the use of legal sanctions. Time-series data on Department of Defense court-martial rates are examined:

1. To locate those periods when commanders' preferences for using legal sanctions were greatest, and hence organizational reaction to deviance was strongest.

2. To discover if war produces periods of heightened court-martial activity in the military, and if these corresponded to heightened activities in each branch.

3. The degree to which branch court-martial rates are related is tentative evidence for a general control climate in the military. If it turns out

that the branches are more dissimilar than they are similar with regard to court-martial rates, the case for a general institutional control pattern is weakened.[1]

4. To see if there is a relationship between the *severity* of court-martial, and the frequency of sanctioning.

Do commanders' preferences for harsh over mild forms of court-marital bear any relation to movements in the general level of court-martial activity? If so, were commanders becoming more selective in their use of harsh sanctions during certain periods? If not, was there a general pattern of indiscriminate harshness? If there is a relationship between severity and frequency of sanctions, does it hold for the entire military system or only for specific branches of the service?

There are three issues here. The first involves specifying the timing of sanctioning in the branches. The second asks if differences in sanctioning rates for each branch were more notable in peace or war. Third, does the rate of sanctioning influence the harshness of the sanctions imposed?

THE RESEARCH PROBLEM: BRANCH OR INSTITUTIONAL CONTROL PATTERNS?

Branch and systemic changes in the American military over four decades afford an indirect measure of the degree to which the military system may be better described as merely a complex organization charged with martial tasks, or as a distinctive military institution that has superficially taken the form of a modern complex organization.

The resolution of the problem of branch distinctiveness vs. institutional determinism addresses three crucial issues in the literature of military sociology, complex organizations, and social deviance. First, to what degree is the military distinct from other types of complex organizations? A "martial model" of the military would answer this question in terms of identifying the distinct characteristics of military settings. Most military sociologists agree that, in one form or another, the preparation for (and conduct of) battles is what gives the military its distinct organizational character.[2]

If this is indeed the case, a martial model of military institutions would stress the "military" part, and would tend to understress the institutional aspects of military arrangements. An alternative view is to emphasize the institutional similarities between armies and corporate or state enterprises.[3] In this view, institutional structure is the determinate social force. Commanders, when viewed as office holders, appear to share the same concerns and interests as do their corporate counterparts: personnel training, turnover, morale, promotion, retention and motivation, worker effectiveness and the like.

These concerns compose the standard menu of managerial and leadership fare that are studied in both schools of business and the military academies (OML/ USMA, 1975). But for the distant battlefield, in this perspective, soldiers are essentially workers, and executives are similar to commanders without benefit of military regalia, customs and traditions.

While both organizational and institutional perspectives stress some aspects of both military and civilian environments, and understate the importance of others, the essential debate as to whether or not the military is similar to, or different from, its host society is intense[4] as are the social implications of policy decisions derived from either point of view.[5]

To shed some light on the degree of similarity or difference between the military and its host society, I propose still a third vantage point which stems from insights gained from those who study social deviance. If the rate at which varied populations of soldiers were stigmatized by their commanders over time reflects the character of the institution wherein they are found, I should expect that the presumably martial character of the military would emerge most strongly during time of war. That is, court-martial rates should be higher in war than during peace.

I will address the varied ways that the military has reacted to "threats from within" by producing sanctioning patterns of differing severity that have emerged during and after wars. A general sketch of the contextual issues concerning the control options available to commanders is offered in the notes.[6]

COURTS-MARTIAL

A court-martial is a trial in a military setting. It is convened by, and on behalf of, the commanding officer who represents higher authority in the military system—although career enlisted men may sit on court-martial boards if requested. The type of court-martial corresponds to the severity of the offense and also to the direct involvement of the higher echelons: a General court-martial requires the convener's rank to be that of a General officer, while a Special court-martial can be called by an officer of field grade (Major or higher), and a Summary court-martial may be called by a junior officer—usually a Captain, sometimes a Lieutenant.

The court-martial is a formal instrument of control applied by officers to enlisted offenders for violations of what is essentially the entire U.S. criminal code, i.e., burglary, housebreaking, writing a bad check, assault, murder, etc. in addition to offenses which have a uniquely military meaning, i.e., offenses for which there is no civilian counterpart. For example, absence without authority

(AWOL), disrespect toward a superior officer, missing a movement, failing to obey a command, malingering, communicating a threat, desertion and treason.

Officers, of course, may occasionally face court-martial, but this is as uncommon as it is newsworthy. Rivkin explains:

> When an officer commits some offense for which an enlisted man would be tried by court-martial, it is the Army's policy to give him an opportunity to resign. This type of "punishment" is considered to be such a grave rebuke to the officer's honor that the authorities truly think of it as worse than a court-martial conviction (1970, 252).

In addition, many problems in large civilian organizations are crimes in military settings. For example being drunk on duty, being late for work, being improperly attired or failing to keep one's self, work area, or living quarters in line with supervisor's expectations. In brief, many civilian *folkways* are laws in the military and carry legal and quasi-legal sanctions when they are violated.

Control in military settings, moreover, covers a wider range of activity than do the comparatively narrowly defined civil codes. The rules are codified in the Uniform Code of Military Justice (UCMJ) and interpreted through the use of the Manual for Courts-Martial (USGPO, 1969) which serves as a practical guidebook for administratively documenting an offense, providing rules of procedure, and contains examples which demonstrate the proper processing of cases.

Court-martial sanctions[7] in the military system are customarily expressed as a rate in relation to force strength: the number of personnel on active duty. Since a military head count includes the officer corps—and since few officers face court-martial—the rates per 1,000 personnel somewhat understate the amount of legal sanctioning in proportion to the size of the officer fraction-of-forces. This fraction, however, has remained relatively stable (between 10% and 12% of the total force) and therefore does not affect trends (SAUS, 1948, 1954, 1976). Chart 2.1, examines court-martial rates for the military system, that is, for the Department of Defense (DOD).

The chart shows the decisions of commanders to select court-martial sanctions over alternative methods of imposing discipline and control. Four major trends characterize the period under review.

1. The greatest increases in court-martial rates occurred after World War II. Between 1945 (134 per thousand) and 1948 (541 per thousand), the overall court-martial rate quadrupled.

2. Since 1948, the military has relied less on the use of court-martial as a means of social control.

   The decline is dramatic. The 1970 rate is only about 1/10th of the 1948 rate. During World War II roughly one man in slightly over five on ac-

tive duty received a court-martial; in 1948 slightly more than one out
of two were court-martialed; in 1953 roughly one out of three; during
the Vietnam War roughly one in ten, and thereafter, roughly one in
twenty.

CHART 2.1. DEPARTMENT OF DEFENSE COURT-MARTIAL RATES
PER 1,000 ACTIVE DUTY STRENGTH: FISCAL 1941–1979.

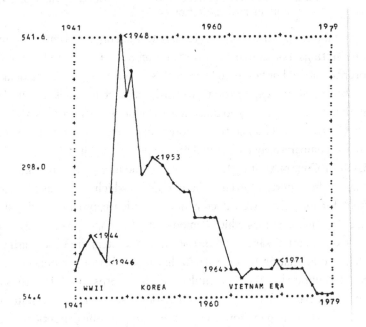

KEY: *In 1948, for every 1,000 active duty servicemen, 541.6 received some form of court-martial.
In 1979, the figure was 54.4*
Source: *See chapter endnote 8.*

The overall decline in court usage suggests that long term institutional, as opposed to branch, forces are at work. A typical enlisted
member entering the military after 1948 faced a decreasing likelihood
of facing a military court. This trend persists through war and peace.

3. Court-martial rates are more stable during than before or after a war.
   This suggests that, whatever else wars may produce, they do not generate a substantial increase in the average rate of court-martial. The
   military does not assume "martial" sanctioning patterns during war.
   Black's assertion is not supported by actual court-martial data.

4. When one looks only at the three wars: court-martial rates were highest
   during the Korean War (1953–330 per thousand), followed by World

War II (1944–181 per thousand) and Vietnam (1971–120 per thousand). However else these wars may have differed, it is clear that the Korean War saw the greatest relative use of the courts.

BRANCH COMPARISONS

Court-martial rates within the respective branches tended, with a few exceptions, to follow the patterns for the military system. The between-branch correlation (R) for overall court-martial rates in the branches are shown in Table 2.1.

TABLE 2.1. BETWEEN-BRANCH COURT-MARTIAL RATES.
CORRELATIONS: 1941–1979, AND FOR THE AIR FORCE; 1949–1979.

SERVICE BRANCH	ARMY*	NAVY*	MARINES*	AIR FORCE**
Navy	.738	X	X	X
Marines	.689	.843	X	X
Air Force	.355	.588	.530	X

*The overall measure of correlation (R) for each of the traditional branches (Army, Navy, Marines) for 1941–79.
**The overall measure of correlation (R) for all service branches (Army, Navy, Air Force and Marines) for 1949–79.
Source: See chapter endnote 9.

Between-branch court-martial rates tended to be more strongly associated over time within the traditional branches (Army, Navy, Marines), which were more similar to each other than any of them were similar to the Air Force. The branches also differed with regard to their relative use of court-martial sanctions, and the swiftness with which the declines were observed.

With regard to extreme movements in court-martial rates, the army—in 1948—experienced a court-martial rate roughly three times that of the other branches (Army, 390.3; Navy, 111.3; Marines, 119.9), with regard to the relative frequency of courts-martial over the entire period of observation, the Marines had the highest court-martial rates, on average, followed by the Army, Navy and Air Force.

The general decline in court-martial rates is also clear for each branch. Some sense of the magnitude of the decline can be realized by examining when the rates peaked for each branch, and what the minimum values were.

TABLE 2.2. BETWEEN BRANCH COMPARATIVE RANGES AND MAGNITUDES OF COURT-MARTIAL RATE EXTREMA: 1941–1979.

RATES ARE PER 1,000 BRANCH STRENGTH.

BRANCH	ARMY	NAVY	MARINES	AIR FORCE
Maximum	390	117	128	74
Year	1948	1950	1950	1949
Minimum	10	14	25	2
Year	1979	1978	1979	1978

Source: See chapter endnote 9.

The table shows that the overall court-martial rate in each branch reached maximum between 1948 and 1950. Rates then declined fairly regularly for all branches to their respective minima in 1978-79. Thus, while the aftermath of World War II saw extreme sanctioning activity, the aftermath of the Vietnam War saw a minimal use of the courts.

TYPES OF COURT-MARTIAL

There are three types of court-martial in the United States military: the General, Special and Summary. As is true in civil society, the most severe kinds of crimes—and the most severe sanctions—occur least frequently. General court-martial, the most severe sanction, accounts for a minority of all courts-martial, with a large part of the remainder being Intermediate Level sanctions, and the bulk of all courts-martial being of the Summary type. This generalization, of course, may vary widely at different times, and across branches as well. Extreme variations in court-martial rates, or shifts in the distribution of court-martial types, reflects the changing preferences of commanders to use the courts as well as their emphasis on harsh or milder forms of punishment.

The different types of court-martial are reviewed below, along with the relation each type of sanction has to the formal authority structure (the chain of command) in the military.

The higher the rank of the convening officer who presides over a court-martial, the more severe the possible sanctions, and, in general, the less frequent are such events. There are, of course, exceptions which will be treated shortly.

FIGURE 2.1. HIERARCHY, NAME AND MAXIMUM SANCTION

LEVEL OF COMMAND	NAME	MAXIMUM SANCTION
High	General Court-martial	Death or any punishment contained in the Manual for Court-martial, United States
Intermediate	Special Court-martial	Six months confinement at hard labor, six months forfeiture of 2/3 pay, and Bad Conduct Discharge.
Low	Summary Court-martial	One month confinement at hard labor, 45 days confinement without hard labor, forfeiture of 2/3 pay for 1 month.

Source: Based on Sherman, 1973.

THE SEVERITY ISSUE

While the overall rate of court-martial represents the degree to which commanders use the court system, each type of court-martial differs in severity. Thus, there are two distinct issues involved: sanction severity and frequency.

Any relative movement in the composition of the overall court-martial rate indicates a sanction preference and helps specify the severity with which commanders discipline the troops. This raises two questions:

1. When court-martial rates were increasing (post-World War II—all branches); in 1953 (for the Army and Marines); in 1967–1975 (for the Marines), was most of the increase due to relatively mild (Summary) or harsh (Special and General) court-martial sanctions?

2. While the use of the court-martial has declined quite substantially in the military, is the same true for the *relative* harshness of the sanctions?

The first issue concerns the distribution of court-martial sanctions when both harsh and mild types are increasing—during "sanction waves" when commanders are revealing an *absolute* preference to use the military courts. The second issue concerns relative sanctioning: when commanders prefer one type of sanction over the other under circumstances where less overall sanctioning is taking place.

Both questions address a central concern as to the nature of organizational reaction to social deviance by examining the degree to which commanders elect to punish their soldiers when it is fairly common (or rare) to use legal channels. These issues can be clarified and put into proper perspective through the use of a 2x2 table which explores the possible sanction climates and frequency relations in the military.

FIGURE 2.2. HYPOTHETICAL SANCTION CLIMATES AND FREQUENCIES, SEVERITY OF COURT-MARTIAL

	Severity	
Frequency	High	Low
High	1	2
Low	3	4

CHART 2.2. U.S. ARMY SUMMARY COURTS-MARTIAL AS A PERCENT OF ALL COURT-MARTIAL ACTIVITY: FISCAL 1941–79.

LEGEND:	X-AXIS	Y-AXIS
Series Name	Year	Percent Summary*
Number Of Ordered Pairs	39	

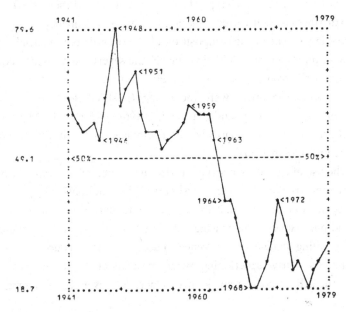

Expressed as a percent of the overall court-martial rate.
Source: See chapter endnote 10.

TYPE 1 sanctioning climates (high severity and frequency) would be characterized as featuring intensive use of the courts with the typical sanction being severe.

TYPE 2 climates would be characterized as those with extensive court use and the typical court-martial being of the Summary type.

Both TYPE 1 and TYPE 2 climates exhibit a substantial use of the military courts. They differ in the typical severity of sanctions imposed.

TYPE 3 climates would feature less frequent court use with disproportionately high dispositions.

TYPE 4 climates would be relatively mild, with few punitive sanctions and little reliance on the courts.

BRANCH COURT-MARTIAL PATTERNS

The U.S. Army

I will first examine the behavior of commanders in the U.S. Army. Chart 2.2 presents the percentage of all courts-martial of the Summary type. Since the Summary court-martial is the mildest of the three types, when expressed as a percentage of the overall rate of court-martial in the Army, the chart nicely shows the relationship between rates of mild and harsh sanctioning.

A display of this type shows the historical movement in the *relative* severity of sanctions. The chart provides evidence for a major shift from a mild sanction climate (1941–63) where the use of the Summary Court was modal, to a harsh climate after 1964 (when harsher sanctions were more typical than Summary Courts-martial).

The shift in sanction modality after 1964 is also illustrated by examining the overall numerical differences in the rates of harsh and mild sanctioning in the Army, which were used to construct Chart 2.2. Table 2.3 shows the differences between the rate of harsh sanctioning, i.e., Special + General Court-martial rates, minus the rate of the milder Summary Court-martial.

A negative value means mild sanctions (Summary Cms) were most frequent, whereas a positive value means that harsher sanctions were modal. The data splits sharply into two segments as suggested in Chart 2.2. Thus, for the Vietnam Era and beyond there was a clear shift from a TYPE 2 sanction climate (lots of court use, mild sanctions typical) to a TYPE 3 climate (less court use, harsher sanctions being typical). Other things being equal, a soldier brought before the courts after 1964, in the Army, faced a greater likelihood of getting a harsh court-martial, than did his comrades serving in the two earlier wars, or during the interim period of peace prior to Vietnam. Since I lack social-psychological data on how commanders actually perceived their decisions to sanction their charges after 1963, I can only note that, however varied their motivations may have been, the shift to severity is clearly documented.

TABLE 2.3. DIFAR: THE DIFFERENCE BETWEEN HARSH AND MILD COURT-MARTIAL RATES IN THE U.S. ARMY. FISCAL 1941–79.

(Special + General) minus Summary Court-martial Rate

YEAR	DIFAR*	DFNAV*	DIFMC*
1941	-14	8	10
1942	-12	2	2
1943	-11	3	0
1944	-9	7	-11
1945	-10	2	4
1946	-3	-14	-1
1947	-30	-1	-6
1948	-231	-4	0
1949	-33	-1	-5
1950	-52	-9	-3
1951	-43	-8	-5
1952	-19	-20	-3
1953	-16	-21	-1
1954	-10	-25	-4
1955	-5	-16	-5
1956	-6	-12	-1
1957	-12	-16	1
1958	-14	-16	-10
1959	-15	-20	-13
1960	-13	-17	-14
1961	-14	-17	-14
1962	-14	-16	-12
1963	-4	-8	-4
1964	9	3	7
1965	9	2	7
1966	10	3	6
1967	16	4	7
1968	23	3	7
1969	31	2	3
1970	20	2	7

1971	12	1	-3
1972	6	-1	1
1973	10	-1	1
1974	14	3	16
1975	10	4	17
1976	8	3	11
1977	5	0	7
1978	5	1	8
1979	4	-1	3

*Rounded
Source: See chapter endnote 10.

In 1964, of all courts-martial convened, harsher outcomes were realized: harsher than, on average, was the case until 1964 and the trend continued well after the Vietnam War had ended. In addition, on average, the courts were being used less. Thus the increase in harshness suggests that the sanctions were being selectively applied. The higher echelons in the army were becoming increasingly involved in the court-sanctioning of soldiers.

The Navy

Naval commanders entered World War II with a small preference for harsher sanctions which lasted until 1945 (Summary Cms= 28.0 per thousand; Special + General Cms= 30.4). After the war, both harsh and mild court-martial rates increased to roughly double their 1945 values by 1950—with a slight preference for the milder type of sanction. Stated differently, Naval commanders tended to slightly prefer harsh sanctions, but both rates increased at roughly the same rate until 1950. Unlike the commanders in the Army (who preferred mild sanctions in the post-World War II period), Naval commanders did not show such a marked preference until the decade of the Forties was over. After 1950, and until 1963, there was a preference for Summary Court-martial.

Trends in the Navy are shown in Chart 2.3:

When one examines the wars, sailors who served in the early part of the Vietnam War (1964–68) received slightly more harsh sanctions that those who served in World War II, and those who served during the Korean War received the mildest treatment of all three.

The second relationship (less harsh sanctioning in the Fifties and early Sixties, followed by preference for harsher sanctions during Vietnam and thereafter) is shown more precisely in Table 2.4.

Naval commanders, as shown in Table 2.4, favored harsh forms of court-martial (Special + General Cms) during World War II, (1941–1945) and from 1964 onward. There was a mild counter-movement in preferences near the end of the Vietnam War (1972-73) with oscillating preferences thereafter.

CHART 2.3 U.S. NAVY SUMMARY COURTS-MARTIAL AS A
PERCENT OF ALL COURT-MARTIAL ACTIVITY: FISCAL 1941–79.

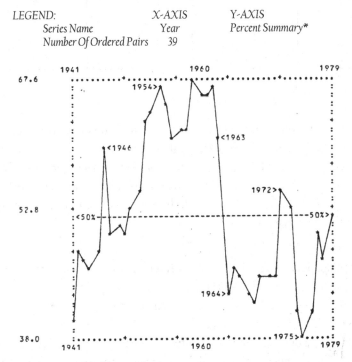

* Expressed as a percent of the overall court-martial rate.
Source: See chapter endnote 10.

As was true in the Army, Naval commanders preferred harsher sanctions after 1963 with two important differences:

1. During World War II harsh courts-martial in the Navy were the norm whereas in the Army milder sanctions were modal.

2. During the late part of the Vietnam War (1972-73) Naval commanders briefly preferred the milder form of court-martial.

In the Navy, martial forces, i.e., those contingencies related to the conduct of war, apparently influenced the sanctioning patterns of commanders. But such forces did not act uniformly across all three wars. For the most part, sailors who served in World War II were sanctioned harshly as were those who served during the Vietnam War—with a mild respite in 1972-73. There was no shift in harshness during the Korean War, however. For the Navy, organizational forces appeared to be stronger during World War II and Vietnam, than was the case for the Korean War.

TABLE 2.4. DFNAV: THE DIFFERENCE BETWEEN HARSH AND MILD COURT-MARTIAL RATES IN THE U.S. NAVY. FISCAL 1941–79.

(Special + General) minus Summary Court-martial Rate

YEAR	DFNAV*
1941	8
1942	2
1943	3
1944	7
1945	2
1946	-14
1947	-1
1948	-4
1949	-1
1950	-9
1951	-8
1952	-20
1953	-21
1954	-25
1955	-16
1956	-12
1957	-16
1958	-16
1959	-20
1960	-17
1961	-17
1962	-16
1963	-8
1964	3
1965	2
1966	3
1967	4
1968	3

1969	2
1970	2
1971	1
1972	-1
1973	-1
1974	3
1975	4
1976	3
1977	0
1978	1
1979	-1

*Rounded
Source: See chapter endnote 10.

The Marine Corps

In examining Marine commanders' preferences for harsh or milder courts-martial it must be remembered that Marine Corps court-martial rates increased (as did the other branch rates) after World War II, and in 1953 (as did the Army's). Unlike the other branches, however, Marine Cm rates increased from 1967 through 1975 when those in the other branches were declining. Stated another way, during these years Marine Corps court-martial rates tended to inflate the Department of Defense rate. Thus, sanctioning in the branches, other than the Marines, was actually less than the overall DOD rate would indicate. The Vietnam War, for Marine commanders, apparently allowed many opportunities for sanctioning the troops. Was this relative expansion of sanctioning in the Marines accompanied by increases in harshness? Chart 2.4 plots the Marine Corps data.

Chart 2.4 helps clarify the previously noted strong association between overall sanctioning activity in the Navy and the Marines (R= .843). As was true in the Navy, Marine commanders were relatively harsh during early World War II, and after 1963. Like the Navy, there was also a respite from harsh sanctioning in 1971.

Beginning in 1964 there was a clear shift to the harsher types of court-martial which persisted until 1975, well after the Vietnam War was over. Thus, during the period 1967–1975 (when Marine Court-martial rates were increasing and those of the other branches were falling) sanction preferences were moving in the direction of increased harshness. Either Marine commanders were responding to organizational, not institutional, imperatives, or the nature of the institution was changing. Table 2.5 identifies the relationship between harsh and severe sanctioning in the Marine Corps.

CHART 2.4. U.S. MARINE CORPS SUMMARY COURTS-MARTIAL AS A PERCENT OF ALL COURT-MARTIAL ACTIVITY: FISCAL 1941–79.

LEGEND:

	X-AXIS	*Y-AXIS*
Series Name	*Year*	*Percent Summary**
Number Of Ordered Pairs		*39*

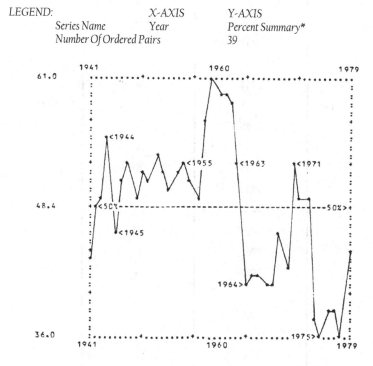

* *Expressed as a percent of the overall court-martial rate.*
Source: See chapter endnote 10.

TABLE 2.5. DIFMC: THE DIFFERENCE BETWEEN HARSH AND MILD COURT-MARTIAL RATES IN THE U.S. MARINES: FISCAL 1941–79.

(Special + General) minus Summary Court-martial Rate

YEAR	DIFMC*
1941	10
1942	2
1943	0
1944	-11
1945	4
1946	-1
1947	-6

1948	0
1949	-5
1950	-3
1951	-5
1952	-3
1953	-1
1954	-4
1955	-5
1956	-1
1957	1
1958	-10
1959	-13
1960	-14
1961	-14
1962	-12
1963	-4
1064	7
1965	7
1966	6
1967	7
1968	7
1969	3
1970	7
1971	-3
1972	1
1973	1
1974	16
1975	17
1976	11
1977	7
1978	8
1979	3

*Rounded
Source: See chapter endnote 10.

CHART 2.5. U.S. AIR FORCE SUMMARY COURTS-MARTIAL AS A
PERCENT OF ALL COURT-MARTIAL ACTIVITY: FISCAL 1949-79.

LEGEND:

	X-AXIS	*Y-AXIS*
Series Name	*Year*	*Percent Summary**
Number Of Ordered Pairs		*31*

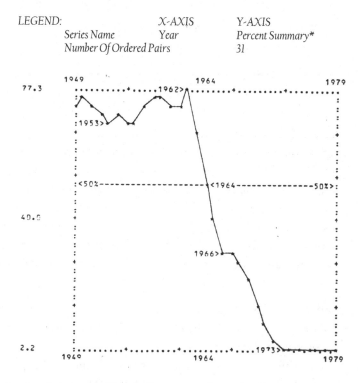

* expressed as a percent of the overall court-martial rate.
Source: See chapter endnote 10.

Marine Corps commanders' harshness preferences broke into three periods:
harsh (1941–43); mild (1944–63); and harsh (1964–79).

Marine commanders used harsh sanctions against the troops during the early
years of World War II, and after 1963. In the interim, to the degree that the absolute size of the difference between harsh minus mild sanctioning rates in the traditional forces can be considered a preference for types of sanctions applied, such
differences were smallest in the Marine Corps (cf. DIFMC, DFNAV and DIFAR).

TRADITIONAL FORCE SANCTION CLIMATES

All traditional forces (Army, Navy, Marines) shifted to more frequent use of
harsher sanctions after 1963. In the Navy and Marines there was a trend to be
relatively harsh on the troops during World War II. The Korean War was free of
sanction shifts: all traditional forces were relatively mild in their court-martial rate

patterns. Overall rates of court-martial in the Marines, however, were increasing during the period 1967–1975, whereas they were falling in the other branches. To examine the relative variation in the cross-branch preferences for harshness, the differences (harsh minus mild court-martial rates) are correlated below (1941–79).

TABLE 2.6. CORRELATIONS OF DIFFERENCES
TRADITIONAL FORCES 1941–79.

	DIFMC	DIFNV
DIFAR	.249	.178
DIFNV	.646	X

Table 2.6 suggests that the Navy was most similar in response to the Marines, and least similar to the Army. On the one hand, this not surprising if one views the Marine Corps as part of the command structure of the Navy. On the other hand, since the ground forces fight a more similar kind of war, one might expect the Marine commanders to have similar sanctioning preferences to commanders in the Army. This was not the case, however. This is further tentative evidence that institutional forces, in this case related to the structure of command, were operative.

The Air Force

Harsh and mild court-martial rates for the Air Force are characterized by their striking uniformity and convergence in 1964, and the virtual disappearance of the Summary Court-martial thereafter. This is shown in Chart 2.5.

Air commanders exhibited a clear, sustained, and almost mechanical preference for milder sanctions (Summary Cms) over harsher options (General + Special Cms) between 1949 and 1964. In addition, for the first fifteen years of Air Force existence as a separate branch, the mild sanction rate on average (Summary Cms) was about three times that of the harsher sanction rates combined (Special + General Cms). In 1964, parity was achieved (3.53 Cms, each type, per 1,000 active duty Air Force personnel). Table 2.7 documents the shift in sanction climate in the Air Force after 1964.

TABLE 2.7. DIFAF: THE DIFFERENCE BETWEEN HARSH AND MILD COURT-MARTIAL RATES IN THE U.S. AIR FORCE, FISCAL 1949–79.
(Special + General) Minus Summary Court-Martial Rate

YEAR	DIFAF*
1949	-34
1950	-36

1951	-20
1952	-21
1953	-19
1954	-17
1955	-14
1956	-16
1957	-18
1958	-15
1959	-12
1960	-10
1961	-9
1962	-10
1963	-4
1964	0
1965	1
1966	1
1967	1
1968	1
1969	2
1970	2
1971	2
1972	3
1973	4
1974	4
1975	3
1976	2
1977	2
1978	2
1979	2

* *Rounded.*
Source: See chapter endnote 10.

After 1964 (the beginning of the Vietnam Era) the Summary Court-martial rate began to diminish at an increasing rate until 1976 when it virtually disappeared (1976 = 8 Summary Cms per 100,000 Personnel). Thus, the *relative* increase in harsh sanctions was more pronounced. In the Air Force, 1964 marked the beginning of a relatively harsh period. Air commanders were simultaneously choosing to use the courts less frequently than ever before, but when they did elect to use the courts the sanctions were disproportionately severe.

Upon examining the *absolute* values of the differences between the sanction types, the disappearance of the Summary Court-martial, and the low level of court use in the Air Force relative to the other branches, it is clear that young Air Force commanders have been much less likely to sanction the troops. To be brought before the court in the Air Force requires the actions of the higher echelons to a greater degree than in the less technical branches.

COMMANDERS' PREFERENCES FOR HARSH SANCTIONS

Military court-martial rates address the frequency of organizational reaction to social deviance in the ranks by using the courts to punish offenders. The distribution of court-martial types reflects the severity of organizational reaction.

The two stages of overall activity in the branches, i.e., the general trend for either a harsh or a mild sanctioning climate, can be further analyzed by examining the sub-periods of greatest movement (up or down) or overall stability. The research question becomes: Did commanders prefer harsh sanctions when use of the courts was extremely common, rare or essentially stable? Figure 2.3 examines five possibilities: (1) A rapid increase in court use. (2) A moderate increase in court use. (3) A rapid decrease in court use. (4) Fairly constant court use. (5) A decline in court use to the minimum value.

To roughly measure the shifts in harshness within a period of court activity, overall branch court-martial rates were examined by their defining characteristics. For example, condition 1 specifies "a rapid increase in court use." All periods of rapid increase were identified. Then, a simple coding scheme was used. If during the period of increased activity, harsh sanctions were increasing faster than milder sanctions, commanders' harshness preference was coded "Yes." If milder sanctions were increasing faster, commanders' harshness preference was coded "No."

FIGURE 2.3. THE MOVEMENT TOWARD HARSH SANCTIONS, BY BRANCH, DURING VARYING DEGREES OF COURT USAGE.

Court-Martial Rate of Movement	Period	Preference for Harshness?			
		Marines	Army	Navy	AF
Rapid Increase	1946–48	No	No	Yes	No*
Mild Increase	1951–53	Yes	Yes	No	No
Rapid Decline	1954–1963	No	No	No	No

| Fairly Stable | 1964–1974 | Yes (1) | Yes | Yes | Yes |
| Drop to Minimum | 1975–79 | Yes | Yes | Yes | Yes |

Notes:
* Air Force was part of the Army in this period.
1. Marine court usage was increasing, not stable, during this period, and was atypical of the overall military pattern.
Source: Derived from examination of branch court-martial rates. See chapter endnote 11.

Figure 2.3 provides answers to a number of questions concerning commanders' preferences for harshness.

1. When court-martial rates were increasing rapidly (1946–48) in all branches, Naval commanders were preferring harsh sanctions; other commanders were not.

2. When court-martial rates were increasing mildly (1951–53) in the military, Marine and Army commanders were becoming relatively harsh; Air and Naval commanders were not.

3. During the period of sustained, rapid decline in court-martial activity (1955–63) all commanders increasingly elected to sanction mildly.

4. During the period (1964–74) of relatively stable court activity, all commanders were becoming increasingly harsh—and decreasingly using the Summary Court-martial—except for Marine Corps commanders who were selecting harsher sanctions and also using the courts to a greater degree: thus both types of sanctioning increased.

5. When use of the courts was sharply declining in all branches (1975–79) all commanders preferred harsh sanctions at the "expense" of Summary Cms. This was most notable in the Air Force.

Commanders' preferences for harshness apparently were negligibly influenced by rapid increases in average court-martial rates. They were moderately influenced by mild increases, however, and not at all harsh on the troops during a rapid decline in a reaction wave. Thus it appears that when the military is undergoing a rather severe adjustment of some sort (before and after a wave of activity) commanders are not disproportionately harsh.

When overall average court-martial rates continued to drop, however, there appeared to be a point (1964), beyond which a continued decline in court activity resulted in increased harshness. This is suggestive of a lower limit on sanctioning activity that apparently serves as a floor above which the higher echelons become increasingly involved in the punishment of soldiers.

It appears that the military has been modernizing as an institution—in that less use of the court system is a measure of such modernization—while certain organizational forces remained salient. Martial goals are most important in the

Marines, and less important in the Air Force. More importantly, however, the institutional patterns transcend the war-peace cycle. For example, upon entering the military services after 1976, a typical member of the enlisted force serving in any of the branches has less of a chance of facing the court, than at any time prior.

The decisions of commanders to mobilize social control resources, however, are not limited to the courts. The next chapter will examine the use of the "Bad Paper" Discharge.

NOTES: CHAPTER II

Materials from this chapter have been modified and published as: "Social Controls and Martial Contingencies: Organizational and Institutional Patterns in the U.S. Military". 1987. *Journal of Political and Military Sociology* Vol. 15(2 Fall), 263-278.

1. This distinction is crucial to an understanding of the degree to which it is plausible to distinguish military reality from the reality of complex organizations in general. The examination of branch and system control patterns affords an unobtrusive examination of social differentiation as well as centralization in complex organizations. These are both divergent outcomes of the division of labor and both are relevant for deviance theory.

   Studies of policing, for example, have shown that centralized police forces which apply universalistic criteria produce higher arrest rates than those less centralized forces using particularistic standards (Wilson, 1978). High arrest rates in this case presume that, other things being equal, police on the beat are innocent of community norms. What if, in theory, the personnel who police used the same rules and were equally centralized? If this were the case, variation in arrest rates could not be attributed to level of bureaucratization. The military case affords this possibility: The same rules are used and the chain of command is equally institutionalized in all service branches.

2. Lang defines the subject matter of military sociology as follows: The subject matter of military sociology is best defined by reference to organized violence. All those situations and structures in which this element constitutes a major and legitimate preoccupation—whether as a readily available means to achieve some social objective or as a potential last resort—are within its scope. (1972, 9). Other sociologists also stress the importance of violence (Biderman, 1967; Janowitz, 1968; Nisbet, 1973; Feld, 1977).

3. Kanter's study of "The Managerial Careers of Air Force Generals" (Kanter, 1976) uses this perspective. In addition, this is a theme of readers used at West Point in Leadership classes (OML-USMA, 1975). It is also the perspective of sociologists of complex organizations (Hall, 1972). Indeed, most comparison studies that focus only on a limited number of relevant substantive foci implicitly *assume* that when samples of civil and military populations are compared, observed differences or similarities are largely attributable to the selected variables in the research design. The ideological possibilities of this type of research await the attention of students of social deviance. For example, attitude polls of students and soldiers, however else they may be flawed, tacitly assume sufficient congruence in the life-world (Schutz, 1973) for comparisons to be credibly made. For a discussion of the problems of comparative research on military institutions see Janowitz (1977b, 1-26).

4. There is a debate as to the degree that military institutions are unique. For students of deviance the issue remains relatively undeveloped. Military sociologists have tended

to view difference or similarity in terms of impact on the civil-military relations in a society (Janowitz, 1971a, 1972; Biderman and Sharp, 1965; Segal, et al., 1974; Little, 1971). The issue is usually defined in terms of civilian control over the military with extreme possibilities ranging from the 'garrison state' (Lasswell, 1941) to total erosion of the values, *esprit*, and traditions (Nisbet, 1973) that have historically come to set the military apart from ordinary occupations. Of recent, from the perspective of the domain of military *values*, Moskos (1975) has called attention to the possible dangers of military service becoming similar to other forms of civilian employment, i.e., a "job" as opposed to a profession.

For the many facets of the convergence-divergence argument see: Babin and O'Mara, 1980; Barber, 1973b; Biderman and Sharp, 1968; Bowers, 1968; Bradford and Brown, 1974; Brotz and Wilson, 1946; Clarkson and Cochran, 1941; Coates and Pellegrin, 1961; Coffin, 1964; Colby, 1937; Collins, 1974; Davis, 1954; Dornbusch, 1955; Feld 1975, 1977; Finer, 1962; Galligan, 1973; Gard, 1971, 1973; Hauser, 1973; Horowitz, 1971; Huntington, 1956, 1960; Hutchinson, 1957; Janowitz, 1966, 1972, 1976, 1977a, 1977b; Janowitz and Little, 1974b; Janowitz and van Doorn, 1970; Kanter, 1976; Kjellberg, 1965; Kluckhohn, 1951; Kourvetaris and Dobratz, 1976, 1977; Krendell and Gomberg, 1975; Lang, 1965b, 1972; Larson, 1974; Lasswell, 1941; Little 1971; Masland and Radway, 1957; Mazuri and Rothchild, 1967; Moskos, 1971c, 1973b, 1977b; Nauta, 1971; Ney, 1966; Nisbet, 1973; Rappoport, 1962; Roucek and Lottich, 1964; Sarkesian, 1972, 1973; Segal 1974; Segal, et al., 1974; Stahl, et al., 1980; Strauss, 1971; Taylor and Bletz, 1974; van Doorn, 1965, 1966, 1968, 1970, 1977a, 1977b; van Gills, 1971; Wamsley, 1972.

5. The many debates on the draft are relevant (Tax, 1967) to the idea that military service places special demands and obligations on citizens. Few researchers, on the other hand, examine the social claims effected *after* such service is performed. In the United States the central issue appears to be the equity of various coercion strategies. Also relevant in this area would be the work of Janowitz (1977b) on the developing nations where he argues cogently that the civilianization of forces poses threats to the democratic order. For a richer examination of the many issues raised by the draft see: Beusse, 1975; Blair and Backman, 1976; Blum, 1972; Bucky, 1973a; Carmichael and Mead, 1951; Cutright, 1974; Evans, 1969; Feld, 1975; Fisher and Disario, 1974; Fisher and Hartford, 1973; Fritzsch, 1972; Glass, 1970; Hackel, 1970; Holbrook, 1971; Janowitz, 1977a, 1973b, 1975a, 1976; Janowitz and Moskos, 1974, 1979; Karpinos, 1972, 1975b; Latham, 1974; Lee and Parker, 1977; Leigh and Berney, 1971; Levy, 1972; Marmion, 1971; McNall, 1973; Miller and Tollison, 1971; Millet and Trupp, 1981; Moskos, 1967; Murray, 1972; O'Sullivan and Meckler, 1974; Smith, 1948; USARI, 1977; U.S. Senate, 1978; van Doorn 1975b; Vitola, 1977; Wamsley, 1969a, 1969b; White, 1968.

The social implications of the 'draft-debates' for the deviance creation process have, unfortunately, not received much attention from students of social deviance. Nor have the ideological underpinnings of much of the current research. There are at least three reasons for this: 1. Much of the research takes the problematic aspects of varied populations as "given"—as an outcome instead of as a process of competing interest groups (Rubington and Weinberg, 1981); 2. Psychiatric language and vocabularies (Mercer, 1965) often form the dominant background from which inclusion and exclusion decisions are made; and, 3. There is a tendency for individual deficiencies to be seen in lieu of structural issues (Mills, 1943; Ryan, 1976). For sociologists of the military there seems to be a reluctance to envision changes in the purposes to which the state uses the military form and the social acceptability of these shifts.

To illustrate, consider the issue of Black participation in the armed forces. During World War II, when Blacks were excluded from participation in the military authority structure and largely from the combat role as well, the "issue" of minority participation was seen in terms of *military effectiveness*, i.e., Can they competently serve? Can they fight? Can they lead? With desegregation of the forces—and Blacks increasingly filling military roles—*other criteria* involving the purposes to which the military was being put emerged. During the Vietnam War, there was little question as to whether or not Blacks were 'capable' of military performance: indeed they were disproportionately serving in the combat arms.

An astute observer might note the "historical trick" played on Black soldiers who were denied the heroic recognition they would have received *if* the Vietnam effort were seen as credible. In this case, I would argue, the characteristics of *the audience* not the actors had radically shifted. The social meaning of being a veteran has much to do with the social climate wherein wars are conducted and less to do with the martial qualities of the troops.

For more information on Black participation in the U.S. armed forces see: Badillo and Curry, 1976; Bahr, 1970; Barbeau, 1970; Berfun and Meeland, 1958; Beusse, et al., 1976; Borus, 1972; Browning, 1973; Butler, 1976; Cox and Krumholtz, 1958; Cutright, 1974; Dalfiume, 1966; Davenport, 1947; DOA, 1971; Dwyer, 1953; Hall, 1947; Hastie, 1942, 1943; Hausrath, 1967; Janowitz and Moskos, 1974; Leigh and Berney, 1971; Mandelbaum, 1952; Mason, 1947; McGonogal, 1973; Millet and Trupp, 1981; Moskos, 1966, 1969, 1971b, 1973b; Mueller, 1945; Murray, 1972; Nail, et al., 1974c; Nordlie, 1973; OASD-EO, 1971; Prattis, 1943; Schnexnider, 1973a, 1973b; Star, 1958; Stillman, 1968, 1969; Sutton, 1973; Terry, 1984; USARI, 1977; U.S. Senate, 1978; Vitola, 1974; Weigert, 1974; Weil, 1947; White, 1968; Willis, 1972.

6. Maintaining Order: The Commander's Options

Conformity to the norms of complex organizations can be achieved in a number of ways ranging from, and including, internalization of appropriate norms to the application of sanctions to rule violators. Perhaps the most widespread, and obvious technique used by commanders to decide which type of controls are appropriate, is based upon the surveillance of their charges through the informal friendship networks which mingle with, and ultimately center on, the formal "chain of command" which places the commander at the apex of a formal group responsible to him alone.

In this chapter I am concerned with the decision of commanders to use explicitly legal controls—the military courts—to insure compliance in the ranks. Such decisions are of interest because military commanders have, in fact, many more options than do their control agent counterparts in other settings and legal sanctions are a last resort drawn from a rather rich and varied array of possibilities.

These include:

A. Restrictions: Imposed by direct word of mouth, or through the use of NCO subordinates. These can include, but are not limited to quarters, base or certain travel limitations requiring a pass or permission. Also included are restrictions of physical movement, for example being required to stand at attention for longer than normal periods.

B. Punishments: Administered under Article 15, which can include reductions in grade, punitive or disciplinary duties such as housekeeping tasks, confinement, or physical activities.

C. Classification: A soldier's occupational classification can be changed by commanders. Extra assignments are possible, occupational classifications can be modified, temporary duties given as incentives (for training, for example) or withdrawn (a commander must approve all personnel actions involving a soldier). Soldiers can be re-assigned, re-located, transferred, upgraded or downgraded in the occupational structure without a trial. The politics of "strength utilization" as a social control concern has been ignored by most researchers. For example, the "unit manning document" is an excellent control tool used by the personnel division in accord with the wishes of commanders. Since few occupational specialties are "fully manned" to authorized strength, for example, there are always shortages and imbalances within some skill-fields. So a soldier of a given rank may, in fact, actually perform duties requiring more or less responsibility and grade. Conformers not only get "choice duty" within a given job setting, but non-conformers get to do the least desirable tasks. In the daily round of work, this can mean that someone gets to fill the coffee-pot, and someone else has to clean the latrine. In more extreme cases, certain soldiers are sent to the front, and others avoid such assignments. Manpower utilization decisions, additionally, are quite invisible to most troops and are usually attributed to "luck" or "the way things are" (Stevenson, 1976). The fact that personnel commanders routinely make *manpower utilization decisions* (and use these precise terms), however, belies the likelihood of random assignments.

D. Bad Paper Discharge (discussed in Chapter III). Military institutions are also structured so that a commander's perceptions of appropriate soldierly behavior are easily disseminated through mandatory monthly "Commander's Briefings to the Troops," in base or post newspapers, and by word of mouth.

7. Technically, sanctions are imposed by the commander after the suggestions of the court are written up for his decision. In a strict sense, to be court-martialed is to be accused. Acquittal rates, however, in the U.S. Army are historically low (Gale, 1969) and get smaller as the severity of the offense increases. For all practical purposes, to be brought before the court is to be convicted. Critics of the military have interpreted this to mean that military justice is, in fact, not justice at all (Sherrill, 1970). Apologists for the military have noted that the procedural guarantees of the military court far exceed those in civilian settings for the same type of offense (Borro, 1973). A more neutral stance would likely be that the military is a conscientious bureaucracy as well as a coercive one. A historical-legal perspective (Moyer, 1972) would support this view. I thus take court-martial rates to be synonymous with conviction rates. This is also in keeping with common usage by enlisted men in the services. When it is said that a man is to be court-martialed; it is to mean that he will be convicted by a military court.

When the decision is made to use the courts, the commander has all the evidence—and legal advice as to "what will stand up." Simply put, acquittals (all other things being equal) should be expected to be even rarer than they are—and probably can be attributable to the inexperience, or idealism, or professionalism (depending on one's view) of the non-career JAG officers who defend the troops at a Summary Court.

Perhaps the most important reason for low acquittal rates is the fact that social control in the military is cumulative. Deviance amplification (Lofland, 1969) is much more likely than in civilian life. There are few "first time" offenders with regard to military rules. By the time in a soldier's social control career, i.e., his past experience with control agents, reaches the courts he is likely to have broken a number of rules.

The argument is put forth by Bryant (1974b) that military training requires *all* soldiers to break *some* rules. To the degree that this is the case, the ritualistic function of court activity is underscored. For a fuller understanding of the military justice system consult: Berger, 1946; Bishop, 1968, 1974; Black, 1976; Borro, 1973; DoA, 1960, 1970; Finn, 1971; Fulton 1971; Harding and Richards, 1971; Hughes-Morgan, 1977; Jacobs, 1978; Jernigan, 1973; Karlen, 1973; King, et al., 1972b; Landing, 1973; Lermack, 1972; McCallum, 1946; McDonaugh, 1945a; Moyer, 1972; Pearlman, 1976; Radine, 1977; Rivkin, 1970; Sherrill, 1970; Starr, 1973; Szasz, 1973; Technical Report, 1977; USGPO, 1973, 1974; U.S. Senate, 1962, 1966, 1078; Veterans Administration Report, 1971.

8. Court-Martial Rates

TABLE 2.8. DEPARTMENT OF DEFENSE COURT-MARTIAL RATES PER 1,000 ACTIVE DUTY STRENGTH IN THE MILITARY SYSTEM, 1941–1979.

Year	DoD Court-Martial Rate*
1941	114
1942	149
1943	152
1944	182
1945	136
1946	134
1947	251
1948	542
1949	443
1950	480
1951	296
1952	301
1953	330
1954	299
1955	289
1956	271
1957	264
1958	250
1959	208
1960	212
1961	213
1962	204
1963	175
1964	116
1965	114
1966	100
1967	105
1968	104
1969	116

1970	115
1971	120
1972	111
1973	110
1974	112
1975	104
1976	80
1977	62
1978	55
1979	54

*Rounded (Fiscal Years).

Note: The Department of Defense does not record system court-martial statistics. Data were obtained for each branch. During the years 1941–1948 the DoD was composed of three branches (Army, Navy, Marines); thereafter, the Air Force joined the system as an independent branch. The rates presented represent courts-martial per thousand active duty strength in the military system. This was computed by summing the branch rates and dividing by three (1941–1948); and, by four thereafter (1949–1979). The overall average rate of court-martial in the DoD is thus presented, per year.

It is also possible to compute overall court-martial rates using a weighted average method, i.e., to divide the total events in the system by total system strength and multiply by 1,000 for the rate. This method produces much lower rates than shown in my chart. It also assumes that men serve in the system, not in branches. This becomes a crucial factor when the high strength, low punishment, Air Force is combined with the low strength, high punishment Marines, for example. To demonstrate, consider 1978 (the lowest year of court activity for the Air Force, and also one of the lowest years for the other branches as well). My average DoD court-martial rate (all branches) is 55.17 per 1,000 DoD strength. The overall rate (weighted average method) is 10.18. But Air Force Strength in 1978 was 573,421; whereas Marine strength was 172,426. The court-martial rate per 1,000 Airmen was 1.73 per 1,000 Air Force Strength. The court-martial rate in the Marines per 1,000 Marine Strength was 28.9. Obviously, when the Air Force was part of the Army (before 1949) the weighted average figure is even lower than the average annual overall rate I report. There is obvious ideological mileage to be gained by using a weighted average method if one wishes to produce low rates per 1,000 troops in the system.

Discounting the fact that court-martial rates are incidences, not prevalences, and that the "true" event rate may be elusive and subject to ideological interpretation, the *pattern* for the DoD is clear whichever method is used. This can be proven by assuming that my method is an over-estimation, and that the weighted average method is an underestimation of the elusive "true" event rate. The *range of variation* using either method is over a factor of 10 (as measured from the minimum to the maximum observed values in the rates).

Sources: Departments of: The Air Force (DAF, Letters of 23 Dec 81 and 8 Jul 82); The Army (DoA, USA J: Letter of 6 Jul 82); The Navy (DN,HQJAG: Letter of 26 Jan 82), and Defense (DoD-OASD, Letter of 14 Jun 82—Manpower, Reserve Affairs and Logistics).

9. Branch Court-Martial Rates

TABLE 2.9. BRANCH COURT-MARTIAL RATES PER 1,000
ACTIVE DUTY STRENGTH BY BRANCH (*): 1941–1979.

Year	Army*	Navy*
1941	48	41
1942	54	61
1943	62	61
1944	69	80
1945	59	58
1946	39	70
1947	107	112
1948	390	111
1949	127	117
1950	164	121
1951	103	85
1952	97	74
1953	116	73
1954	97	71
1955	90	56
1956	88	54
1957	92	65
1958	82	65
1959	66	55
1960	62	54
1961	69	51
1962	68	47
1963	60	39
1964	42	24
1965	43	24
1966	35	25
1967	35	25
1968	38	20
1969	50	17

1970	40	17
1971	36	20
1972	32	14
1973	27	15
1974	28	16
1975	21	17
1976	13	16
1977	11	16
1978	10	14
1979	10	17

Rounded (Fiscal Years).

(BRANCH COURT-MARTIAL RATES—CONTINUED)

Year	Marines*	Air Force* (1)
1941	76	
1942	100	
1943	88	
1944	98	
1945	55	
1946	75	
1947	96	
1948	120	
1949	125	74
1950	128	67
1951	66	43
1952	77	54
1953	98	54
1954	87	43
1955	104	39
1956	89	41
1957	68	40
1958	73	31
1959	62	25

1960	75	22
1961	75	19
1962	71	18
1963	63	14
1964	43	7
1965	43	5
1966	37	3
1967	42	3
1968	42	3
1969	47	3
1970	54	3
1971	61	3
1972	62	4
1973	65	4
1974	64	4
1975	64	3
1976	49	2
1977	33	2
1978	29	2
1979	25	2

*Rounded (Fiscal Years).
Source: Chapter endnote 8.
(1) Note: The Air Force became an independent service branch in 1949. The Army Air Corps court-martial rates are thus included in the Army figure until 1948. Thereafter independent Air Force figures are reported.

9. Branch Preferences For Harshness

TABLE 2.10. BRANCH PREFERENCES FOR HARSHNESS

2.10.1. U.S. ARMY MILD SANCTIONING RATES

Year	Summary*	All*	Percent Summary
1941	31	48	64.2
1942	33	54	61.0
1943	36	62	59.0
1944	39	69	56.3
1945	34	59	58.1

1946	21	39	54.1
1947	69	107	64.2
1948	311	390	79.6
1949	80	127	63.2
1950	108	164	65.8
1951	73	103	70.8
1952	58	97	59.7
1953	66	116	56.8
1954	54	97	55.3
1955	48	90	52.9
1956	47	88	53.4
1957	52	92	56.3
1958	48	82	58.6
1959	41	66	61.5
1960	38	62	60.7
1961	41	69	60.0
1962	41	68	60.5
1963	32	60	53.3
1964	17	42	39.3
1965	17	43	39.3
1966	13	35	36.3
1967	9	35	26.6
1968	8	38	20.0
1969	9	50	18.7
1970	10	40	25.5
1971	12	36	32.8
1972	13	32	40.9
1973	9	27	32.1
1974	7	28	24.2
1975	5	21	25.3
1976	3	13	19.7
1977	3	11	24.1
1978	3	10	25.2
1979	3	10	30.7

*Rounded (Fiscal Years).

2.10.2. U.S. NAVY SUMMARY COURT-MARTIAL DATA

Year	Summary*	All*	Percent Summary
1941	17	41	40.8
1942	30	61	49.5
1943	29	61	48.6
1944	37	80	45.9
1945	28	58	47.9
1946	42	70	60.3
1947	57	112	50.4
1948	58	111	51.7
1949	59	117	50.6
1950	65	121	53.7
1951	47	85	54.8
1952	47	74	63.1
1953	47	73	64.4
1954	48	71	67.4
1955	36	56	64.9
1956	33	54	61.3
1957	41	65	62.0
1958	40	65	62.5
1959	38	55	67.6
1960	36	54	65.9
1961	34	51	66.2
1962	31	47	67.3
1963	24	39	61.0
1964	10	24	43.7
1965	11	24	46.2
1966	11	25	44.9
1967	11	25	42.7
1968	9	20	42.5
1969	8	17	45.2
1970	8	17	45.7
1971	9	20	45.6

1972	8	14	55.2
1973	8	15	53.0
1974	7	17	41.3
1975	6	17	37.9
1976	7	16	41.3
1977	8	16	50.4
1978	7	14	47.8
1979	9	17	52.0

Rounded (Fiscal Years).

2.10.3. U.S. Marine Corps Court-Martial Data

Year	Summary*	All*	Percent Summary
1941	33	76	43.7
1942	49	100	49.1
1943	44	88	49.9
1944	55	98	55.8
1945	25	55	46.3
1946	38	75	50.9
1947	51	96	53.1
1948	60	120	50.0
1949	65	125	52.1
1950	65	128	51.1
1951	35	66	53.5
1952	40	77	51.8
1953	44	88	50.4
1954	45	87	52.1
1955	55	104	52.6
1956	46	89	51.1
1957	33	68	49.3
1958	41	73	57.1
1959	37	62	60.8
1960	44	75	59.3
1961	45	75	59.8

1962	41	71	58.3
1963	33	63	52.8
1964	18	43	41.5
1965	18	43	41.8
1966	16	37	42.4
1967	17	42	41.4
1968	17	42	41.2
1969	22	47	46.7
1970	23	54	43.1
1971	32	61	52.7
1972	31	62	49.4
1973	32	65	49.3
1974	24	64	37.9
1975	23	64	36.7
1976	19	49	38.5
1977	13	33	39.0
1978	10	29	36.0
1979	11	25	44.3

*Rounded (Fiscal Years).

2.10.4. U.S. Air Force Court-Martial Data

Year	Summary*	All*	Percent Summary
1949	54	74	73.0
1950	52	67	77.2
1951	31	43	72.6
1952	37	54	69.8
1953	36	54	68.1
1954	30	43	70.2
1955	27	39	67.7
1956	28	41	69.7
1957	29	40	72.5
1958	23	31	74.8
1959	19	25	75.0
1960	16	22	73.5
1961	14	19	74.5

1962	14	18	77.2
1963	9	14	65.1
1964	4	7	50.0
1965	2	5	40.7
1966	1	3	30.3
1967	1	3	30.9
1968	1	3	28.7
1969	1	3	23.0
1970	0**	3	14.8
1971	0**	3	11.0
1972	0**	4	6.1
1973	0**	4	3.9
1974	0**	4	3.2
1975	0**	3	4.4
1976	0***	2	4.3
1977	0***	2	2.2
1978	0***	2	2.9
1979	0***	2	2.6

* *Rounded (Fiscal Years).*
** *More than 1 per 10,000.*
*** *More than 1 per 100,000.*
Source: Chapter endnote 8.

10. Traditional Forces Court-Martial Rates By Type

TABLE 2.11. BRANCH COURT-MARTIAL RATES BY TYPE.
TRADITIONAL FORCES COURT-MARTIAL RATES
ARMY, NAVY, MARINES: 1941–1948

2.11.1. SPECIAL COURTS-MARTIAL

Year	Marines*	Year	Navy*	Year	Army*
1941	38.8	1941	22.7	1941	12.8
1942	44.4	1942	26.8	1942	19.3
1943	40.0	1943	28.4	1943	22.5
1944	38.9	1944	39.0	1944	27.2
1945	24.9	1945	22.8	1945	21.6

1946	30.4	1946	20.5	1946	10.5
1947	35.9	1947	42.7	1947	31.1
1948	48.2	1948	43.5	1948	63.2

2.11.2. SUMMARY COURTS-MARTIAL: 1941–1948

Year	Marines*	Year	Navy*	Year	Army*
1941	33.0	1941	30.7	1941	16.6
1942	49.3	1942	33.1	1942	29.6
1943	43.9	1943	36.5	1943	29.1
1944	54.5	1944	38.9	1944	36.8
1945	25.3	1945	34.3	1945	28.0
1946	38.3	1946	21.1	1946	42.3
1947	51.2	1947	68.5	1947	56.5
1948	59.9	1948	310.8	1948	57.6

2.11.3. GENERAL COURTS-MARTIAL: 1941–1948

Year	Marines*	Year	Navy*	Year	Army*
1941	3.7	1941	1.4	1941	4.4
1942	6.7	1942	4.6	1942	1.9
1943	4.0	1943	3.6	1943	2.8
1944	4.3	1944	4.4	1944	3.1
1945	4.5	1945	7.7	1945	3.2
1946	6.5	1946	7.4	1946	7.5
1947	9.3	1947	12.9	1947	7.1
1948	11.8	1948	10.2	1948	16.3

*Rounded (Fiscal Years).

2.11.4. Special Court-Martial Rates, All Branches: 1949–1979

Year	Marines*	Year	Navy*
1949	47.8	1949	47.8
1950	48.8	1950	49.2
1951	26.7	1951	35.8
1952	31.7	1952	24.8
1953	36.7	1953	23.3
1954	33.3	1954	20.5
1955	42.5	1955	17.9
1956	36.1	1956	19.2
1957	29.4	1957	23.9
1958	27.7	1958	22.9
1959	21.6	1959	16.9
1960	28.4	1960	17.7
1961	29.3	1961	16.7
1962	28.4	1962	14.8
1963	28.3	1963	14.6
1964	24.1	1964	13.0
1965	24.2	1965	12.5
1966	20.4	1966	13.4
1967	23.1	1967	14.1
1968	22.7	1968	11.4
1969	22.8	1969	8.8
1970	27.8	1970	8.9
1971	26.7	1971	10.5
1972	28.0	1972	6.0
1973	29.9	1973	6.6
1974	37.7	1974	9.4
1975	37.7	1975	40.0
1976	28.0	1976	8.8
1977	19.0	1977	7.7
1978	17.5	1978	7.1
1979	13.3	1979	7.9

Rounded (Fiscal Years).

2.11.5. RATES OF SPECIAL COURTS-MARTIAL

Air Force*	Year	Army*
16.4	1949	38.2
12.9	1950	48.0
10.2	1951	25.1
14.9	1952	33.8
14.8	1953	42.7
10.4	1954	36.7
10.7	1955	35.0
10.4	1956	33.7
9.4	1957	34.6
6.7	1958	30.0
5.2	1959	22.8
5.0	1960	22.2
4.1	1961	25.4
3.5	1962	25.2
4.2	1963	26.1
3.0	1964	24.0
2.4	1965	24.4
2.1	1966	21.1
2.0	1967	24.3
2.0	1968	28.9
1.9	1969	39.0
2.4	1970	28.1
2.6	1971	21.9
3.1	1972	16.7
3.3	1973	16.3
3.3	1974	18.5
2.5	1975	13.3
1.5	1976	8.8
1.5	1977	6.5
1.5	1978	6.2
1.9	1979	5.2

*Rounded (Fiscal Years).

11. Summary Courts-Martial Rates

TABLE 2.12.1. BRANCH COURT-MARTIAL RATES BY TYPE - CONTINUED
SUMMARY COURTS-MARTIAL RATES, ALL BRANCHES: 1949–1979

Year	Marines*	Year	Air Force*
1949	65.1	1949	54.2
1950	65.2	1950	51.7
1951	35.1	1951	31.5
1952	39.8	1952	37.4
1953	44.4	1953	36.5
1954	45.2	1954	30.3
1955	54.6	1955	26.7
1956	45.5	1956	28.2
1957	33.4	1957	28.7
1957	41.4	1958	23.3
1959	37.4	1959	18.7
1960	44.2	1960	15.9
1961	44.8	1961	13.8
1962	41.3	1962	13.9
1963	33.1	1963	9.1
1964	17.8	1964	3.6
1965	18.1	1965	2.0
1966	15.7	1966	1.1
1967	17.2	1967	1.0
1968	17.3	1968	1.0
1969	21.7	1969	.7
1970	23.4	1970	.5
1971	32.3	1971	.4
1972	30.5	1972	.2
1973	31.8	1973	.2
1974	24.2	1974	.1
1975	23.4	1975	.1
1976	18.7	1976	.1
1977	12.9	1977	0**

| 1978 | 10.4 | 1978 | .1 |
| 1979 | 11.2 | 1979 | .1 |

Rounded (Fiscal Years).
**More than 1 per 100,000.*

TABLE 2.12.2. BRANCH COURT-MARTIAL RATES BY TYPE - CONTINUED
RATES OF SUMMARY COURT-MARTIAL

Army*	Year	Navy*
80.1	1949	59.2
107.8	1950	65.1
72.7	1951	46.5
57.6	1952	46.8
65.7	1953	47.1
53.8	1954	48.1
47.8	1955	36.0
46.8	1956	32.8
51.8	1957	40.5
48.1	1958	40.4
40.7	1959	37.5
37.6	1960	35.7
41.2	1961	33.7
41.3	1962	31.4
31.8	1963	23.5
16.7	1964	10.4
16.8	1965	10.9
12.8	1966	11.1
9.3	1967	10.7
7.6	1968	8.6
9.3	1969	7.5
10.2	1970	7.9
11.7	1971	9.2
13.0	1972	7.8
8.6	1973	7.8
6.7	1974	6.9

5.2	1975	6.3
2.6	1976	6.5
2.5	1977	8.1
2.5	1978	6.7
3.4	1979	8.8

Rounded (Fiscal Years).

TABLE 2.12.3. BRANCH COURT-MARTIAL RATES BY TYPE - CONTINUED GENERAL COURTS-MARTIAL RATES, ALL BRANCHES: 1949–1979.

Navy*	Year	Army*
10.0	1949	8.4
7.0	1950	8.0
2.5	1951	4.8
2.5	1952	5.1
2.7	1953	7.2
2.7	1954	6.9
1.6	1955	7.5
1.5	1956	7.2
1.7	1957	5.6
1.4	1958	4.0
1.0	1959	2.7
.8	1960	2.2
.5	1961	2.1
.4	1962	1.8
.5	1963	1.8
.4	1964	1.8
.2	1965	1.5
.2	1966	1.3
.2	1967	1.3
.3	1968	1.6
.3	1969	1.6
.5	1970	1.8
.5	1971	2.1
.3	1972	2.1
.3	1973	1.9

.3	1974	2.3
.3	1975	2.1
.4	1976	1.9
.3	1977	1.5
.2	1978	1.3
.2	1979	1.7

Rounded (Fiscal Years).
Source: Chapter endnote 8.

Chapter III. Organizational Reaction: "Bad Paper" Discharges

> In reacting to any situation of potential "trouble," different regimes might well make different assessments of, or, we might also say, invoke difference tolerance limits. These assessments will most likely be influenced by various factors not yet mentioned—including the regime's overall existing strength and degree of legitimacy, the other problems it simultaneously faces, its commitment to certain goals, its current reading of public opinion, and its perceptions of, and dealings with, diverse and possibly competing special interest groups.
> — E. M. Schur, *The Politics of Deviance*, (1980, 72–73)

This chapter will follow the movement of organizational reaction rates to social deviance in one institution: the U.S. military. The central question is this: If organizational reaction to deviance indicates the tolerance limits of commanders with regard to certain *kinds* of behavior performed by soldiers, how have such limits changed over time?

Under examination are the rates at which soldiers are discharged under "less than honorable" conditions. Such discharges remove the soldier from the organization, but also leave a stigma that follows into civilian life. For this reason discharges under conditions of stigma are called "Bad Paper Discharges." They are virtually irreversible, and terminal concerning the soldier role. Even in those rare instances where the type of discharge has been changed by subsequent litigation (appeals and court contests), the soldier is never re-admitted to the ranks.

The unit of analysis in this chapter is the entire military system, i.e., the Department of Defense (DoD). While discharge data by branch of military service are, in fact, unavailable (only the overall rates of discharge are reported by the

DoD) my concern is not with the situated, contextual determinants which individual soldiers face. Nor with those forces which may influence larger groups of troops, or even the service branches themselves.

Indeed, there are likely to be some differences in branch-specific discharge patterns, as there would be expected to be, for example, by theatre of operations, military occupational specialty, tenure in the ranks, or any combination of these factors. I have chosen to ignore all of these (and many others) for three reasons. First, the military-as-an-institution is a legitimate object of study. Second, military service requirements neatly divide members of the host society into two mutually exclusive groups: those who serve and those who, for whatever reason, do not. Cohorts of citizens thus are called to perform *military service*, broadly defined, and my interest in this chapter focuses on the kinds of discharge decisions which were made as varied numbers of citizens were called to arms.

Third, the variation in the rates at which the service branches produce populations of discredited personnel is likely to be small when measured against the overall pattern of discharges in four decades. This, however, is an assumption which is based on the quite notable secular trend for all service branches, discussed in Chapter II, toward an *institutional* pattern of court usage. Whether or not, in fact, discharge outcomes resulting from military service may be more branch or system specific is, of course, an empirical question. A partial answer is provided in Chapter IV (Containment and Expulsion) and Chapter VII (The Volume of Deviance in the Army).

THE DISCHARGE SYSTEM: THE SOCIAL CREATION OF VETERANS

When a soldier completes his contractual stay of military service he is issued a discharge document removing his soldierly status and attesting to the "general character and quality" of the service rendered. The five types of discharge correspond to the military's general assessment of the soldier's performance[1] and determine his subsequent eligibility for privileges and benefits granted veterans by the state. Military discharges are given to enlisted men under both "honorable" and "less than honorable" conditions (Starr, 1973).

Table 3.1 lists the types of military discharge, condition designations, and the ranges of the rates per one thousand discharged enlistees.

"Bad Paper" refers to the stigma associated with three of the five types of discharge. Two of these, Bad Conduct and Dishonorable Discharge, are the outcome of a court-martial.

The table shows that as the severity of the stigma associated with the differing types of discharge increases, the number of such discharges decreases.

The characteristics of each discharge are summarized below.

56

TABLE 3.1. DISCHARGE TYPES, CONDITIONS OF DISCHARGE, AND RANGES OF RATES PER 1,000 ENLISTED DISCHARGEES (DoD) (ALL BRANCHES) FISCAL 1941–79.

Type	Conditions	Range Per Thousand
Honorable	Honorable	931–986
General	Honorable	20–84
Undesirable	Less Than Honorable	1–49 Admin. "Bad Paper
Bad Conduct	Less Than Honorable	1–20 "Bad Paper" (Court-martial)
Dishonorable	Less Than Honorable	.5–12 "Bad Paper" (Court-martial)

Source: Letter/DoD/OASD: 1982

ADMINISTRATIVE DISCHARGES: COMMANDERS' ASSESSMENTS OF CHARACTER, PERSONA, AND COMPLIANCE

The Honorable Discharge: Given to over 90% of all enlisted veterans, denotes proficiency in the performance of duties. Starr (1973, 169) notes that a soldier with one or two minor infractions of military discipline (i.e., Article 15s for minor offenses) will usually be given an Honorable Discharge. Such dischargees are entitled to all veteran benefits and re-enlistment eligibility.

The General Discharge: Granted under "honorable conditions" with regard to veterans benefits, but without appeal rights. The "Discharge Authority", i.e., commanding officer of a base or post, in these cases has classified the soldier's service as "neither sufficiently meritorious to warrant an Honorable Discharge, nor sufficiently egregious to warrant a discharge "Under Less Than Honorable Conditions" (1973, 169). Since type of discharge, i.e., honorable or less than honorable, is noted, and also coded, on a man's discharge document (DDform214), stigma can be detected in the formal screening process for employment in government positions and it is also likely in tight labor markets, for any position requiring scrutiny of a veteran's character of military service.

General Discharges are usually given for unsuitability. This category includes any individual characteristic not readily changeable by punishment, but detrimental to the soldier role. Specifically, deviants so classified are seen to have medical and psychiatric conditions. The official categories for "unsuitability" (Rivkin, 1970, 315) are:

- inaptitude.
- character and behavior disorder.

- apathy.
- alcoholism.
- enuresis (bedwetting).
- homosexuality—homosexual tendencies, desires, or interests, without homosexual acts.

All of these dispositions involve judgments concerning the *persona* of soldiers in the eyes of commanders. They are typifications (Kitsuse: 1962) which are seen to discredit the uniform but only seriously enough to warrant its forced and premature removal. General dischargees are seen to have social deficiencies derived more from an assessment of their essential *being* than from outright rule violation. These soldiers have broken the soldierly mores and something is 'being done" about it. The line being drawn here is a social statement concerning the military's intolerance of certain *attributes*.

These classifications are statements concerning what *kind* of person is considered non-remediable to military authorities. They define the range of acceptability for soldierly being. Steps will be taken to remove any individual who does not fall within this range. General dischargees are entitled to full veterans' benefits as they may be available upon discharge, without review from the Veterans Administration. General dischargees are not, however, eligible to re-enlist. Both general and honorable dischargees, having served under honorable conditions, are not stigmatized upon returning to civilian life. The line so drawn is designed not so much to punish the veteran as to hasten his creation.

The Undesirable Discharge: This disposition carries heavy penalties in civilian life. It is most frequently given for drug abuse, and frequent acts of misconduct, but also for homosexual acts, conviction by civil authority of an offense involving "moral turpitude" or imprisonment for more than one year (Starr, 1973, 169–70). Rivkin (1970, 313–15) notes that Undesirable Discharges denote "unfitness' which the military categorizes in the following manner:

1. Frequent incidents of a discreditable nature with civil or military authorities.
2. Sexual perversion including but not limited to –
   A) Lewd and lascivious acts.
   B) Indecent exposure.
   C) Indecent acts with, or assault upon, a child.
   D) Other indecent acts or offenses.
3. Drugs/chemicals, etc.
   A) Drug addiction, habituation, or the unauthorized use, sale, possession, or transfer of any narcotics, hypnotics, sedatives, depres-

sants, hallucinogens, or other known or habit-forming drugs and/
or chemicals or the introduction of such drugs and/or chemicals
into any Army installation or other Government property under
Army jurisdiction.

B) The unauthorized sale or transfer of marijuana.

C) The unauthorized use or possession of marijuana.

4. An established pattern of shirking.

5. An established pattern showing dishonorable failure to pay just debts.

6. An established pattern showing dishonorable failure to contribute adequate support to dependents, or failure to comply with orders, de-
crees, or judgments of a civil court concerning support of dependents.

7. Homosexual acts—as opposed to desires, tendencies or interests.

These *behavior patterns* (Clinard and Quinney, 1973) are defined as outside the
limits of morally acceptable soldierly *conduct*. Only one (No. 4, "shirking") is job-
related, i.e., concerned with the performance of soldierly work. The rest concern
off-duty behavior, i.e., patterns of sexual behavior, family responsibilities, substance abuse and prior interactions with the legal system. In the latter case, prior
punishments from military or civilian authorities have been meted out.

In addition to unfitness and unsuitability, Undesirable Discharges can also
be given for "Misconduct" which includes Fraudulent Entry, Civilian Crimes,
AWOL and Desertion.[2]

Those who receive an Undesirable Discharge are entitled to veterans benefits
only by petitioning the Veterans Administration which will determine on a "case
by case" basis if eligibility criteria are met. This is done for *each* benefit and requires a substantial amount of time. Thus, these veterans are virtually excluded
from consideration for benefits although there is no legal obstacle to their being
granted.[3]

The Undesirable Discharge forces a premature release from the soldier role.
When this occurs, the typical transition from military to civilian status—which
a discharge represents—places the soldier into a new social category: that of the
stigmatized veteran. In the eyes of their commanders, such soldiers have trans-
gressed norms more serious than presenting deficient personas but less serious
than criminality.

Honorable, General and Undesirable Discharges are granted by the commanding officer (the "Discharge Authority") of a post or base. They are a commander's way of releasing those who: 1) have fulfilled their military obligation
with approval (Honorable), 2) cannot meet the requirements due to inability or

inaptitude (General), and 3) fail to meet the behavioral requirements appropriate for soldiers (Undesirable).

These three types of discharge are administrative in that they require no further action other than that of the commander, and in this sense they are routinely issued and thought of as a normal prerogative of command: those rights privileges and responsibilities that are associated with the office of a military leader. In this case, the formal certification of the character of services rendered by enlistees. Of the three types of administrative discharges given, only the Undesirable Discharge is considered bad paper. The other two types of bad paper discharge are explicitly designed to be *punitive*. These are described below.

THE PUNITIVE DISCHARGES: CRIMINALITY

There are two types of expressly punitive discharge that are the result of prior court-martial action: The Bad Conduct Discharge (BCD) and the Dishonorable Discharge (DHD). These are given under "less than honorable" conditions and are the last in a sequence of formal sanctions applied by military authorities (i.e., the "Convening Authority" in a court-martial) which affect a soldier while he remains in, and after he leaves, military service. That is, soldiers who receive BCDs and DHDs also receive other "in-service" sanctions—usually a fine, reduction grade, and/or confinement—in *addition* to a bad paper discharge.

DISHONOR

The DHD is the only *mandated* type of bad paper discharge—for murder and spying (USGPO, 1969). It is given for very serious crimes against the person and property as a maximum sanction, at the discretion of the court, as well as for other offenses which have a civilian analogue (such as assault and rape). It is also given (USGPO, 1969) for some that are more nebulous in terms of their warranting such severe consequences, such as writing a bad check (over $100.00); missing a movement (by design); disobeying a lawful order from an officer; for wounds which are self-inflicted, and desertion (protracted absence).

While I do not have data on variation in the composition of DHD types over time and how these may have changed, i.e., the relative distribution of spies, bad check writers and deserters, etc., I am willing to assume that DHD offenders unambiguously represent cases where commanders felt the need to use the maximum sanctions available. Less grievous dispositions are handled with the Bad Conduct Discharge (BCD).

BAD CONDUCT

The BCD is given for crimes against person and property that are less severe than offenses which would warrant a DHD such as AWOL, disobeying the lawful order of the NCO; property damage under $100, and most minor thefts as well as, for example, missing a movement (by neglect), and writing a bad check (under $100.00). Both forms of punitive bad paper can also be given for repeat offenses which, in and of themselves, need not have been sufficiently grievous to warrant either form of maximum sanction, but rather which occurred within one year of the present charge. The Manual for Courts-Martial (USGPO, 1969) specifies two prior offenses make a defendant eligible for a BCD; and, three for a DHD. In this manner the military expels repeat offenders, and in doing so, creates *felons* in the literal sense.

The movement of bad paper discharge rates represents the varying distribution of *management decisions* concerning the moral fate of certain enlistees in the military. The decisions to expel and stigmatize (versus retain, reform or punish) are judgments concerning the severity of controls deemed necessary by commanders, for which the responsibility is theirs alone. The resultant patterns are the aggregative product of summed individual decisions which characterize the changing punitive climate in the military.

This point was well made in a study concerning the use of psychiatric selection criteria in the U.S. Navy. Although a different concern was at issue in this research, the conclusion holds true for a precise statement of the *control requirements* of the officer corps vis-à-vis enlisted personnel. J. A. Plag, et al., note:

> The failure of Naval personnel to make a satisfactory adaptation to the demands of service life may be manifested in a variety of atypical behaviors. *All* of these are readily reduced, however, to *line decisions* which are ultimately made with regard to whether an enlistee is, or is not, recommended for re-enlistment by his *Commanding Officer*. (Emphasis mine). Plag, et al. (1970, 8).

It should be noted that there are very few known cases where the disposition of a dischargee moves in a direction counter to the collective judgments of his superiors in the chain of command—as embodied in the judgment of his commander. When this does occur it is exceptionally rare and usually requires the marshalling of external organizational support as might be the case when the ACLU or an activist group might take the case as being representative of a larger *issue* with which they are already concerned and are attempting to politicize. Unless such organizations are willing to make a test case, the word of the commander is final for the vast multitude of discharge actions (Bishop, 1974; Jacobs, 1978).

Chart 3.1 examines Bad Paper applied through administrative and legal channels for the Department of Defense. Bad Paper discharge rates are expressed in terms of a percentage of total troop strength, i.e., the number of events divided by the total number of soldiers on active duty on a yearly basis multiplied by one hundred.

This indicator is not distorted by fluctuations in force size brought about by expansion and contraction. I have chosen to report expulsions with bad paper as a percent of strength for stylistic reasons. One percent of strength is, of course, equal to a rate of 10 per 1,000: which is accepted usage for social rates standardized to a common population base (Matras, 1973).

The distribution of Bad Paper Discharges (BPDs) in the military has three peaks with considerable fluctuation. There are, however, a number of striking similarities concerning the movement of the BPD rate toward the three minima

CHART 3.1. DEPARTMENT OF DEFENSE. BAD PAPER DISCHARGE RATES (UNDESIRABLE + BAD CONDUCT + DISHONORABLE DISCHARGES) AS A PERCENTAGE OF TOTAL TROOP STRENGTH: 1941–1979

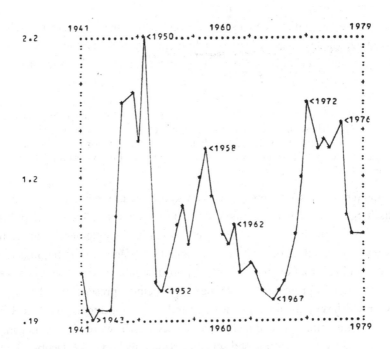

Key: For every 100 active duty soldiers in 1950, 2.2 received BPDs.
Note: Tabular data appear in chapter endnote 4 (Fiscal Years).

and its rapid acceleration thereafter to reach maximum values. For each war the BPD rate reached bottom in the early stages of mobilization (1943, 1952, 1967). Thereafter, the rate began to increase. There were some notable differences between the wars in terms of acceleration and the corresponding size of the post-war increases.

VARIATION IN THE BAD PAPER DISCHARGE RATE

The Bad Paper Discharge (BPD) rate was at its lowest when the military was in the process of mobilizing for war. For World War II and Korea, the quite dramatic increases in the BPD rate: tenfold and fivefold, respectively, were essentially post-war occurrences. The fivefold increase during the Vietnam period, however, occurred during wartime. Vietnam Era soldiers thus received disproportionately more bad paper than the veterans of Korea and World War II com-

CHART 3.2. TYPES OF PUNITIVE BAD PAPER IN THE DEPARTMENT OF DEFENSE EXPRESSED AS A PERCENTAGE OF TOTAL STRENGTH: 1941–1979.

PAIR	SERIES	SERIES	SYMBOL
1	Year	BCD	A ‹Bad Conduct Discharges
2	Year	DDH	B ‹Dishonorable Discharges

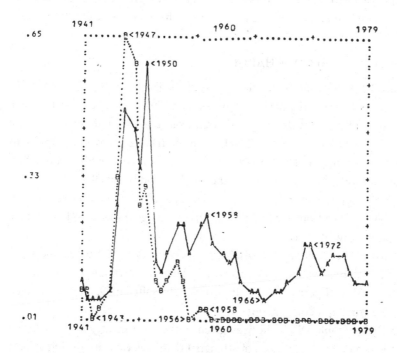

Key: For every 100 active duty soldiers in 1962, .01 received a DHD; in 1947, .65 received a DHD.
Note: Tabular data appear in chapter endnote 5 (Fiscal Years).

bined: more than did the post-Korean peacetime soldiers, but not as much as the soldiers who served in the post-world War II period. Since bad paper discharges differ in severity and mode (administrative vs. punitive) the distribution of discharges by *type* is quite important as it reflects the relative emphasis on court and commander initiated reactions to deviance, as well as the distinction between criminality and other sanctionable conduct.

COURT SPONSORED BAD PAPER

Of the three types of bad paper discharge, two—the Dishonorable and the Bad Conduct discharge—are imposed by the courts. These sanctions differ from normal court-martial dispositions in that they are expressly designed to expel a soldier from the ranks *in addition* to imposing penalties which are served while he remains in uniform. An examination of the patterns of court imposed bad paper discharges addresses the issue of when, and to what degree, commanders saw fit to expel felons from the military.

The two types of punitive discharge are the outcomes of a court-martial process, and they are strongly associated with each other (R= .808) over time. This is consistent with the findings on court activities, in general, discussed in Chapter II (Courts-martial). There are, however, significant differences in magnitude and frequency. I will first examine the movement of the more severe of the two sanctions: The Dishonorable Discharge.

THE DISHONORABLE DISCHARGE

Chart 3.2 shows that the maximum use of the DHD was in the post-World War II period. During the period 1946–1948, the DHD was the most frequently used type of punitive discharge. Viewed from the 1943 minimum (.02% of strength—which represented 1871 DHDs) the DHD rate grew quite rapidly to .65% of strength in 1947 (10,275 DHDs). This represented roughly a thirty-fold rate increase and a fivefold increase in the absolute number of DHDs.

The DHD rate, however, fell almost as quickly as it had risen reaching a low in 1952—well into the Korean build up—(.07% of strength) that stood quite near, but slightly below, its 1945 value (.08% of strength).

The use of the Dishonorable Discharge has been somewhat dated and short lived when one reviews the forty-year period. The concentration of DHDs in the post-World War II period, and their virtual disuse after 1959, allows for some interesting cross-war comparisons.

The Dishonorable Discharge was given with much greater frequency during the Korean War (max= .15% of strength) than was the case during World War II (max= .08% of strength); or during the Vietnam War (fewer than .02%

of strength during the entire war: 1964–1973) and thereafter. While post-World War II soldiers were treated much more harshly than their comrades who served during the war, the reverse was true for post-Korean troops who received proportionately fewer DHDs during the period of peace than were meted out to their brothers in arms who had served during that conflict. In addition, those who served in the entire post 1960 military received fewer Dishonorable Discharges than did those who served during World War II. The burden of maximum "dishonor," however, was experienced by the post-World War II peacetime army and those who served in the Korean War, as the raw and percentaged data in Notes 4 and 5 will attest.

THE BAD CONDUCT DISCHARGE

Overall, the Bad Conduct Discharge (BCD) rate followed the DHD rate with two notable exceptions in direction and one in magnitude.

During the years 1949-50 the BCD rate almost doubled to its 1950 maximum while the DHD rate was declining.

The BCD rate rose steadily from its 1966 minimum (.06% of strength) to maximum in 1972 (.18% of strength; roughly a three-fold increase)—essentially during the Vietnam War—when the DHD rate was negligible.

Excepting the burst of post-World War II activity—which more or less corresponded with a like pattern in the DHD rate—the BCD rate was essentially cyclical. The absolute and relative movements of the BCD rate are best understood by referring to the comparative movements of the DHD rate as detailed below.

MOVEMENTS IN PUNITIVE BAD PAPER

In 1945, the BCD and DHD rates stood at relative parity (.07% and .08% of strength, respectively). By 1947 the BCD rate had increased roughly seven-fold (.50% of strength). This was comparable to the eight-fold increase in the DHD for the same period. This twin movement in *both* severe rates of punitive discharge clearly marks the aftermath of World War II as a period of highly punitive sanctions. After 1947, the punitive discharge rates moved in different directions. While the DHD rate continued to decline, the BCD rose rapidly between 1949 and 1950 to its maximum (1950= .59% of strength). The BCD rate fell quite sharply thereafter, reaching a minimum in 1952—well into the Korean buildup—as did the DHD rate.

The punitive discharge rates rose into the end of the Korean War (1954), and declined together thereafter; with the decreases in the DHD being much more substantial—leading to an eventual damping of that rate. After 1958, for all practical purposes, the BCD rate "became" the punitive discharge rate as the DHD rate had essentially vanished.

After 1958, the BCD rate began an eight year gradual decline to minimum in 1966 (.06% of strength) and a six year gradual increase to .18% of strength, 1972). The decline in this case was larger than the three-fold increase. Thus, each maximum of the BD rate, after the high in 1950, was somewhat less than its predecessor, documenting a long term decline in the rate with cyclical periods of activity.

When the overall trend of the BCD rate is examined in terms of the three wars, the greatest amount of BCD activity occurred during Korea (fiscal 1954= .24% of strength), followed by the Vietnam War (1972= .18% of strength) and World War II (1945= .07% of strength). Stated differently: the Vietnam War BCD rate was roughly twice the World War II rate, which was, in turn, roughly one third of the rate prevailing during the Korean War.

PEACETIME PUNITIVE COMPARISONS

Then one examines BCD rates during peacetime a somewhat different picture emerges which is influenced by the extreme BCD activity in the post-World War II period. Post-World War II soldiers received more BCDs than any group of soldiers who served in any of the wars; and more than any other group of peacetime soldiers as well. Also, BCD rates tended to be higher after a war than during one—except for the Vietnam War where the 1972 maximum (.18% of strength) stood higher than any post-Vietnam peacetime value.

With the relative composition of punitive bad paper discharges in mind, I will now examine the overall movement of Bad Paper Discharges broken into its two components: administrative and punitive. Chart 3.3 examines Administrative discharges (Undesirable Discharges) and punitive bad paper. The overall movement in punitive bad paper represents the military's reliance on legal controls whereas the Undesirable Discharge rate reflects commanders' decisions to bypass the requirements of court-martial. In effect, this is a decision to purge the ranks of certain kinds of deviants in a more expedient manner than would be the case in a formal trial procedure. While it is, of course, true that both types of bad paper must sum to 100%, i.e., all bad paper, and thus only one type need be plotted, I have graphed both rates for ease of visual comparison.

Two clear trends are common to the period under review.

1. With the passage of time there was a notable increase in the use of administratively given Undesirable Discharges.

With the exception of the years 1946–48—when punitive discharges were at their height (and modal)—Undesirable Discharges were the most frequent form of bad paper discharge.ff

CHART 3.3. DEPARTMENT OF DEFENSE: THE CONTRIBUTION OF
COURT AND COMMANDER IMPOSED BAD PAPER DISCHARGE TYPES
TO ALL BAD PAPER GIVEN. EXPRESSED AS A PERCENT OF THE BPD
RATE. 1941–79.

	X	*Y*	
PAIR	*SERIES*	*SERIES*	*SYMBOL*
1	*YEAR*	*ADPAP*	*A ‹ADMIN. BAD PAPER*
2	*YEAR*	*CPAP*	*B ‹COURT PAPER*
NUMBER OF ORDERED PAIRS		*39*	

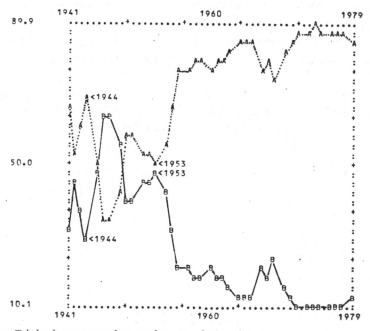

Note: Tabular data appear in chapter endnotes 4 and 5 (Fiscal Years).

Looked at somewhat differently, after 1951 both punitive and administrative rates were relatively stable and roughly equal (UDR= .26% of strength; PDR=
.22% of strength). From 1953 on, the administrative rate *rose more rapidly* than the
punitive rate declined. This produced an excess of administrative paper after
1953.

This excess can be used to chart the relative reliance of commanders on administrative versus punitive discharges. Ergo, I used a "net" rate calculated by
subtracting the punitive discharge rate (BCDs + DHDs) from the administrative
discharge rate (UNDs). This is plotted in Chart 3.4.

The logic of *subtracting* discharge rates is theoretically grounded in the notion
that commanders, in fact, have a dispositional choice with regard to expulsions

with stigma. Did they use the courts? Did they use other than court channels? The issue of differing target populations, i.e., the non-substitutability of offender types, will be explicitly treated in Chapter VI (Containment and Expulsion) and Chapter VII (The Volume of Deviance in the Army).

Chart 3.4 can be read as an indicator of commanders' willingness to expel wayward soldiers through administrative (Undesirable Discharge) as against court (BCD + DHD) channels. There has been an unmistakable upward secular trend for commanders to increasingly rely on the Undesirable Discharge in lieu of processing through the military courts. The sole exception to this trend occurred during the end, and aftermath, of World War II (1945–1948) when "felonizaton" of the troops became the norm for those receiving bad paper. NB: all punitive discharges are felony class, that is: federal crimes. The numerical value of "net"

CHART 3.4. DEPARTMENT OF DEFENSE. ADMINISTRATIVE (UNDs)
MINUS PUNITIVE DISCHARGE (BCDS + DHDs) RATES EXPRESSED AS
A PERCENTAGE OF STRENGTH. 1941–1979*

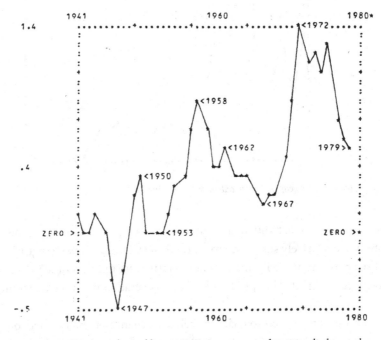

KEY: *For every 100 active duty soldiers in 1947, .5 more received punitive discharges than received administrative discharges; in 1972, 1.4 more received administrative discharges than received punitive discharges.*
*Note: The 1980 value set to unity to locate the zero difference point.
Sources: Chapter endnote 4 and 5 (Fiscal Years).

represents the difference from parity, or the size of the increase of administrative over court imposed bad paper.

When one examines the distribution of bad paper discharges during and after each war, a *common reactive pattern* emerges: for each war a turning point is reached before war's end which apparently sets the pattern for the duration and thereafter.

For the early part of World War II (1942, 1943) punitive and administrative discharge preferences were roughly equal, and 1944 saw a mild increase in administrative discharge rates. By 1945, there was a clear punitive trend which lasted until sometime in 1948. Korea showed the same pattern of relative stability during 1951–1953; by 1954 the pattern was set—with a reversal of the severity of the sanctions vis-à-vis the World War II experience. The gradual increase in the undesirable discharge rate continued until the rate reached maximum in 1958. This was followed by a nine-year move toward equality of the rates which stopped in 1967—three years into the Vietnam War.

This characteristic of the BPD rate made the early part of the Vietnam War similar to the wars which preceded it. In 1967, commanders could (following the logic that all wars are similar) take one of two paths: to equalize the rates, or to prefer one over the other. Some oscillation occurred before a trend was established. After 1969 the pattern was clear—commanders were not going to the courts. They began to purge the ranks via an increasing reliance on the Undesirable Discharge. In 1972, when the rate differential reached its maximum—while the war was still being waged—more administrative bad paper was issued than at any other time during the period under review.

SUMMARY: THE STRUCTURE OF BAD PAPER

The Bad Paper Discharge (BPD) Rate is composed of three components. The first (Undesirable Discharge) is administratively applied, while the second (Bad Conduct Discharge) and third (Dishonorable Discharge) require a court-martial. The latter are expressly punitive. I can thus speak of overall trends in the bad paper discharge (BPD) rate; in administrative paper (UDs); and in punitive paper (BCDs + DHDs). These trends were:

1. The Bad Paper Discharge (BPD) Rate has fluctuated widely, but had three peaks. The variation in the Bad Paper Discharge Rate centered around three maxima (1950, 1958, 1972). Commanders' preferences for Bad Paper Discharges reached their peaks during three *quite different* social contexts. The first peak (1950) was the climax of a disproportionate amount of *punitive* bad paper given after World War II. The second (1958) occurred within a clearly defined "peace" period. The

third (1972) occurred during the latter part of the Vietnam War. This last wave was smaller than the first, but larger than the second.

2. There has been a long term decline in the use of punitive bad paper. This was caused by two major shifts in the punitive components (DHD + BCD) of bad paper.

   A) The DHD rate peaked (1947) and then declined to virtual disuse. In 1947, when the DHD reached maximum (.65% of strength), it was the most common form of *punitive* bad paper *as well as* the *typical* form of bad paper discharge. By 1959, the DHD rate was fewer than two hundredths of 1 percent of strength.

   B) The BCD rate declined in a cyclical manner: each of its peaks (1950, 1958, 1972) was progressively smaller than its predecessor. Each peak in the BDC rate coincided with the maximum of the overall Bad Paper Discharge Rate.

3. Administrative bad paper usage has been increasing regularly. The increase in commanders' preferences for the Undesirable Discharge have been steady and rapid. After 1953, the UDR has been growing faster than the punitive component of bad paper has been shrinking—resulting in a partial replacement of punitive with administrative bad paper.

Of the three types of bad paper, administrative paper (i.e., Undesirable Discharge) is the most interpretive—and negotiable—statement concerning soldierly conduct. The UD involves a more direct, personal statement on the part of a commander than do the punitive forms of paper since the "rule of law," as this is normally meant concerning systems of law, i.e., evidence, trial, witnesses, judicial procedure, etc., is waived. Simply put, the commander has much more *discretion* than in punitive proceedings—although the ultimate decision is, of course, his in all types of sanctioning.

Theoretically, there always have been more ways of reacting to social deviance in military settings by labeling such individuals "Undesirable" and expelling them, than there are of adjudicating them felons. While the rate at which these types of decisions have been made is historically variable, the *long term* trend is toward the identification of troops who are seen by commanders as apparently having difficulties presenting themselves as soldiers. This change in emphasis with regard to organizational reaction is directed against offenders defined as less than criminal, and is becoming increasingly important in the modern military.

NOTES: CHAPTER III

1. The following is quoted from Landing (1973, 35):

> The five types of discharge are intended to reflect the character of an individual's service. The discharge categories—Honorable, General, Undesirable, Bad Conduct and Dishonorable—complement four official denominations of character of service: Honorable, Under Honorable Conditions, Under Other Than Honorable Conditions, and Dishonorable. The Honorable and Dishonorable Discharges correspond to the Honorable and Dishonorable character of service designations: the General Discharge corresponds to the Under Honorable Conditions designation: and the Bad Conduct and Undesirable Discharges correspond to the Other Than Honorable Conditions designation. The character of service appears in the service record, Form DD 214, given to the serviceman at separation. The type of discharge appears only in the discharge certificate, a separate document.

2. Rivkin (1970: 315-316) summarizes the grounds for Misconduct, Fraudulent Entry, AWOL, and Desertion as follows:

> Fraudulent Entry: involves common misrepresentations, most are *concealments*: concealment of prior service, alien identity, civil court conviction of more than one year, criminal record, juvenile offender status, medical defects, AWOL or Desertion from prior service, other disqualifications. Conviction by civil court: "If an individual has been convicted by a civil court, state or federal, of a crime for which penalty under the UCMJ would be confinement for more than one year, the Army *may* discharge him. If the crime is one of "moral turpitude" which usually means a sex offense, the Army may discharge him even if the penalty imposable would be less than a year in jail. The soldier may be retained in the service if he has received a decoration, or for any other reason the discharge authority considers sufficient. AWOL and Desertion are grounds for an administrative discharge for misconduct.

Rivkin also notes, "It is emphasized that none of the above grounds for discharge is mandatory upon a commander. In all administrative discharges the commander is given the broadest possible discretion to retain soldiers in the Army, even after a board of officers has recommended discharge."

3. Paul Starr (1973, 176) notes:

> According to the law, benefits are available to all veterans who received discharges "under conditions other than dishonorable". Anyone who received a Dishonorable Discharge is unambiguously excluded from benefits, as is someone issued a Bad Conduct Discharge by general court-martial. Undesirable Discharges and Bad Conduct Discharges issued by a special court-martial constitute the "gray area". "A veteran who seeks benefits from the VA applies to his local office, where he will be asked for his discharge papers. If the applicant has a Bad Conduct Discharge, the VA will advise him that his application must be sent to the regional office for an eligibility determination. At the regional level an "adjudicator" will examine the applicant's entire file, supplied by the military service involved, and then rule whether the veteran engaged in moral turpitude or persistent and willful misconduct." (Starr, 177). "Ordinarily, the VA keeps no statistical records on benefit applications from veterans with undesirable and bad conduct discharges. A Study of a five-month period in 1972, however, noted that only 1,305 applications for educational benefits were received from men with bad discharges. Of these, ninety-one were approved. During this same period more than 4,000 veterans with bad discharges applied for unemployment compensation. (Although the benefits are dispensed by the Labor Department, eligibility determination are made by the VA.) Of the 4,000 men who applied, 3,400 were found ineligible. Ninety-seven of the cases involved veterans with drug related

discharges: six of these were approved. As one VA official remarked after seeing these statistics, Undesirable and Bad Conduct Discharges are effectively the same as a Dishonorable Discharge in terms of eligibility for veterans' benefits." (Starr, 179).

In addition to the letters cited from the Department of Defense, materials in this chapter were drawn from DoD (1972, 1978, and 1979).

4. Department of Defense Discharge Data

TABLE 3.2. DoD DISCHARGE DATA (FISCAL YEARS)

Strength (BODDD), Number of Undesirable Discharges (UDs), Bad Conduct Discharges (BCDs), and Dishonorable Discharges (DHDs). 1941–1979.

Year	BODDD	UD	BCD	DHD
1941	1801000	6447	1807	1488
1942	3859000	6187	2427	2574
1943	9045000	10676	4959	1871
1944	11452000	25488	6432	4824
1945	12124000	19505	8769	10033
1946	3030000	10411	7963	10254
1947	1583000	10082	7840	10275
1948	1399000	11477	6145	8402
1949	1615000	14036	5735	4243
1950	1460000	19170	8616	4501
1951	3249000	8387	4286	2864
1952	3685000	8528	4278	2683
1953	3555000	10617	5985	3606
1954	3302000	17597	7831	5002
1955	2935000	20041	6764	2758
1956	2806000	16291	7392	369
1957	2796000	27075	6452	995
1958	2601000	30717	6653	588
1959	2504000	23196	4838	369
1960	2476000	16227	4149	304
1961	2484000	14594	3572	163
1962	1808000	13202	2774	173
1963	2700000	13541	2461	97
1964	2687000	13743	2330	98

1965	2655000	13178	2088	55
1966	3094000	10544	1784	72
1967	3377000	9741	2565	65
1968	3548000	11707	2886	34
1969	3460000	12392	3662	187
1970	3066000	20911	3964	375
1971	2715000	29139	4737	325
1972	2323000	36345	4167	356
1973	2253000	29049	2906	434
1974	2162000	29336	2988	315
1975	2128000	27015	3587	193
1976	2081000	30721	3435	229
1977	2074000	18104	2349	190
1978	2069000	15054	1823	160
1979	2049000	14759	1914	291

Source: Chapter endnote 3.

5. Department of Defense Computations

TABLE 3.3. DoD UNDESIRABLE DISCHARGE RATE (UDR) AS A PERCENTAGE OF STRENGTH: 1941–1979.

Year	UDR*	BCDR*	BCDR*	CMOUT*	BPRAT*
1941	0.36	0.1	0.1	0.18	0.54
1942	0.16	0.06	0.06	0.13	0.29
1943	0.12	0.05	0.05	0.08	0.19
1944	0.22	0.06	0.06	0.1	0.32
1945	0.16	0.07	0.07	0.16	0.32
1946	0.34	0.26	0.26	0.6	0.94
1947	0.64	0.5	0.5	1.14	1.78
1948	0.82	0.44	0.44	1.04	1.86
1949	0.87	0.36	0.36	0.62	1.49
1950	1.31	0.59	0.59	0.9	2.21
1951	0.26	0.13	0.13	0.22	0.48
1952	0.23	0.12	0.12	0.19	0.42
1953	0.3	0.17	0.17	0.27	0.57

1954	0.53	0.24	0.24	0.39	0.92
1955	0.68	0.23	0.23	0.32	1.01
1956	0.58	0.16	0.16	0.17	0.75
1957	0.97	0.23	0.23	0.27	1.23
1958	1.18	0.26	0.26	0.28	1.46
1959	0.93	0.19	0.19	0.21	1.13
1960	0.66	0.17	0.17	0.18	0.84
1961	0.59	0.14	0.14	0.15	0.74
1962	0.73	0.15	0.15	0.16	0.89
1963	0.5	0.09	0.09	0.09	0.6
1964	0.51	0.09	0.09	0.09	0.6
1965	0.5	0.08	0.08	0.08	0.58
1966	0.34	0.06	0.06	0.06	0.4
1967	0.29	0.08	0.08	0.08	0.37
1968	0.33	0.08	0.08	0.08	0.41
1969	0.36	0.11	0.11	0.11	0.47
1970	0.68	0.13	0.13	0.14	0.82
1971	1.07	0.17	0.17	0.19	1.26
1972	1.56	0.18	0.18	0.19	1.76
1973	1.29	0.13	0.13	0.15	1.44
1974	1.36	0.14	0.14	0.15	1.51
1975	1.27	0.17	0.17	0.18	1.45
1976	1.48	0.17	0.17	0.18	1.65
1977	0.87	0.11	0.11	0.12	1
1978	0.73	0.09	0.09	0.1	0.82
1979	0.72	0.09	0.09	0.11	0.83

*Rounded (Fiscal Years).
* Rounded (Fiscal Years).
** Less than 1 per 10,000 strength.
***More than 1 per 100,000 strength.

5. DoD Percentage Computations – Continued.

TABLE 3.4. ADMINISTRATIVE (ADPAP) AND PUNITIVE (CPAP) BAD PAPER AS A PERCENT OF THE BPD RATE: 1941–1979.

Year	ADPAP*	Year	CPAP*
-1941	66.18	1941	33.82
1942	55.30	1942	44.70
1943	60.98	1943	39.02
1944	69.37	1944	30.63
1945	50.92	1945	49.08
1946	37.36	1946	63.63
1947	35.76	1947	64.24
1948	44.10	1948	55.90
1949	58.45	1949	41.55
1950	59.37	1950	40.63
1951	53.98	1951	46.02
1952	55.06	1952	44.94
1953	52.54	1953	47.46
1954	57.83	1954	42.17
1955	67.79	1955	32.20
1956	77.38	1956	22.62
1957	78.43	1957	21.57
1958	80.92	1958	19.08
1959	81.67	1959	18.33
1960	78.47	1960	21.53
1961	79.62	1961	20.38
1962	81.75	1962	18.25
1963	84.11	1963	15.89
1964	84.99	1964	15.01
1965	86.01	1965	13.99
1966	85.03	1966	14.97
1967	78.74	1967	21.26
1968	80.04	1968	19.96
1969	76.30	1969	23.70

1970	82.82	1970	17.18
1971	85.20	1971	14.80
1972	88.93	1972	11.07
1973	89.69	1973	10.31
1974	89.88	1974	10.12
1975	87.83	1975	12.27
1976	89.34	1976	10.66
1977	87.70	1977	12.30
1978	88.36	1978	11.64
1978	87.00	1979	13.00

*Rounded (Fiscal Years).
Source: Chapter endnote 3.

CHAPTER IV. CONTAINMENT AND EXPULSION

Soldiers identified as having broken military rules may be punished while remaining in uniform, or expelled from the organization with stigma. These possibilities have differing implications for deviance theory and may bear on the accuracy of the kinds of assumptions commonly made concerning the utility of soldiers. This chapter concerns the decisions made by commanders to manage deviant populations by containing or expelling them.

Time series data on court-martial rates for the Department of Defense (DoD) are divided into two broad categories with regard to whether or not stigmatized soldiers were punished within the confines of the military system—or punished and expelled. The dispositions of enlisted offenders who have appeared before the courts for various types of offenses are examined in light of utilitarian and normative explanations of organizational reaction to deviance.

These patterns are then compared with the rates of expulsion via administrative Bad Paper Discharge and the overall trend in expulsions and containment through commander and court channels is analyzed.

CENTRAL ASSUMPTIONS FOR DEVIANCE MANAGEMENT

If, following Kai T. Erikson,

> Each society regulates the flow of deviant persons to and from the boundaries of the group, and in this way governs the amount of deviance in the structure at any given time...(1966, 27).

decisions to expel or contain deviant soldiers define the *deployment pattern* used by military commanders. That is, the containment or expulsion of different offender-types provides a measure of how the tolerance of the leadership may vary with regard to different kinds of behaviors seen as deviant.

Such decisions are part of a changing *ethos of control*: a collective mood which characterizes commanders' assessments of what is, and what is not, considered acceptable soldierly conduct. The deployment pattern measures the degree to which certain managerial decisions were made with regard to expulsion.

Numerous social forces may operate to identify certain soldiers as objects for punishment. All may be classified, however, as fitting into one of the three general requirements for a deviance creation process: action, interaction, and reaction (Scarpitti and McFarlane, 1975).

Action refers to the universe of deviant acts. Soldiers may vary in the frequency with which they break the rules. Interaction concerns the process wherein control agents interpret the actions of soldiers and classify them; as well as the role played by social negotiation, rules of procedure, and consensus in identifying "what was done" and how serious it may be to the interests of the group. Reaction involves the social processing of identified offenders and an assigning of punishment (because of "what was done") by the group's representatives to the offender. Reaction to deviance occurs at the very end of a complex social process. My data address the dispositions that have been made by commanders concerning expulsion from the organization.

While I have no way of knowing which social forces act to single out certain soldiers for punishment, or what is going through the minds of commanders who initiate a given reaction pattern, I can accurately gauge the *kinds* of decisions that were made concerning containment and expulsion, and how these varied. This permits speculation as to the possible functions that various containment and expulsion strategies may serve in the military.

Containment and expulsion patterns, however, are subject to constraints having their origin in certain distinctive properties of the military system, as well as normative limitations concerning the symbolic importance of the soldier role.

For example, while mobilization for war places a premium on the value of soldiers to the organization, it also escalates the demands made upon them. In like manner, a peacetime army is set to drill, practice and endlessly prepare for military tasks without benefit of a martial context.

While the military, at war, may require more from the troops than they can produce, such organizational expectations are consonant with the ideals of soldiering. *Soldiers*, after all, fight, take risks, expose themselves to hardship, and follow rules and procedures uncommon in civil contexts.

A soldier in the peacetime army, on the other hand, is asked to behave as if his daily tasks have martial urgency which, of course, they do not. These conditions create constraints on commanders charged with punishing rule-breakers.

Variable rates of expulsion over time may drain the organization of scarce manpower or may suggest laxity or indecision with regard to which norms should be enforced by making an expulsive example. Which set of conditions generates more stress for the military is partially resolved by examining the degree to which the kinds of social controls vary across the peace-war cycle, as well as some of the normative and utilitarian constraints which may be operative.

MANPOWER SCARCITY

The recruitment and training of soldiers is costly and time consuming. In addition, manpower utilization proceeds from an assumption uncommon in a market economy, namely that the burden of the development of a soldier's potential *lies with the organization*, not the individual. This was well stated by Janowitz (1972, 166):

> Once a person is admitted into the institution, there is no question that the organization must incorporate him into a functioning role.

One might expect, especially during a war, that commanders would be reluctant to expel soldiers who, in other regards, are able to perform useful work. In addition, the constraint against expelling scarce manpower may work at cross purposes with the apparent need for groups to identify certain types of offenders so as to set examples for potential rule breakers in the ranks. Thus it is possible that the relative size of the stigmatized population may be influenced by the manpower exigencies of war.

CONTAINMENT AND EXPULSION

To the degree that wayward soldiers are contained within the system, they occupy the status of remediants. That is, they serve a fixed period of time in jail, under restriction, at disciplinary assignments, or in a reduced grade. After such time is spent in the remedial role, they re-enter the population of normal soldiers and continue their military careers or obligations.

The soldier role, however, contains a set of behavioral prescriptions (and proscriptions) as well as an implied future claim to the use of organizational resources, status, privilege and benefits based upon conforming to a commander's expectations concerning behavior, bearing, and performance.

To the degree that soldiering is *not* a lifetime pursuit, all who serve in the military have some stake in how members of the host society may come to view their stay in uniform, that is: soldierly conduct is ultimately evaluated in civilian contexts. In this way, commanders are assured that at least part of their sanctioning power is grounded in the allegiance citizens have to the authority of the state.

Soldiers, likewise, are simultaneously constrained as well as protected by the uniforms they wear. True, they must adhere, more or less, to military rules but they are also granted certain license (in time of war) from civil constraints and from numerous middle class conventions as well. For example, greater tolerance in the use of alcohol, male subcultural activities (athletics and marksmanship), male adventure activities (geographic displacement from "roots" and family) and, individualism, as these relate to what most men of similar age experience at home, school or factory (for a discussion see Nisbet, 1976).

While the coercive aspects of the soldier role are well documented—especially as these relate to combat or images of the battlefield—the autonomous aspects of the role are less emphasized. Moskos (1971), for example, has suggested that the enlisted ranks are the last bastion of the "all male subculture," and Beck (1971) has noted that the military can perform essential welfare functions because it is not *primarily* identified as a welfare institution. Additionally, Janowitz (1972) has stressed the adult socialization functions of serving in the enlisted ranks.

Changes in the kinds of deviants expelled by the military may indicate that soldiering varies in the amount of coercion required. The military may also become more or less protective of soldiers at different times. Expulsion rates may also indicate a change in the choice of punishment selected.[1]

For the organization the decision of commanders to expel or contain wayward soldiers contains an evaluative statement concerning the implied remediability of such troops, their value to the organization, and the willingness of the organization to be protective. That is, to withdraw permanently the option for certain soldiers to return to the ranks.

It is my thesis that patterns of containment and expulsion reflect managerial decisions concerning the organizations' response to perceived threats from within. The data address the basic issue of deviance management. How stable have the relative distributions of expelled and contained deviants remained over time? Do certain types of offenders face a different likelihood of being expelled? If so, what does this tell us about the possible functions served by such decisions?

Specifically at issue here are the possible functions of *punishment* in the military system. According to van den Haag, punishment serves three utilitarian functions through incapacitation, reform and deterrence (van den Haag, 1975). The normative, or group boundary defining, properties of punishment are also at issue here (Durkheim, 1960; Mead, 1918).[2]

THE STRUCTURE OF CONTROL

Time series data are available on the overall rate of courts-martial in the Department of Defense, and the rate at which *some* of these trial outcomes result in expulsion. Since all punitive bad paper discharges require court action, subtracting the punitive bad paper rate from the court-martial rate gives a rough approximation of the prevalence of containment.[3]

When the line is drawn to expel a soldier from the system, the military reaches the absolute limit of its control: soldiers so classified are barred permanently from the ranks. How frequently are such lines drawn? What are the magnitudes involved? Are courts-martial essentially a way of instilling internal order which *requires* a substantial number of offenders to remain captives of the organization while serving out their punishment? Or is it possible that expulsion from the ranks allows commanders to rid the organization of deviants it would normally have to remediate?

There are three possibilities with regard to command punishment styles.

1. *Containment*: commanders may opt to punish their troops in a manner which keeps soldiers *inside* the system. This creates a deviant population which can be managed, displayed, or otherwise used to inform conformers of the boundaries beyond which transgressors will be punished. The costs of such decisions are, of course, borne by the military system but manpower so classified remains under military control. The existence of a fairly large number of those in various stages of remediation and punishment would suggest that such sanctioning is primarily for "internal consumption." This population of deviants may be necessary for the purposes of establishing normative boundaries in the system—as well as for the more utilitarian purposes of reform, deterrence and incapacitation—and thereby suggests the possibility that such outcomes may serve to socially support the authority of the commanders in some manner.[4]

2. *Expulsion*: commanders may opt to literally discharge their norm-breakers and by so doing absolve the organization the social cost of maintaining them. Such preferences are clearly *not* cost effective, in the manpower allocation sense. The economic costs of retention and punishment are recoverable through future service, duties performed, and tasks accomplished. On the other hand, the costs of expulsion are final and permanently lost to the organization.

   Expulsion, however, makes reform and incapacitation *impossible*. In fact, from the point of view of social control in the military, expelling a soldier can only be conceived of as a punitive attempt to deter those still remaining under military control.

3. *Balanced Organizational Reaction*: commanders may opt for equal amounts
of both containment and expulsion to meet differing contingencies.

Chart 4.1 examines the percentage contribution of expulsions (punitive bad
paper discharges) resulting from courts-martial.

The chart shows:

1. Those who face the military court are overwhelmingly retained in the
   system. At the height of expulsiveness (1947) over 95% of those court-
   martialed remained within the system. Stated another way, the entire range of variation in the expulsion rate was less than 5 per 100
   courts-martial.
2. Expulsions have dropped dramatically after 1947. In 1952, the expulsion rate was .63%; it only rose sporadically to, or slightly above, 1%
   during 1954-55 and 1957-58. After 1969, expulsions increased steadily,
   but did not exceed 2.2% at maximum (1976).

CHART 4.1. DEPARTMENT OF DEFENSE COURT EXPULSIONS
(PUNITIVE BAD PAPER DISCHARGES) AS A PERCENT OF THE COURT-
MARTIAL RATE: 1941–79.

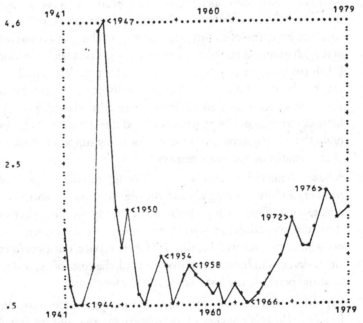

KEY: *For every 100 court-marital events in 1947, 4.6 resulted in a Bad Paper Discharge; in 1972, the
figure was 1.7, and in 1976, it was 2.2. Source: Chapter endnote 5.*
NOTE: *The court-martial rate is already standardized per 1,000 strength (Fiscal Years).*

3. Commanders clearly did not use a balanced strategy of containment and expulsion with regard to offenders facing court-martial. The military does not expel the overwhelming majority of those, by its own definition, who have committed a serious offence in that a court-martial is an indicator of such gravity.

4. The relative movement in expulsions did follow a pattern with regard to the early stages of mobilization for war. In the early years of a war (1942–44; 1951–52; 1964–66) rates of expulsion weakened to their minima (1944, 1952, and 1966), and strengthened thereafter—well into the post war aftermaths. Movements in expulsions were greatest following World War II, essentially negligible after Korea, and relatively high after Vietnam.

To examine the absolute movements in expulsion activity, I have created an indicator (VARM) which measures the variation in court expulsions as a percentage of the court-martial rate as measured from its minimum value. The values for VARM are reported in Note 6.

There are two major findings:

1. With regard to the expulsion of serious offenders, there is a moderate inverse relation between VARM and strength (R = - .288). This suggests that, on average, expulsions for serious offenses appear to be constrained by manpower considerations.

2. There were notable differences across wars. When one looks at increases in the rate of expulsion for each war and its aftermath, World War II commanders were reluctant to expel when the war was being waged, and the highest rates of expulsion occurred thereafter. There is a strong case to be made for the scarcity of manpower argument for the Second World War.

During the Korean War, expulsiveness increased at roughly mid-war, and continued to rise about one year into the aftermath. Then the rate fell slowly and stabilized, with some oscillation. Commanders were clearly not disproportionately expelling peacetime soldiers for serious offenses.

The pattern for the Vietnam War, with regard to expulsions for serious offenses, was distinctive considering that military strength was virtually identical to that of Korea. First, expulsion rates increased steadily from 1966 to 1972. By 1969, the Korean War maximum was exceeded, and expulsions were higher than during World War II. Second, the wind down of the Vietnam War (fiscal 1973–74) saw a distinct difference from the trends for the earlier wars where commanders were expelling at higher rates after the wars, than during their last moments. Third, the pattern for expulsiveness for World War II and Korea was such that after the maximum was reached, there were sharp and moderate declines respectively. After 1974, however, expulsiveness increased until the maximum was reached in 1976. The 1976 rate of expulsions was higher than at any time during the Vietnam War, the decade of peace which preceded it; during the Korean War, or during World War II. Expulsiveness was only greater in 1946–47.

The argument that expulsions for serious offenses are related to what may be called "surplus manpower" basically stands up for World War II and its aftermath, but is less compelling for Korea; is only weakly supported for the peacetime army (1954–64); and clearly doesn't explain the move toward containment in 1973–74 at the end of the Vietnam War.

If one assumes that serious offenders pose a threat to the values of the military system, and for this reason they must be cast out from the ranks, it is clear that, other things being equal, the threat was greatest in fiscal 1941, 1947, 1954 and 1976. This view is obtained when one ignores the *movement* in expulsion rates and focuses on those periods when the values from minimum were largest.

In this view the threat was greatest before and immediately after World War II; at the end of the Korean War, and in the All-volunteer post Vietnam military (1976). Such a threat from within is largely addressed by expulsive decisions made by commanders in the *peacetime* military.

EXPULSIONS FOR LESS SERIOUS OFFENSES

Soldiers may also be expelled from the military, without using the courts, through the commanders' use of the administrative discharge, for less grievous, and essentially non-criminal conduct. Does the pattern for Undesirable Discharge follow the war-peace cycle? Is it related to those periods when serious rule-breakers were being expelled? Chart 4.2 examines variation in the rate of Undesirable Discharge (Administrative Bad Paper) as a percentage of the overall Bad Paper Discharge Rate for the Department of Defense. The graph is constructed by subtracting the minimum value for Administrative Bad Paper (1947 = 35.8% from the value for each year under observation (1941–79). All values are therefore positive and movements toward or away from minimum activity are indicated by the direction of the plot and the respective values identified for each year.

There are two major findings.

1. There is a mild inverse relation between strength and movements in the Undesirable Discharge contribution to all Bad Paper Discharges (R = .240).

This is somewhat smaller than that observed for court expulsions (VARM = -.288) but does offer some evidence that manpower constraints are operative.

2. The trend in the increase of Administrative Bad Paper is only reversed *during* wars.

This occurs earlier in some wars than others, however. The only notable steady decline in Administrative Bad Paper, i.e., a steady decline for at least three years—as opposed to an oscillation—occurred during 1944–47; 1950-53; and during 1966–69. The aftermath of each successive war saw increasing amounts of such discharges issued. In fact, after 1971 more Undesirable Discharges were issued than at any time prior.

CHART 4.2. VARU: VARIATION IN THE PERCENTAGE CONTRIBUTION OF THE UNDESIRABLE DISCHARGE TO THE TOTAL OF ALL BAD PAPER GIVEN IN THE DoD, AS MEASURED FROM THE MINIMUM VALUE: 1941–79.

	X-AXIS	Y-AXIS
SERIES NAME	YEAR	VARU
NUMBER OF ORDERED PAIRS	39	

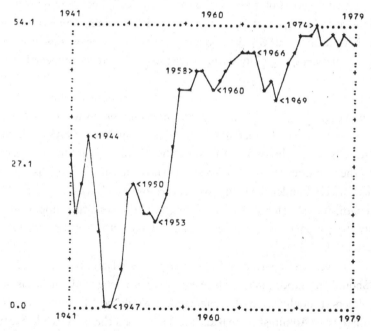

Source: *Chapter endnote 7 (Fiscal Years)*.
Note: *The BPD Rate is standardized per 1,000 strength.*

If the *kind* of offender that receives an Undesirable Discharge can be seen as a threat to military values, the system was under increasing attack in 1944, 1958 and 1974: the years when the rates were at their peak. Such threats are clearly a peacetime phenomenon, with the very glaring exception of the observed peak in

Administrative Bad Paper occurring in fiscal 1944. More on this peculiarity to follow shortly.

One conceivable interpretation may be that perhaps there were simply too many men in the system and that something had to be done to reduce force size. This is unlikely to have been so during World War II, while it might have been plausible in 1958, and perhaps in 1974. An examination of the size of the maximum discharge population, i.e., when the greatest numbers were discharged from the service, reveals that demobilization reached maximum in 1946, 1955 and 1970; much too early for this type of argument to account for the peaks in Undesirable Discharges in peacetime, and too late to account for the World War II observation in 1944.

A partial explanation for the steady rise in administrative bad paper may be that commanders are using such discharges in lieu of the courts. Could it be that *some* of the vast numbers of soldiers who have historically been contained within the system after facing court-martial are increasingly coming to be thrown out without benefit of a trial? My data do not permit a direct answer as post court-martial readjustment or recidivism rates for those who are not expelled are not available.

The actual contribution of the court system to expulsions via the punitive discharge, however, has been shown to vary from its minimum value (VARM). The use of administrative bad paper also varies from its minimum (VARU). Is there any relation between the two? It turns out that there is a mild inverse relation between the two rates (R = -.389). This association, it will be noted, is stronger than that observed under the manpower constraint which was -.288 for VARM and strength; and -.240 for VARU and strength. This is tentative support for the *possibility* that commanders are effecting a trade-off with regard to the type of expulsion used.

It is possible that this trade-off is related to the relative frequency of court usage? Should one expect, in a given year, that after having made the decision to expel soldiers through the courts, commanders would be reluctant to use their discretion to issue Administrative Bad Paper? Stated another way, while it is true that, on average, court usage has been declining—and administrative Bad Paper increasing—to the degree that commanders make the decision to use *either* mode of expulsion, might they be relatively reluctant to use the bad paper option after having used the courts?

To find out, the data on movements in court expulsiveness (VARM) were broken into two periods:

1. Those years when VARM was increasing, and 2) Those years when VARM was decreasing.

Starting with 1942, the value of VARM (the movement in court expulsiveness relative to its minimum value) was compared with the value for the previous year, i.e., 1942 was compared with 1941; 1943 with 1942; and so on. The value for the relative movement in Administrative Bad Paper from its minimum (VARU) is also provided. It is thus possible to measure the movements in administrative bad paper against increases or declines in court expulsions for a given year, and for a series of years.

There were 21 years when court expulsions were increasing relative to the value for VARM in the previous year. This is shown in Table 4.1, with the value for Administrative Bad Paper (VARU) expulsions also given.

From the data in Table 4.1 I found that the overall association between VARMI and VARU when court expulsives was increasing was R = -.562, a notable inverse relationship. Commanders were reluctant to use Bad Paper Administrative expulsions in those years that they were *also* using the courts to expel.

Table 4.2 examines those years when VARM was declining relative to its value for a previous year. There were 17 such years.

The overall association between declining court expulsiveness (VARMD) and Administrative Bad Paper movement (VARU) was R = .007. Commanders, in those years when they were less prone to use the courts, were independently issuing Administrative Bad Paper.

TABLE 4.1. YEARS WHEN COURT EXPULSIONS WERE INCREASING (VARMI) AND THE VALUE FOR ADMINISTRATIVE BAD PAPER EXPULSIONS (VARU).

Obser.	Year	VARMI*	Year	VARU*
1	1944	.04	1944	33.61
2	1945	.65	1945	15.16
3	1946	3.98	1946	.61
4	1947	4.06	1947	0
5	1950	1.38	1950	23.62
6	1953	.32	1953	16.78
7	1954	.81	1954	22.07
8	1957	.51	1957	42.67
9	1958	.62	1958	45.17
10	1962	.30	1962	46.00
11	1964	.28	1964	49.23
12	1967	.25	1967	42.98

13	1968	.30	1968	44.28
14	1969	.46	1969	40.54
15	1970	.74	1970	47.06
16	1971	1.05	1971	49.44
17	1972	1.26	1972	53.18
18	1974	.87	1974	54.12
19	1975	1.21	1975	51.97
20	1976	1.72	1976	53.59
21	1979	1.48	1979	51.25

*Rounded (Fiscal Years).
Source: Chapter endnotes 6 and 7.

TABLE 4.2. THOSE YEARS WHEN COURT EXPULSIVENESS WAS
DECLINING (VARMD) AND THE VALUE FOR ADMINISTRATIVE BAD
PAPER EXPULSIONS (VARU).

Obser.	Year	VARMD*	Year	VARU*
1	1942	19.54	1942	.38
2	1943	25.22	1943	0.0
3	1948	8.33	1948	1.42
4	1949	22.69	1949	.90
5	1951	18.23	1951	.25
6	1952	19.30	1952	.13
7	1955	32.04	1955	.63
8	1956	41.63	1956	.13
9	1959	45.91	1959	.50
10	1960	42.71	1960	.35
11	1961	43.87	1961	.21
12	1963	48.36	1963	.05
13	1965	50.26	1965	.21
14	1966	49.28	1966	.10
15	1973	53.93	1973	.85
16	1977	51.94	1977	1.49
17	1978	52.61	1978	1.26

* Rounded (Fiscal Years).
Source: Chapter endnotes 6 and 7.

DISCUSSION

These data on the responsiveness of administrative to court expulsions are necessarily crude. They are presented, however, in search of any institutional trend which may hold without regard to the war-peace cycle. They address the following question:

> If one looks only at expulsions for severe offenses, i.e., court expulsions (all other things being equal), were commanders also expelling soldiers for less serious shortcomings?

When commanders increasingly relied on the courts, i.e., court expulsions were increasing from their historical minimum value, declining amounts of non-court Administrative Bad Paper was also being given. Declining court issued expulsions, however, had a negligible relation to such bad paper.

This suggests a striking possibility. To the degree that commanders can be thought to select expulsion options for the sake of expulsion per se, the functional substitutability of these options is only partial, and in one direction only: that being in the direction of increased severity of offense.

SUMMARY

Expelling a soldier with stigma is a deterrence strategy presumably necessary to instill order among those remaining in the ranks. Such soldiers thrown out of the military are expelled by the courts or via the administrative discharge. When the courts are used, only a tiny fraction of all those facing them are thrown out. The bulk are retained in the system for punishment.

Since World War II, the manpower scarcity argument as a possible constraint on the rate of court expulsions has been less persuasive with each passing war, and cannot, of course, explain the use of the courts to contain soldiers during peacetime. Commanders have, however, been increasingly issuing Administrative Bad Paper Discharges since the end of the Second World War. They clearly have been reluctant to do so, however, during war: when the greatest declines in administrative paper were clearly noted.

The data clearly show that with regard to expulsions, there is no quota-like relationship involving the *number* of soldiers expelled from the military. There is, however, a certain rigidity in the *type* of expulsion used. When the courts are increasingly used to expel, on average, the administrative bad paper discharge rate contracts.

This affords a speculative possibility. Court expulsions are for extremely grievous offenses, while an administrative expulsion with stigma is given for less serious shortcomings. While a soldier issued administrative bad paper could never have been expelled through the courts, he certainly could have *faced* the courts and been kept within the ranks for punishment. Stated another way, the offense requirements of court warranted expulsions preclude those who would qualify for administrative bad paper, but the expulsion option of commanders could certainly include those whose court disposition falls short of expulsion. Provided, of course, that the courts are not *already* being used to expel.

Court expulsions in the military, however, involve the decision of commanders to use this channel. When commanders were disproportionately doing so they issued correspondingly less administrative bad paper. They did not, however, issue more bad paper when court expulsions were declining, except in 1944: the only year for which increases in bad paper discharges were associated with low levels of court expulsions. If one were to speculate that, perhaps, the courts were clogged at certain times (and thus commanders reluctant to tax the legal system for expulsions) this would not explain the relative stability of the administrative discharge rate when court expulsions were declining. In fact, the vast majority of court action does not result in expulsion, but rather in an increasing number of deviants contained within the system.

It is difficult to construct a utilitarian argument for such a deployment pattern in light of the fact that, on average, those given bad paper discharges are less serious offenders than those contained within. When the more grievous offenders, however, are disproportionately expelled through the courts, commanders expel the less serious at lesser rates. This relation is not a perfect one, but it is quite suggestive that the *ethos of control* operates so as to permit a moderate amount of functional substitution to occur among offender types. It is as if commanders become unwilling to issue bad paper discharges at those times when the courts are imposing quite severe punitive expulsions.

NOTES: CHAPTER IV

Materials from this chapter have been modified and published as: "The Containment and Expulsion of Wayward Soldiers in the U.S. Military" 1988. The Social Science Journal Vol. 25(2), 195-210.

1. While increases in rule enforcement are a good indicator of an increasingly coercive environment, increases in expulsiveness are an indicator of an increasingly punitive one. Whether or not a soldier is being protected or punished by his commander depends, in large part, on the moral authority of the military at a given time. Such punitive expulsions are not conceptually equivalent to coerciveness. An institution may be coercive, but not necessarily punitive. For example, if the military is held in high regard by the host society, a stint in the brig and honorable discharge would be much less punitive for a soldier than a bad paper discharge for a lesser offense. In this regard, the sometimes quite high rates of court-martial in the military discussed in Chapter II, for example, may be rites of passage provided that they do not result in permanent stigma in the civilian society. Expulsions with stigma, on the other hand, are intentional attempts to label certain kinds of offenders in a permanent manner. In this sense all expulsions with stigma are clearly punitive, whether or not they fit the expressly punitive official

designation, as is the case for the "punitive discharges" for criminality, or are of the administrative type for less than criminal offenses.

2. Mead (1913), for example, has argued that hostility to crime is common not because crime is physically damaging, but rather because it runs counter to the values that society cherishes. Being able to locate a type of offender that emerges during war would be one unobtrusive measure of increasing collective sentiments on the part of commanders.

3. While a soldier can face court-martial a number of times, he can only be expelled once. My data show incidence rates, not prevalence statistics, and as such are measures of the level of court processing activity in a given year. For the purpose of measuring the degree of containment, my data show that a certain percentage of courts-martial result in expulsion: the remainder stay in the ranks.

4. This argument has relevance if, and only if, containment rates are fairly high. If large numbers of soldiers face the courts and are kept in the military to be punished, it is clear that such troops cannot readily escape from the system by using the courts. In a recent motion picture (A Soldier's Story, 1984) a drill instructor tells his recruits: "I've got you turkeys now, but your ass belongs to the Army." The point is that the ability of the organization to enforce compliance is pervasive.

5. PEROUTCM: Punitive Bad Paper Discharges and the DoD Court-Martial Rate.

TABLE 4.3. PEROUTCM: THE PERCENT CONTRIBUTION OF PUNITIVE BAD PAPER DISCHARGES TO THE DoD COURT-MARTIAL RATE: 1941–79.

Fiscal Year	PEROUTCM*	VARM*	VARU*
1941	1.61	1.11	30.4
1942	.87	.38	19.5
1943	.50	0.0	25.2
1944	.54	.04	33.6
1945	1.14	.65	15.2
1946	4.48	3.98	.6
1947	4.56	4.06	0.0
1948	1.92	1.42	8.3
1949	1.40	.90	22.7
1950	1.87	1.38	23.6
1951	.74	.25	18.2
1952	.63	.13	19.3
1953	.82	.32	16.8
1954	1.30	.81	22.1
1955	1.12	.63	32.0
1956	.63	.13	41.6
1957	1.01	.51	42.7

1958	1.11	.62	45.2
1959	1.00	.50	45.9
1960	.85	.35	42.7
1961	.70	.21	43.9
1962	.80	.30	46.0
1963	.54	.05	48.4
1964	.78	.28	49.2
1965	.71	.21	50.3
1966	.60	.10	49.3
1967	.74	.25	43.0
1968	.79	.30	44.3
1969	.96	.46	40.5
1970	1.23	.74	47.1
1971	1.55	1.05	49.4
1972	1.75	1.26	53.2
1973	1.35	.85	53.9
1974	1.37	.87	54.1
1975	1.71	1.21	52.0
1976	2.21	1.72	53.6
1977	1.99	1.49	51.9
1978	1.75	1.26	52.6
1979	1.98	1.48	51.3

* *Rounded.*
  Source: Chapter III

Chapter V. The Physical and Social Risks of War

Participation in military organizations exposes soldiers to two fundamental risks: death or injury if they perform their duty and social ostracism if they do not. There are, of course, less central, although sometimes equally debilitating, work associated contingencies that soldiers share with other workers in times of war and peace. These include exposure to disease, accidents, isolation, drink and drugs.

What distinguishes civilian occupational hazards from soldiering, however, is the structure of the soldier role itself. Stouffer et al. have noted:

> The soldier role involves placing a man in a position where he must fight or bear the institutionally sanctioned consequences. (1965, Vol. 1).

While it is not the case that all soldiers fight, many do: and all are faced, to some degree, with this possibility; and all come under varying degrees of organizational control imposed by commanders.

This chapter seeks to explore the relationship between the rates of physical risk associated with battle and the application of social controls by the officer corps. It is guided by the implicit expectation of a relation between the use of social control and the risks associated with battle, and the concern of deviance theorists with the capacity of social organizations to create, and limit, the size of deviant populations under varying circumstances.[1]

SOCIAL RISK AND CONTROL

My first concern is the historical movement of *one* type of severe organizational reaction to social deviance on the part of military commanders: the issuance of Bad Paper Discharges[2] during times of war. The rate at which bad paper is given is viewed as the level of social risk faced by cohorts of troops who served in three wars.

While commanders are aware, to some degree, of social control activities within their domains, in that matters of troop discipline are the routine stuff of staff meetings and ubiquitous briefings, commanders are not usually aware of the activities of fellow officers outside their immediate base, post, command or immediate jurisdiction, much less of the control rates in branches of service other than their own.

Nor can they be, even theoretically, so aware. This poses a dilemma. The structure of the authority system in the military—while essential for social control (McDonagh, 1945a; Janowitz and Little, 1965)—oftentimes retards the "upward and downward flow" of even crucial tactical information (Lang, 1968). Thus, social risk should be viewed as an *emergent phenomenon*, rather than as a policy mandate.

Stated another way, for an individual soldier—as for a civilian before a judge—the merits of a specific case may result in a wide range of possible dispositions. Commanders are doubtless concerned at this point, as well, with drawing an accurate line between the needs of their organizations and what they feel (for whatever reason) is appropriate justice in a given instance. For the military system, however, the rates of such dispositions indicate the degree to which certain populations of enlisted men are deemed by their commanders to be candidates for sanctioned expulsion.

The utility of such individuals as symbolic objects is derived by induction since alternative decisions—less costly to the military, individual soldiers, and the host society—are foregone when bad paper is issued. Additionally, since I have already shown in Chapter IV (Containment and Expulsion) that the more serious offenders are kept within the system, and there is an obvious scarcity of manpower during time of war, it follows that expulsions during war must serve important functions.

Following the thinking of Maury D. Feld, who notes that military service deliberately sets a price on human life (1977, 8), expulsion with stigma sets a deliberate cost on certain types of soldierly non-conformity. Unlike the few medical or criminally mandated stigmatized discharges, however, bad paper is largely a discretionary outcome[3] of commanders.

It is, of course, possible that the social risks of war, as here defined, serve no function at all for the military: that a certain number of troops are bound to run afoul of the rules in any complex organization, and little should be made of this other than it is a fact of organizational life. Were this the case, there would be no reason to expect variation in the rates of control across three wars, and it is also doubtful that much importance could be inferred from an essentially static rate of ostracism.

This premise is central to my line of argument. I assume that commanders produce deviant populations of varied size due to a waxing and waning *collective sense* of the urgency of applying the necessary amounts of stigma to maintain order in the system. My data do not provide the rationale used for such actions, nor suggest the mechanisms whereby such an implied sense of urgency may be communicated to and among those in control of the troops.

I assume, furthermore, that patterned variation in the BPD rate reflects a management characteristic of those in control. It is quite possible to argue otherwise: 1) One can assume the officer cadres are passive agents. 2) One can argue that the BPD rate is influenced by forces more central to the military than the will of its commanders. 3) One can argue that soldierly behavior precipitates organizational reaction in the form of bad paper.

I have chosen to ground my arguments in the presumed symbolism associated with rates of social control. That is, I accept that: 1) the amount of deviant behavior in a group is always larger than the population of identified offenders, 2) the behavior of the officer corps is central to the identification of labeled offenders—thus they are unlikely to be passive, 3) there is no social force more central to the operation of a military organization than the behavior and decisions of its commanders, at least to the degree that such behaviors and decisions influence the rates of social controls applied. The will of commanders is, of course, insufficient to achieve purely military objectives (no commander wishes failure at his appointed tasks) but it is difficult to conceive of discretionary command decisions being unrelated to it.

Lastly, it may be argued that commanders are responding to increased *rule breaking* on the part of the troops during time of war. This possibility is examined in Chapter VII (Organizational Reaction and the Volume of Deviance in the Army).

While court actions carry the symbolism of law; medical dispositions the illusion to illness; and informal controls the taken-for-granted mores of the group; bad paper represents the discretionary use of command authority. Further support for this interpretation is to be found in the fact that the vast (and an increasing) majority of all bad paper is administratively issued (see Chapter III).

THE PHYSICAL AND SOCIAL RISKS OF WAR

I am especially concerned with rates of social ostracism during times of war. The risks to life and limb are available as casualty statistics of which there are two types: 1) battle deaths and, 2) wounds resulting from enemy action. Both statistics exclude deaths and injuries caused by accidents and disease not related to enemy action.

Soldiers also face collective *social risks*: the likelihood that their behavior will run afoul of military regulations and that their temporary stint in the services may result in permanent stigma by way of a bad paper discharge. Table 5.1 examines the physical and social risks faced by three populations of soldiers in three wars. Each type of physical and social harm done to soldiers is expressed as a percentage of strength "at risk", i.e., the total number of troops on active duty during a given war.[4]

The physical risks of war are contingencies bound up with performance of the soldier role. Ostracism rates, on the other hand, are social costs imposed on soldiers for a given level of discipline and order.

THE FINDINGS

When one looks at the physical and social risks of three wars it is clear that there was a progressive decrease in physical risk and a progressive increase in social risk. For World War II, three soldiers were either killed or wounded (74.0% of total risk) for each bad paper discharge given (26.0% of total risk). The risks were at relative parity during the Korean War (49.9% of risk due to deaths and wounds; 50.1% of risk attributable to bad paper); for each soldier killed or wounded one bad paper discharge was given. During the Vietnam War, for every soldier killed or wounded (34.6% of risk) roughly two bad paper discharges were given (65.4% of total risk). Wartime service in the U.S. military is causing less proportionate physical harm and significantly more social stigmatization of soldiers.

The physical risks of soldiering are, of course, greatest during time of war and at such times the *rate* of sanctioning via the Bad Paper Discharge is also the lowest. Presumably military commanders have to devote less time to formal control of the troops when physical risks communicate to all the gravity of the situation and serves to underlie the purposes for which the military institution exists. In fact, my analysis is based on this very possibility. Indeed, the presence of physical risk may enable commanders to sanction less frequently for certain types of deviance than would otherwise be the case.

TABLE 5.1. PHYSICAL AND SOCIAL RISKS OF WAR

WWII	Korea	Vietnam	‹Name of War
1 Dec 41–31 Dec 46	25 June 50–27 Jul 53	4 Aug 64–27 Jan 73	‹Calendar Years
1942–47 (1)	1951–54 (2)	1965–73 (3)	‹Fiscal Years
-- Physical Risks --			
291,557	33,259	45,000*	‹Battle deaths (4)
670,846	103,529	304,000*	‹Wounds – not mortal (5)
-- Strength -- (See Note 6)			
16,353,659	5,764,143	8,811,000*	
-- Computation of Physical Risks --			
1.8	.6	.5	‹Battle deaths as a percent of strength
4.1	1.8	3.5	‹Wounds – not mortal as a percent of strength
5.9	2.4	4.0	‹Total deaths and wounds as a percent of strength
-- Social Risks --			
2.1	2.4	7.5	‹Bad Paper Discharges as a percent of strength (7)
8.0	4.8	11.5	‹Combined physical and social risk as a percent of strength
-- Percentage contribution of physical and social risk to total risk based upon percent of strength --			
22.4%	12.3%	4.5%	‹Battle deaths
51.6%	37.6%	30.1%	‹Wounds
74.0 %	49.9%	34.6%	‹Subtotal
25.9%	50.1%	65.4%	‹Bad Paper
99.9%**	100.0%	100.0%	‹Total physical and social risk (deaths+ wounds+Bad Paper)

Rounded as given (Source: Statistical Abstract of the United States. Various years.)
**Does not add to 100% due to rounding error.*

(1) *This base will overestimate the WWII Bad Paper Discharge Rate as it includes a fiscal period when the rates were increasing after the war ended.*
(2) *This base allows a good estimate of Korean Bad Paper Discharge Rates as only a few days separate the war period from the fiscal accounting period.*

(3) *This base will underestimate the Vietnam Bad paper Discharge rate as the fiscal year falls 6 months short of the calendar year.*
(4) *Inflicted by enemy action. Excludes accidents and injuries not related.*
(5) *Inflicted by enemy action. Excludes accidents and injuries not related.*
(6) *Strength is the number of personnel on active duty for the duration of a war (calendar year method).*
(7) *Source: Strength statistics from Janowitz and Moskos, 1979. Bad Paper rates from Chapter III.*

DISCUSSION

The finding that physical and social risks have been inversely related suggests a number of interpretations. One possible interpretation is that perhaps the number of rules to be applied to wayward soldiers has changed such that there are more categories[5] available to label real or imagined offenders. That is, more ways were available to label soldiers in a later war, than were available in a prior conflict: a change in the number of deviant categories. Over the last three wars, however, the types of bad paper available remained constant at three.

Moreover, historical evidence shows, if anything, a homogenization of the number of rules in the military system. After 1950 the Uniform Code of Military Justice was promulgated by all four service branches. The number of rules has remained fairly constant. There is no evidence that: prior to 1950 any service branch differed significantly in the number of ways it could classify deviants, i.e., an offense in the Army is not essentially different from one in the Navy, nor do Air Force commanders use a different set of rules than those used by officers in the Marine Corps.

There is some evidence, however, that the *severity* of sanctioning has been changing across wars. Table 5.2 shows the distribution of types of bad paper expressed as a percentage of all bad paper given. In terms of severity: the Dishonorable Discharge (DHD) is the most severe sanction; the Bad Conduct Discharge somewhat less severe, and the Undesirable Discharge the least severe.

Were it true that bad paper is merely a fact of organizational life, why are commanders becoming less prone to punish harshly, and more likely to expel wayward soldiers with each successive war?

Perhaps the wartime reaction patterns reflect a general tendency that begins during peacetime. While it is somewhat peculiar to view the military in such a light, the argument would be stated as follows: Different *kinds of people* staff the enforcer ranks in time of peace who are wont to punish disproportionately, i.e., that the peacetime officer cadres[6] are more punishment prone due to their lack of experience in wartime settings or perhaps that wartime armies are less unruly[7] than their peacetime counterparts, or some combination of both circumstances.

These possibilities are extremely unlikely, however, since both apologists for the military and its critics agree that maximum stress in the system exists when a war is being waged due to the heightened reality of the combat role within the institution. Combat is commonly seen as a major contributor to generating fear of death and injury among the troops, of eroding morale and the effectiveness of soldiers, as well as to oftentimes decrease the willingness of civilians to serve in the ranks.

It is also highly unlikely that changes in the types and qualities of leaders could occur in such a rapid manner as to explain the cyclicality of the BPD rate over four decades, much less its movement across wars. True, leadership style is substantively important in squads and during military training (Selvin, 1960) but as a *system level concept* it must apply to broad changes in the types, frequencies and severity of social controls applied.

TABLE 5.2. TYPES OF BAD PAPER DISCHARGE FOR THREE WARS EXPRESSED AS A PERCENT OF ALL BAD PAPER GIVEN (FISCAL YEAR METHOD)

WAR	Type of Bad Paper Discharge as a Percent of All Bad Paper Given						
World War II	UD	BCD	DD	Total	UD%	BCD%	DD%
1942	6187	2427	2574	11188	55.3	21.7	23.0
1943	10676	4959	1871	17506	61.0	28.3	10.7
1944	25488	6463	4824	36744	69.4	17.5	13.1
1945	19505	8769	10033	38307	51.0	22.9	26.1
1946	10411	7963	10254	28628	36.4	27.9	35.8*
1947	10087	7840	10275	28197	35.8	27.8	36.4
TOTAL:	82349	38390	39831	160570	51.3	23.9	24.8
KOREA							
1951	8387	4286	2864	15537	54.0	27.6	18.4
1952	8528	4278	2683	15489	55.1	27.6	17.3
1953	10617	5985	3606	20208	52.5	29.6	17.8*
1954	17597	7831	5002	30430	57.8	25.7	16.4*
TOTAL	45129	22380	14155	81664	55.3	27.4	17.3
VIETNAM							
1965	13178	2088	55	15321	86.0	13.6	.4
1966	10544	1784	72	12400	85.0	14.4	.6
1967	9741	2565	65	12371	78.7	20.7	.5

1968	11707	2886	34	14627	80.0	19.7	.2*
1969	12392	3662	187	16241	76.3	22.5	1.2
1970	20911	3964	375	25250	82.8	15.7	1.5
1971	29139	4737	325	34201	85.2	13.9	1.0*
1972	36345	4167	356	40868	88.9	10.2	.9
1973	29049	2906	434	32389	89.7	9.0	1.3
TOTAL:	173006	28759	1903	203668	84.9	14.1	.9*

Note: (*) *Does not equal 100% due to rounding error.*
Source: *Data from Chapter III.*

It is possible that the broad upward trend in administrative sanctioning (discussed in Chapter III) could be partially a product of changes in the social qualifications of officers and troops (discussed in Chapter VI). The very existence of such a trend, however, argues against the cyclicality of the bad paper discharge rate as being attributable to *rapid* changes in social composition which, by and large, were never experienced (the possible affect of *slow, but steady changes* in social qualifications on the BPD rate is explored as an hypothesis in Chapter VI).

A definitive resolution of this issue, however, depends on which indicators are selected to measure selectivity in the system. In any event, whether one selects educational criteria (Chapter VI) or Selective Service disqualification ratios—see Note 8—the fluctuation of the BPD rate is more substantial than would be expected by either measure of troop quality and qualifications. Both indicators show protracted stability in qualifications of enlistees when the BPD rate was oscillating significantly.

If rapid increases in the rate of Bad Paper Discharge occur within the context of a fairly stable number of rules, fairly high admissions standards for the enlisted ranks, and are being generated by a seasoned cadre of professional officers, what can account for the observable relation between physical and social risk if it cannot be attributable to a social characteristic of either the enlisted force which is punished, or the officer cadres who are responsible for rule enforcement?

One last possibility concerns relative anomie. This argument would stress the possibility that extreme contractions in force size may generate uncertainties as to which rules to enforce and some ambiguity over the degree of sanctioning required, i.e., the chaos and immediacy of mobilization and contraction may somehow influence the collective decisions of commanders to utilize Bad Paper as a sanctioning vehicle.

This form of argument concerns the amount of time necessary for control agents to acclimate themselves to the role requirements of command: the taken for granted, learned set of meanings that officers use to answer the question as to when, in fact, their charges are stepping out of line and 'something must be done.'

While my data cannot suggest what goes on in the minds of commanders, severe expansions and contractions of force size, of necessity, must produce co-

CHART 5.1. FLUCTUATIONS IN FORCE STRENGTH, DEPARTMENT OF
DEFENSE, BY FISCAL YEAR: 1941–1979. (MILLIONS).

SOURCE: Chapter III.

	X - Axis	Y–Axis
Series Name	Year	BOD*
Number of Ordered Pairs		39

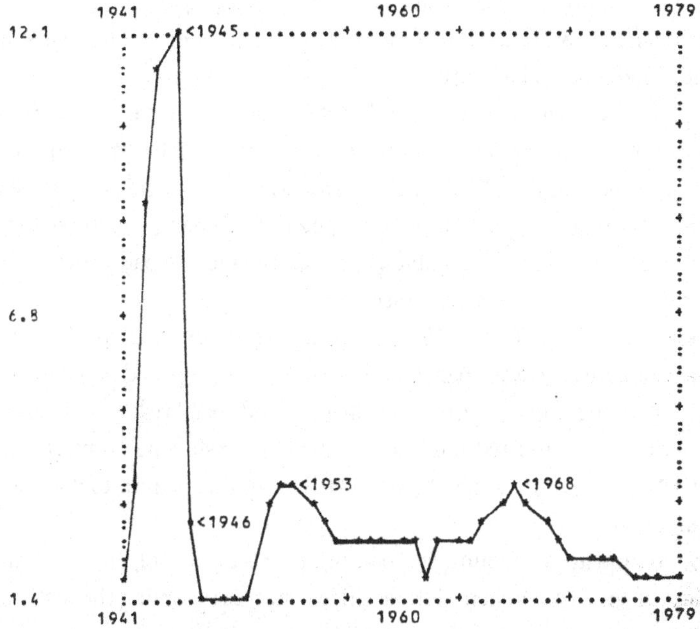

Rounded (Fiscal Years).

horts of officers who are relatively inexperienced in applying controls (during mobilization for war) and may produce (during demobilization) a career force mentality. There may be a difference with regard to the willingness to sanction enlistees on the part of those officers who remain in the service after a war that would distinguish them from their short tenured comrades who have left the forces to become civilians.

While I do not have the required social-psychological data on perceptions of wartime and post-war officer cadres with regard to sanctioning the troops, this would lead to the *type* of argument where ostracism rates would be influenced by changes in force strength. Chart 5.1 shows military strength: the number of personnel on active duty in the Department of Defense.

The analysis involves locating the periods of maximum fluctuation in force strength and seeing if these contain a BPD rate maximum.

The characteristic expansions and contractions of forces surrounding each war are quite clear with relative stability between conflicts and a gradual reduction in force size after the Vietnam War. Periods of rapid expansion (1942–1945; 1950–1953; and 1964–1968) do not correspond with the maxima for the Bad Paper Discharge Rate (1950, 1958, 1972) in any way that can be seen to be due to rapid expansion alone. In like manner, the contractive periods (1946–1947; 1953–1956; and 1968–1972) do not contain the maxima for the Bad Paper Discharge Rate in a manner consistent with the argument that rapid demobilization is associated with notable increases in Bad Paper.

It is not very likely that expansion and contraction could have been disruptive enough to influence observed sanctioning patterns. In fact, the strength profiles for the Korean and Vietnam Wars are *virtually identical* in magnitude and shape. Thus, degree of expansion and contraction—and indeed changes in the size of the military system—have had a negligible impact on the rates of bad paper. Further evidence in favor of such an interpretation is that the correlation coefficient for the BPD rate in the DoD (1941–79) and military strength was -.145 for all bad paper; -.246 for administrative paper, and .094 for court imposed bad paper.

I suggest that the shifting patterns of physical and social risk associated with military service in the enlisted ranks are related to the shifting normative basis upon which such service rests and particularly how this manifests itself in the officer cadres.

Soldiering appears to require the potential for sacrifice of life and limb in the interests of the state. When such sacrifice is not forthcoming the institution must develop alternative methods for instilling belief in its legitimacy[9] such that the requisite degree of conformity will be elicited. One such strategy is to rely more heavily on rule enforcement and punishment.

Much research has been conducted to document the deleterious effects of casualties on survivors during a war. All of it, unfortunately, is either cast in terms of the analysis of individuals,[10] or focuses on the situated context of the loss to immediate others, i.e., comrades, squads, or battalions: with well documented accounts of the resultant demoralization and disorganization of units (Keegan, 1976; Lang, 1968; Lewy, 1978; Savage and Gabriel, 1976), the erosion of military effectiveness (Sarkesian, 1980) and the like.

The disruptions caused by combat, however, are least likely to have a direct effect on *most* members of the forces—especially increasingly large numbers of soldiers in modern war who are not combatants. Such deaths are an abstraction which may, in fact, permit the organization to function more effectively by instilling very real fears and allowing them to operate as a method to ensure conformity within the ranks.

There is also the possibility that public death, i.e., death caused by the deployment of war hardware (Elliot, 1973), may have different meanings and serve different control functions for soldiers actually in a battle, than for those removed from the killing zones (who may be threatened with being sent to the former). My interest concerns the impact of casualty rates and social control activities on soldiers who are neither killed, maimed, nor actually stigmatized, that is, *on the other soldiers in the system* who must face physical and social risk. The plots of such rates suggest, in part, the risks that were so faced by differing cohorts of troops who participated in three wars.

SUMMARY

By conceptualizing bad paper as a social risk faced by enlisted populations at the discretion of the officer cadres I have shown that such risk (and therefore the discretionary use of command authority) has been increasing with each passing war as physical risk—in an actuarial sense—has been declining.

While I have not addressed all the possible sources for variation in the BPD rate, I assume that the central determinants are social in nature. It has something to do with the kinds of interpretations made by commanders to ostracize their charges. Moreover, these appear to be clearly related in an inverse manner, over three wars, to the level of physical risk in the system.

Chapter II has shown that, in addition, the increasing prevalence of bad paper during peacetime. This suggests that the sanction preferences of the officer cadres may be an important determinant of this phenomenon and that the social characteristics of soldiers as well may partially explain the general pattern of increased discretionary sanctioning. The next chapter will address this possibility.

NOTES: CHAPTER V

Materials from this chapter have been modified and published as: "The Physical and Social Risks of Military Service During War" 1991. Michigan Sociological Review No. 5, Fall, 66-89.

1. Few theorists have dealt explicitly with deviance in military settings. I have found two insights, however, fruitful. Erikson (1966) has suggested that the number of deviants that a community can afford to recognize is likely to remain stable over time. This must, however, be qualified in military settings. What determines if the community will set its agents to work at full, or reduced capacity? Clearly the central purposes to which that community is committed ought to be important. Of equal importance is the degree

to which such purposes are threatened by waywardness, and if perhaps there are larger social imperatives that may override the need to sanction on the part of community leaders.

One fruitful approach may be seen in the containment theory of Walter Reckless. Reckless posits a set of non-causal constraints in the social environment that retard rule breaking and a set of internal constraints concerning the self image of the potential deviant (Reckless et al., 1956, 1957). While I am not concerned with the behavior of individuals, as is Reckless, his theory, when applied to social organizations, suggests the possibility that control agents have a collective stake in the levels of control they apply which may transcend both the personalities, and motivations, of the agents themselves as well as those whom they punish. In short, there are functional alternatives to a given level of social control and these are known by the environment wherein control is practiced. So, for example, it has been documented that the demeanor of adolescents is an important variable in their dealings with civilian police (Wilson, 1977). It is also true that policing "style" is important, i.e., whether universalistic or particularistic criteria are applied (Wilson, 1978). Of overriding importance, however, is the legitimacy of those who police: how they see themselves and how they are seen in their host community. That is, their central purposes. When the police are under attack, they are more attentive to their public front. The point is that there may be functional alternatives for a given level of control. The police may undertake activities other than arrest, or they may "put on the heat" if there is public clamor.

In like manner, those who violate laws face a variable likelihood—depending on the type of crime—of encountering control agents. In the extreme, public clamor for arrests and the prevalence of highly visible crime types (such as street mugging) makes policing legitimate. The emergence of a more serious offender than the mugger, however, shifts the central concerns of law enforcement officers. The mugger then, in this hypothetical example, would become less important as an organizational product than was the case prior to the shift in both public and police attention.

2. For a discussion of the types of military discharge condition designations, and the ranges of the rates per one thousand discharged enlistees, as well as a fuller treatment of the Bad Paper Discharge, see Chapter III.

3. The degree of discretion is important here. While commanders ultimately decide the outcomes of all sanctioning events in the military, the discharges that require the use of the military court require more organizational energies to comply with judicial procedures: this involves the formal military court system, its personnel and extensive administrative documentation of events in a trial. Thus, "trial paper," i.e., punitive discharges such as the Bad Conduct and Dishonorable, require more time and resources than do Undesirable Discharges issued outside of court channels. Increases in the rate of non-trial paper indicate that commanders are opting to avoid the courts to expel soldiers. Stated another way, dispositions are always at the discretion of commanders—in all cases of formal sanctioning—but movements in non-trial paper indicate that men are being expelled when they could have been contained within the system.

4. This is standard demographic practice for estimating the exposure of populations to socially important variables. I am not, of course, implying that the combat fractions, i.e., the percentage of troops who actually faced enemy fire, was the same for all wars. For a discussion of the evolution of combat fractions, the role of risk for officers and their authority, the structure of the killing zones, and the impact of technology on the conduct of wars see Chapters VI and VII.

5. This notion was influenced by my reading of contemporary labeling theory. For a statement of this perspective see: H. Becker, 1964, 1973; G. Becker, 1978; Goode, 1975; Kitsuse, 1962; Lemert, 1974; Scheff, 1977; Schur, 1971.

6. There is a tradition in military sociology, perhaps most notable in the work of Morris Janowitz, to examine the social characteristics of the officer corps as important determinants of the character of military institutions—see Janowitz, 1968. For other studies that see some aspect of the officer corps as being central to understanding military institutions see: Abrahamsson, 1968; Bain, 1973; Barnett, 1967; Bons, 1970; Borgatta, 1955; Brown, 1951; Campbell, 1953; Coates, 1966; Davis, 1954; Dorman, 1976; Dornbusch, 1955; Feld, 1975, 1977b; Gard, 1977b; Gray 1975; Halpin, 1954; Hauser, 1973; Heise, 1969; Horowitz, 1967, 1971; Huntington, 1956, 1960; Johnson and Wilson, 1972; Kerckhoff, 1958; King, 1972a; Larson, 1974; Lewis, 1947; Lovell, 1964, 1977; Marmion, 1971; Marwald, 1959; Masland and Radway, 1957; Miller and Medalia, 1955; Moellering, 1973; Mylander, 1974; Nauta, 1971; Peterson and Lippitt, 1968; Rappoport, 1962; Razzell, 1963; Sarkesian, 1972, 1973; Savage and Gabriel, 1976; Selvin, 1960; Teitler, 1977; van Doorn, 1965, 1968a, 1968b, 1970, 1975a, 1975b.

7. There is a tradition among military writers to examine "the quality of the troops" to seek explanations for wayward soldierly behavior. See Chapter VII for a detailed discussion concerning the inadequacies of individuals who go AWOL or desert. One variation of this theme is to examine the characteristics of "leadership" in military settings wherein, of course, presumed deficiencies in the officer cadres substitute for real or imagined deficiencies in the quality of soldiers available to the armed forces. See Bradford and Brown for a constructivist approach (1974), Savage and Gabriel (1976) and, Loory (1973) for more radical assessments based on different assumptions concerning the role of the officer corps.

8. I have created an indicator for the selectivity of the Department of Defense using Selective Service Data for the years 1941–1973 while a military draft was operative so as to arrive at an independently derived rough measure of DoD selectivity. Each service branch has its own admission standards—and these change according to what are essentially internal manpower requirements. Also, requirements for officership are substantially determined by supply conditions in the "funnel," i.e., the output of the service academies and the capabilities of ROTC, and decisions to award a commission for critically needed skill categories such as medical, dental, technical and clergy. In the table below I have presented a rough indicator of selective service selectivity. The data were gathered from the Statistical Abstract of The United States and from Historical Statistics of the United States from Colonial Times to the Present. In all cases the "longest data stream" method was used. That is, when there was a discrepancy for a given year, the data source which was most recent was used or the data source with the most consistent reportage surrounding the year in question was used.

KEY TO SYMBOLS:

CLASS = Number of civilians classified by the Selective Service System (in millions).

DISQ = Number of Disqualifications (all reasons, in millions).

SI = Selectivity Index: the ratio of Disqualified to Classified. Note a small index reading, e.g., .07 in 1941, implies that it was fairly easy to qualify for military service. A higher value, e.g., .65 in 1946, implies that disqualifications were rather common and thus standards were high.

TABLE 5.3. DOD SELECTIVITY UNDER THE SELECTIVE SERVICE SYSTEM

Year	CLASS*	DISQ*	SI*
1941	14.7	1.1	.07
1942	28.5	2.4	.08
1943	22.1	3.4	.15
1944	8.7	1.4	.16
1945	8.8	1.3	.15
1946	3.5	2.3	.65
1947	3.7	2.2	.60
1948	8.9	.2	.03
1949	8.9	.5	.06
1950	9.2	.9	.10
1951	8.6	1.3	.15
1952	9.0	1.5	.17
1953	9.7	1.8	.19
1954	10.2	2.0	.20
1955	10.6	2.1	.20
1956	11.1	2.3	.21
1957	11.7	2.6	.22
1958	12.4	2.9	.24
1959	13.2	3.1	.24
1960	14.1	3.3	.24
1961	14.9	3.3	.23
1962	15.4	3.6	.23
1963	16.0	3.6	.22
1964	16.8	4.1	.25
1965	18.0	4.6	.26
1966	19.0	5.0	.26
1967	19.9	4.9	.25
1968	20.8	5.2	.25
1969	21.8	5.6	.26
1970	22.7	6.0	.26
1971	16.1	3.6	.23
1972	15.0	2.9	.19
1973	14.8	2.4	.16

*Rounded (Fiscal Years).

In general, standards (using this measure) increased—and became quite high into World War II; plummeted as quickly as they rose after the war was over; rose steadily from 1949 to 1958; and remained essentially stable from 1958 through 1970, and then dropped steadily until the draft ended. A marginal soldier thus had a better chance of serving during WWII than after it; of serving during the Korean War than after it; and of serving in the late part of the Vietnam War, than in the beginning. If one were to argue that the actual standards used were lowered (something this indicator does not measure) during a war, one would have to show that there was a disproportionable decline in the eligible population, i.e., in the numbers of those classified. To some degree this is the case (due undoubtedly to deferments of all kinds), but it is clearly not the case from 1952 to 1970 when the eligible population was steadily increasing. Thus, while actual standards may have been lowered, the eligibility fraction was increasing. From 1955 to 1970 the selectivity index remained fairly stable. There is no evidence that standards for admission to the military have been steadily dropping.

9. R. B. Smith has argued that wars since WWII have been seen as increasingly legitimate (Smith, 1973) and that each war has seen increasing levels of disaffection both in the services and at home. Hofstetter and Moore (1979), on the other hand, have suggested that the legitimacy of the military as an institution has little to do with its popularity—as commonly measured by public attitude questionnaires which attempt to discern the occupational appeal of the services and the willingness of civilians to volunteer for military duty. While civilians may, or may not, find the military an attractive occupation, most Americans feel that the military is necessary and important. None of the above research, however, has addressed the internal requirements for order within the military.

10. By this I mean that the unit of analysis is the individual; his fears, anxieties, morale, general attitudes and the like. I do not wish to minimize the traumatic effects of military service—especially combat—on individuals, nor to judge the adjustment strategies that soldiers must use to survive hostile physical and group environments. My point is, however, that public death may have social control implications on survivors which are used for the purposes of the organization. Martyrdom is a case in point: a martyr fires the enthusiasm of believers and, I would argue, grants legitimacy to their surviving spokesmen who may make social claims they would otherwise likely not have. Nor would these claims, without the spectacular event, likely be seen as valid. The casualties of war lend credibility to the institution of soldiering and thus require commanders to use fewer artificial or socially imposed controls to insure order.

CHAPTER VI. ORGANIZATIONAL REACTION AND THE OFFICER–ENLISTED DISTINCTION

> The soldier, by his initial act of enlisting (or allowing himself to be drafted, if a draft exists) has submitted to legitimate authority. Then, in his work and training, he submits each day to the authority of officers and noncommissioned officers, and to a plethora of rules, regulations and customs. Again and again, he is made to do things which he does not want to do—rise at dawn, endure cold and heat and filth and fatigue, and accept unquestioningly the often arbitrary commands of his superiors. The first rule of the soldier, dinned into him from the first day of his service, is to obey. If this conditioning process has been effective, the soldier will continue to submit to the orders of legitimate authority, even though the orders be contrary to his fundamental instincts of self-preservation.
> —William Hauser (1980, 188–189)

The military system of social control *requires* the submission of enlisted men. The above quotation—with all its behavioral implications—captures the basic premise of "command": that the requisite submission of the enlisted force is essential for the exercise of legitimate authority.

It is my thesis that such legitimate authority as may be possessed by the officer corps is, in part, *generated* by the social distinctions between officers and men. The officer–enlisted distinction is *central* to social control in the military, and movements in the rates of such activities indicates a change of some sort in the nature of the officer–enlisted distinction.

That is, social forces which weaken the distinctiveness of officers with regard to their subordinates would be expected to induce higher rates of organizational reaction to deviance than would otherwise be the case.

While those *in* control differ in structural location from those who *are* controlled, this organizational imperative which separates officers from men may not be supported by: (1) the actual work performed by commanders and troops, (2) the educational attainments of officers and men, (3) the risks faced by both groups, and (4) recent changes in the technology of war.

I hypothesize that any constellation of social arrangements which lessens the distinctiveness of officers with regard to their charges erodes the legitimacy of a system of control based on caste distinctions and that organizational reaction to deviance will be highest at such times. In that the office of commander carries with it an imperative to discipline soldiers for the purpose of maintaining order, I further hypothesize that the level of such activity will be lowest when the officer–enlisted distinction is seen as legitimate.

I propose what may be called a status conservation argument to explain patterns of organizational reaction to deviance in the military. The basic line of argument is as follows:

1. The legitimate authority of officers increases as the social distance between them and the troops increases.

2. When the social distance between officers and men is fairly substantial, officers can rely on informal—as opposed to formal—controls to maintain order.

3. Officers face a crises in legitimacy when the social distance between them and their charges declines.

4. At times of declining distinctiveness, rates of organizational reaction to deviance will increase most notably.

METHODOLOGY

Rather than attempting to address all the possible sources of endogenous and exogenous strain which may be associated with the increased use of formal sanctions by commanders, I shall focus my attention on two of the most important external factors: the war-peace cycle, and the selectivity of the Department of Defense with regard to its admissions standards. The most important internal factor I take to be the social distinctiveness of the officer corps with regard to the enlisted population.[1]

The research problem is to isolate those periods of most extreme organizational reaction, and to suggest alternative interpretations based on the limitations of the available data. The findings will then be presented in light of a contrast of extremes, by comparing high and low rates of organizational reaction.

The analysis proceeds by examining patterns of court activity and bad paper discharges. If there is stability in reaction rates across war-peace periods, I assume that this signifies the operation of institutional processes not central to the presence or absence of the stresses of war. In this manner the *ethos of control*, my short hand notation for the collective sentiments, propensities, and predispositions regarding sanctioning on the part of the officer corps, becomes an organizational property. It is, however, grounded in—and requires—substantial variation in control patterns. Lacking such variation, I can only speak of institutional trends.

The *ethos of control* requires distinct deployment patterns against varied kinds of deviants. These patterns may be harsh or mild; they may favor containment or expulsion; and may be implemented through the courts or through the discretionary use of administrative channels on the part of commanders. After locating the periods which characterize a particular pattern, it is then possible to examine some of the factors which may be associated with the changing types of dispositions issued by the officer corps.

TURNING POINTS IN DEPLOYMENT PATTERNS

There are three major trends in organizational reaction to social deviance in the military which suggest major changes in the deployment patterns used by commanders.

1. While commanders since 1948 (the year of maximum court activity) have become less reliant on the courts to punish wayward soldiers, 1964 marked an increase in harshness when the courts were used.

2. While the vast majority of soldiers who face the courts are kept inside the system for punishment (this amounts to over 95% of all decisions in 1947—the height of expulsiveness), 1966 saw a reversal of this trend and the courts were increasingly used to expel.

3. While all forms of bad paper discharge have tended to be used less during wars than after them, this pattern did not hold for Vietnam.

All three measures of organizational reaction to deviance, *taken together*, delimit a zone in time (1964–1972) where it is clear that deployment patterns had changed—at least with regard to the war-peace cycle. Relative to World War II and Korea, Vietnam Era commanders were less prone to keep deviant soldiers in the military, they were disproportionately expelling through the courts and with administrative bad paper, and they were more punitive. My analysis will center on this quite notable period of transition. What force, or combination of forces, may have acted to produce this rather atypical set of *wartime management decisions* on the part of commanders?

MOBILIZATION FOR WAR

The rapid infusion of men and materiel under the control of commanders in a growing complex organization doubtlessly places men and managers under substantial strain. Indeed, the training, indoctrination, processing and movement of civilians into the soldier role has few civilian parallels. Table 6.1 shows military strength for three wars.

TABLE 6.1. MILITARY STRENGTH, DEPARTMENT OF DEFENSE MOBILIZATION TO MAXIMUM PLUS TWO YEARS. WWII, KOREA AND VIETNAM.

Year	Strength (in Millions)*
World War II Period	
1941	1.8
1942	3.9
1943	9.0
1944	11.5
1945	12.1 ‹ Maximum
1946	3.0
1947	1.6
Korean War Period	
1950	1.5
1951	3.2
1952	3.7 ‹ Maximum
1953	3.6
1954	3.3
Vietnam Era	
1964	2.7
1965	2.7
1966	3.1
1967	3.4
1968	3.5 ‹ Maximum
1969	3.5
1970	3.1

*Rounded (Fiscal Years).
Source: Chapter V.

Mobilization for war was clearly most dramatic during World War II, whereas the Korean profile was essentially the same as that observed during Vietnam. This clearly cannot explain the Vietnam Era reaction patterns of commanders, which were significantly different from the pattern for the earlier wars.

SELECTION

Perhaps the DoD was disproportionately accepting candidates for military service during Vietnam that it would otherwise have refused during peace, or during other wars. Project 100,000 (instituted in 1966) was, in fact, an explicit attempt to do just that. In the words of Robert McNamara:

> The poor of America have not had the opportunity to earn their fair share of this nation's abundance, but they can be given an opportunity to return to civilian life with skills and aptitudes which for them and their families will reverse the downward spiral of decay. (Starr, 1973, 190)

Lieutenant General Herman Nickerson, Jr., Deputy Chief of Manpower, U.S. Marine Corps, writing in the *Marine Corps Gazette* (1968, cited in Starr, 193), commented:

> Those of our youth who lack education, those who live in the ghettoes, combine the ills of idleness, ignorance and apathy. Our task is to help cure these ills with education, training, and incentives.

Sociologist Morris Janowitz describes this program:

> As of 1967, under Project 100,000 more than 49,000 men had entered the Armed Forces under "new standards" which *permitted the acceptance of men who had previously been rejected for induction or enlistment.* (Emphasis mine, 1973, 168).

There is considerable controversy, however, assessing the effectiveness of Project 100,000. Each interpretation makes different assumptions concerning the impact the program may have had on the *social control* activities of commanders. To illustrate this, consider what I call "the bottom dog hypothesis": In this extreme view, the military recruits disproportionate numbers of lower SES enlistees who have trouble adjusting to military service. These men disproportionately break military rules. Such soldiers find themselves on the receiving end of their commanders' displeasure and are punished and/or expelled from the military with stigma.

The bottom dog hypothesis is, of course, highly tendentious in at least four regards:

1. First, it blames the victim. High SES, by definition, implies differential access to, and possession of, scarce social skills and resources. Those at the lower reaches of the measure will, of course, be deficient in these qualities. While no

one to the best of my knowledge has argued for an army composed entirely of the upper class, a lower class army is seen in most quarters as especially threatening in terms of military effectiveness and the requisite that, in a democracy, an army should be socially representative (Janowitz, 1975).

2. It assumes that military participation by all social classes is desirable and that disproportionate participation by the underclass is less desirable. The problem of elite infiltration into the enlisted ranks is ignored as are the activities of the officer corps in managing deviance.

3. It assumes that successful adaptation to military rules is a desirable state and that those in the lower orders are less willing, capable, or desirous of such conformity, i.e., it is a statement of managerial ideology.

4. It assumes the neutrality of commanders. Rates of rule enforcement are seen as the result of increases in the size of the bottom dog population.

With the bottom dog hypothesis in mind, it is easier to see how critics and apologists for Project 100,000 talk past one another by selecting evaluation criteria that are mutually exclusive from the point of view of *the operation of the social control system* in the military. This is so primarily because the goals of assimilation and utilization of personnel are inherently contradictory.

To assimilate socially distinct groups of soldiers requires, of necessity, that such differences are minimized, i.e., there is less of a social difference between marginals and the mass, over time. Utilization of manpower, on the other hand, requires a division of labor which distinguishes soldiers from each other—in terms of skill, for example. Thus, a natural outcome of the division of labor (social differentiation) acts contrary to the goal of assimilation (removing social differences).

If the problem is to *assimilate* bottom dogs, one can point to the relative lack of failure Project 100,000 soldiers have had in making it through basic training. The DoD report on the effectiveness of the program (OASD, 1969) takes this tack. Janowitz also notes:

> Almost two years after the program had been launched, the preliminary results were highly successful. Nearly 96 percent of the new standards men successfully completed basic training as compared with 98 percent for all other men.... Perhaps the most sensitive measure both of the progress of new standards men and the response of the various services to these men is their rate of promotion. Of the first group of new standards men who entered the Army during October-December 1966, 84.4 percent were E-3's and above after an average of 16.5 months of service; while for the control group the percentage was 92.6 percent. (1973, 170)

Critics, on the other hand, point to the *utilization* of the new standards men. Starr notes:

> For while the Department of Defense had reduced aptitude require-ments for entering the military, it had no intention of similarly reducing requirements for technical positions within the services. Hence the ma-jority of "New Standards Men" would be barred from the kind of training which McNamara said would 'reverse the downward spiral of decay.' The result was reported in the *Air Force Times*: "According to Defense officials, about 25 percent of the occupations in the military are suitable for the Project 100,000 men." The leading occupation, as might be expected, was combat. In the military as a whole today, 14 percent of all personnel are given combat roles; the rest draw support assignments of one sort or an-other. But among New Standards Men the proportion going to combat proved to be 37 percent (1973; 192).

If, following Janowitz, the military was innovating in the area of adult social-ization by assimilating "bottom dogs" the Vietnam Era organizational reaction rates would cast doubt on such success. What kind of goal could be achieved by training and promoting Project 100,000 soldiers, to only cast them out in dispro-portionate numbers?

If, in fact, such men were not disproportionately cast out, but, as critics con-tend, were disproportionately used as cannon fodder; or served to exempt the middle classes from service as Starr reports:

> The reduction in mental standards, *The New York Times* reported in Oc-tober, "...will probably ease the pressure now building up, because of the manpower demands of the Vietnam War, to begin inducting college stu-dents who are currently being deferred." (1973, 192).

This makes commanders' deployment patterns with regard to social deviance even less understandable. If bottom dogs were replacing the college crowd (an unlikely line of argument due to differences in skill structure and utilization), or if they were not (and thus these men were "making good" as soldiers and dis-proportionately suffering casualties in the combat arms) why were commanders using both the courts and administrative bad paper to expel at increasing rates?

Since the Project 100,000 group *were* disproportionately participating in the combat arms, what function could be served by increasing the burden in stigma faced by this group? If Project 100,000 troops bore both an increased likelihood of facing physical *and* social risks, it would seem that their presence would be well received, both by commanders in need of cannon fodder, and the rest of the troops in whose place they might serve. This was decidedly not the case, howev-er. Starr (1973) reports that many soldiers referred to the Project 100,000 soldiers as the "moron corps" (Starr, 194) and that the program was rapidly scaled down since the cost of "recycling" the new standards men was drawing complaints from the training commands (Starr, 195).

The disciplinary record of the New Standards Men is also cited as evidence of command displeasure with the program. Starr cites a Pentagon study where it was shown that the Project 100,000 soldiers had a rate of court-martial convictions twice that of a control group (3 percent as opposed to 1.4%; Starr, 195). I have shown, however, that the bulk of those court-martialed are not expelled.

Even if one is willing to grant that *all* the extra expulsions after 1964 were attributable to the behavior of the New Standards Men, one would expect expulsions to decline as the project was phased out. This was clearly not the case: expulsions rose, and in fact were highest in 1976 well after the war was over and the last of the marginal men had likely been long since discharged or assimilated.

If the utilization of the New Standards Men, as Starr contends, caused some commanders to question the military's role as a welfare institution (Starr, 190, 195) and others to speak highly of such objectives, as did one officer who told *The New York Times* in 1966:

> These men make the best infantrymen, mortarmen, and mechanics. I'd prefer a company of riflemen with fifth-grade educations over a company of college men anytime (Starr, 192).

Perhaps the uses to which these marginal soldiers were put are secondary to other aspects of the screening process. Table 6.2 provides an indicator or the selectivity of the DoD for the years 1964–72 by examining the ratio of those disqualified to those classified by the selective service system.

The Selective Service System was rejecting roughly 1 in 4 classified during 1964–72 and this rate stayed strikingly stable. There is no evidence that the selective service system has ever disproportionately *included* the sons of the upper class for admission to military service when in fact such men are disproportionately healthy, bright, and capable.

If the argument is made that the local draft boards were choosing to bring in more bottom dogs and thereby exempt the sons of privilege, the above index suggests that it was doing neither: the Vietnam War exempted both extremes of the SES distribution. Since, however, there are fewer at the higher reaches of the distribution than at the lower, exemptions had to be coming disproportionately from the upper middle ranges—to compensate for the sheer volume of those at the very bottom who could not qualify.

TABLE 6.2. REJECTION RATIOS FOR THE SELECTIVE SERVICE SYSTEM.
DEPARTMENT OF DEFENSE, 1964–72.
Those Rejected (all reasons) Over Those Classified.

Year	SI*
1964	.25
1965	.26
1966	.26
1967	.25
1968	.25
1969	.26
1970	.26
1971	.23
1972	.19

*Fiscal Years: Rounded
Source: Chapter V

Additionally, in 1964–66 the "baby boom" children born in 1946–47 were disproportionately becoming eligible for military service and filling the colleges as well. Mobilization for war within such a demographic climate would logically place the sons of upwardly mobile working class families, who were the first to attend college as a result of the expansion of the educational system in the 1960s, into the same pool of candidates as the sons of the more traditional middle class families who became eligible. Americans had never gone to war before with such a relative surplus of formally educated personnel.

SOLDIERLY CAPABILITIES

Assessing the capabilities of the fighting force is an extremely difficult, if not impossible task, because the ultimate measure of soldierly effectiveness lies in the test of battle. All else is simulation, or, more often than not in American society, a reflection of the state of civil-military relations. While there is little conclusive research on the social sources of combat effectiveness (Sarkesian, 1980), none of it can withstand the outcome of an unsuccessful war. No other social institution is evaluated using such polar criteria.[2]

This places contemporary commanders in the uncomfortable position of having to prepare for the eventuality of the next war as the elusive goal of victory becomes increasingly unobtainable. Curiously, most public debate on the effectiveness of soldiers in the American military has been eclipsed by the issue of manpower procurement. This under the assumption that, somehow, armies will function effectively if they are recruited in accordance with the prevailing norms governing the allocation of manpower in the host society.[3]

The arguments for and against the draft, for example, involve the basic issues of voluntarism, equity, cost and civilian control of the military (Barber, 1973b). The case for universal national service—widely seen as an alternative to the draft and the all-volunteer force—seeks to incorporate the ideal of service to the society in the nation's youth so that serving in the military is but *one* option chosen from an array of forced alternative ways to serve the state (Barber, 1973a).

Neither argument addresses either soldierly effectiveness or the kinds of *controls* that would be needed to enforce order in the military after varied combinations of incentives, coercion and patriotism bring civilians to their drill sergeants in requisite numbers to satisfy the proponents of each cause.

The central issue for deviance theory is this: How did the social control system respond to changes in the social attributes of officers and men? For civil-military relations, the central question is: How could the military continue to fill its manpower requirements under circumstances when popular support for its activities was declining?

The capability of soldiers is an elusive quality which appears to wax and wane as the military enjoys public support and chooses to engage in winnable wars. While I do not have data which can establish causal order as to the primacy of each factor's contribution to soldierly effectiveness it should be noted that there have been substantial changes in military skill structure (the occupational aspects of the enlisted force) as well as in the social requirements of officership. These changes may have a direct impact on the kinds of controls used by commanders, without regard to whether or not soldiers are seen as being more or less proficient at their assigned tasks.

THE EVOLUTION OF ENLISTED SKILL STRUCTURE

The occupational distribution of military jobs filled by enlisted men for World War II, Korea, and Vietnam is shown in table 6.3.

The table shows three clear trends with regard to the occupational distributions of the enlisted force.

1. Purely soldierly jobs for which there are no civilian counterparts, e.g., common foot soldiers, members of air crews or naval vessels who operate or load war hardware—not elsewhere classified—have become less common. In World War II (38.8%) roughly 4 out of 10 troops was so classified, whereas in the Vietnam Era (18.3%) roughly 1 soldier in 5 had a unique military occupation.

TABLE 6.3. ENLISTED OCCUPATIONAL DISTRIBUTIONS FOR WWII, KOREAN AND VIETNAM ERAS. DEPARTMENT OF DEFENSE.

Occupational Grouping	WWII	Korea	Vietnam
Tech./Scientific	10.4	12.7	22.1
Admin./Clerical	12.6	18.1	14.7
Mech./Repairmen	16.6	15.3	18.6
Craftsmen	5.9	4.7	5.9
Service Workers	9.6	12.4	13.0
Operatives and Laborers	6.1	6.5	7.4
Military Type Occupations Not Elsewhere Classified	38.8	30.3	18.8
All	100%	100%	100% (rounded)

Source: SAUS, 1976

2. Enlistees with technical/scientific jobs doubled their representation since World War II—from 10.4% to 22.1% of enlisted strength.

3. The redistribution of manpower above the craftsman level was more notable than the redistribution of manpower below the craftsman level, while the number of craftsmen remained fairly stable. Soldiers are increasingly becoming a white collar force.

These broad changes in the evolution of enlisted skill structure *culminated* in the Vietnam Era. It is my thesis that, other things being equal, the white collarization of the enlisted rank served to weaken the social distinctiveness of the officer corps, and thus may serve as a partial explanation for the rather atypical reaction patterns to deviance observed during that war. To test this argument I shall attempt to show that the period 1964–72 was highly atypical with regard to the relative educational qualification of officers and men.

ENLISTED AND OFFICER EDUCATIONAL DISTRIBUTIONS

I am concerned primarily with the rate at which the college educated served in the military as enlisted men relative to the rate at which those in the officer corps acquired college degrees. Table 6.4 focuses on the percentage distributions of educational credentials among officers and enlisted men.

TABLE 6.4. EDUCATIONAL DISTRIBUTIONS, DEPARTMENT OF DEFENSE, OFFICERS AND ENLISTED RANKS 1952–78.

Year	ENLIST	OFF
1952	2.8	46.6
1954	3.2	49.7
1956	2.8	55.5
1958	1.9	56.1
1960	1.5	57.2
1962	1.4	64.6
1963	1.4	69.4
1967	2.2	72.3* ‹ Period
1969	4.9	72.9* ‹ Under
1970	5.8	76.3* ‹ Observation
1971	5.0	73.4* ‹ 1967–71
1973	1.9	82.1
1974	1.7	87.4
1975	1.6	88.8
1976	2.4	91.2
1977	2.7	93.5
1978	2.1	93.6

SYMBOLS: ENLIST: *Percent Enlisted Force with College Degrees*
OFF: *Percent Officer Corps with College Degrees*
SOURCES: *Letters, HQ USAF MPC 1982; DoD/OASD 1982; DoA/AG 1982.*

DISCUSSION

If one looks at the period 1967–71 with an eye to discerning any striking differ-ences between it and the preceding or following years with regard to the rates at which enlisted men with college degrees were present in the ranks, and the rate at which officers acquired college degrees, there are two unmistakable patterns.

1. For the enlisted ranks, the period marked those years when the rate of ex-pansion as well as the absolute number of college graduates in the ranks was highest.

2. For officers, the period was unique in that the rate at which degreed offi-cers were entering the system was relatively stable. This rate was rising steadily in *both* the prior (1952–63) and subsequent (1973–78) periods.

The period 1967–71 was thus *characterized* as the only observable time when college graduates in the enlisted ranks were expanding while the rate of expansion of degreed officers was stable. This is shown graphically in Chart 6.1, where the variable PMAX[4] shows the percentage change in the enlisted degreed fraction of forces as measured from the minimum value. Likewise, the variable POFF[5] shows the percentage change of officers with college degrees as measured from its minimum value.

CHART 6.1. THE PERCENTAGE CHANGE IN COLLEGE DEGREE FRACTIONS AMONG ENLISTED MEN AND OFFICERS AS MEASURED FROM THE MINIMUM VALUES. DoD 1952–78.

	X	Y	
PAIR	SERIES	SERIES	SYMBOL
1	Year	PMAX	A ‹ Enlisted Ranks
2	Year	POFF	B ‹ Officer Corps
Number Of Ordered Pairs		17	

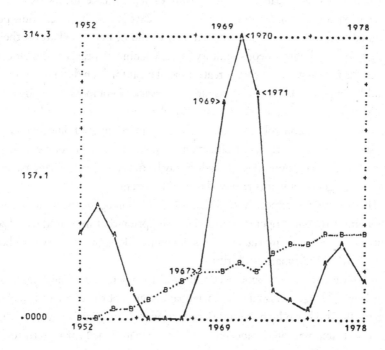

KEY: In 1970 the percentage of enlisted men with college degrees had increased 314.3 percent over the minimum observed value.
Source: Chapter endnotes 4, 5.

SOCIAL HOMOGENEITY AS A THREAT TO THE OFFICER–ENLISTED DISTINCTION

I hypothesize that as the social qualifications of the troops become more similar to officers, the officer–enlisted distinction becomes less legitimate and is a threat to claims (and demands) made by the officer corps on enlisted soldiers with regard to deference, demeanor, respect and proper behavior. A college edu-cated enlisted force might make the officer–enlisted distinction impossible to routinely accomplish as, theoretically, the only distinction (barring seniority) an officer would have with regard to the troops would be his commission. Con-versely, a socially distant officer corps (by virtue of superior educational quali-fications) coupled with a clearly subordinate enlisted structure would enhance the credibility of the distinction.

The former force configuration (i.e., few or no social differences between of-ficers and men) would theoretically require the evolution of new criteria to oth-erwise distinguish officers from men or reliance on some aspects of the extant criteria. It would invariably take a considerable amount of time for such new distinctions to become internalized as sources of legitimate authority.

One expeditious and readily available source would be the sanctioning power assigned to the office—which enlisted men would be denied whatever their ori-gins. A socially homogeneous military force, wishing to preserve the officer–en-listed distinction would have to create a social basis for such differentiation. This could be implemented by emphasizing the *command* component of the office. I would thus expect increased organizational reaction to take the form of com-mander-initiated controls in a military that is increasingly homogeneous with regard to the social origins of officers and enlisted men. Of course, it is quite possible that this proposed relationship may be quite different during peacetime when the urgency of war is removed from the system.

That is, I would expect to find that a socially homogeneous military force is a more punitive one. I operate under the assumption that increased use of social controls serves to secure the positions of commanders, that is, serves to bolster their claims to legitimate authority.

A relevant social analogue occurs in prisons where the social origins of the guards matches quite closely the social background of the captives (Jacobs and Retsky, 1977). That which differentiates prisoners from guards is a social distinc-tion that is imposed on the incarcerated, and is maintained through the office of the guard. But for this distinction, little separates the two populations.

The ease with which personnel for that office are interchangeable has been readily documented by social psychologists who selected those to play guard roles from socially homogeneous groups of college students in an experimental setting. The "guards" quickly assumed all the punitive trappings of captors and acted out the scripts usually associated with such positions (Haney, Banks, and Zimbardo, 1977; see also the "Milgram experiments", Milgram, 1965) for an expla-nation of the principles involved.

It is not difficult to speculate as to what could have happened if the guards had other than experimentally granted legitimacy to act out their aggression *and* the targets in such role playing were not fellow students but more permanently credible social inferiors, outsiders, aliens, or those seen as deserving of less than humane treatment, i.e., were drawn from a population socially subordinate to their captors (see Hilburg, 1979, for an actual historical example of the treatment of "inferiors" by the Nazis).

Following this logic, a socially distinct officer corps would see enlisted men firmly in their place: presumably the moral authority of their social betters would be sufficient to tame the troops and presumably less law enforcement would be necessary. Analogues in this case are readily apparent: 1) in caste societies; 2) in those areas where the rate of social change is very slow; 3) where social mobility is uncommon; 4) where the credibility of the rule enforcers is unquestioned; and, 5) where the social system is very stable.

SOCIAL ORIGINS EXPLANATIONS OF CONTROL PATTERNS

My data do not permit analysis of an order which might discern why commanders chose to shift their emphasis in sanctioning soldiers. It does, however, show that such a shift occurred at a time when officer cadre distinctiveness relative to enlisted men was declining. I can thus specify *when* social origins explanations *may* have the greatest degree of face validity with regard to their imputed role in the process of social control.

It should be mentioned that both adaptations, i.e., extreme social similarity or dissimilarity, are ideal-typical: there are undoubtedly numerous determinants of a given ethos of control—and obviously the *rate* at which homogeneity or heterogeneity with regard to social origins is achieved is centrally important. Gradual movements toward uniformity would be expected to produce less dramatic reaction rates than rapid infusions of status contenders. Table 6.4 documented that the period 1967–71 was decidedly atypical in terms of college degree acquisition rates among enlisted men. This can only be assessed, however, in light of the historical distinctions between officers and men.

Military lore, and history, is rich with the displeasure of soldiers with the treatment they receive by their officer superiors. But it is only in recent times, i.e., since 1940, that the officer corps was *not clearly* of higher social standing. In fact, the historical development of the officer corps has been toward being more socially representative and less elitist in terms of social origins. Historically, the officer cadres were drawn from the upper classes (Janowitz, 1968; Teitler, 1977).

In the contemporary military, while participation in officership has been reaching down the class ladder, the troops, at the same time, have been becoming more socially respectable. The middle-classification of contemporary officers (a step down) has occurred coterminously with a lower-middle classification of the troops (a step upward). In terms of social origins, officers are more prone to be drawn from the middle class (not the upper class), while the troops are more likely to be working class (as opposed to lower class) (Janowitz, 1973; USARI, 1977; Janowitz and Moskos, 1979). Thus, the social homogenization of the *total* force—using social origins criteria—proceeded while the *relative* distinctiveness of the officer cadres was less apparent during 1967–71.

The military *system* has become more socially homogeneous with regard to skill structure while, at the same time, officers are becoming less educationally similar to enlisted men. While the credential gap between officers and men has widened, the contemporary officer is less similar to the troops in terms of his possessing a college degree than was the case since World War II when education was less available to all.

Thus, the absolute differences between the ranks of enlisted men and officers, in terms of social origins, has been narrowing by virtue of the fact that the extremes of both social origin distributions have vanished, i.e., less elite officers and less disreputable enlisted men, but the *relative* differences were most pronounced between 1967–71. While a degree gap has increasingly come to separate the officer from his charges, this was less so during 1967–71; while the poor are increasingly eliminated from service (they can't qualify), and the upper class goes elsewhere, i.e., not into the active officer ranks or for that matter into uniform at all.

CORRECTING FOR "THE MISTAKE" OF AN UNPOPULAR WAR

An alternative explanation for the shift in reaction pattern observed between 1967 and 1971 could possibly be that commanders were as frustrated with the conduct of the war as civilians were due to war weariness (Lang, 1980); disaffection of the troops (Smith, 1971) or some structural deficiencies in the officer corps such as "ticket punching" (Savage and Gabriel, 1976), the rotation system (Bradford and Brown, 1974), or blatant careerism (Savage and Gabriel, 1976). Lewy (1978) captures the civilian sentiment of the period.

But the most important reason for the steady spreading acceptance of the view that the American involvement in Vietnam had been a mistake was probably neither the implausibility of the rationale given for the war nor the preoccupation of both the educated classes and the poor with social reform. The decisive reason for the growing disaffection of the American people was the conviction that the war was not being won and apparently showed little prospect of coming to a successful conclusion. There was a clear correlation between declining support and a mounting casualty toll; the increasing cost in lives, occurring in a war without decisive battles or conquered territory, was the most visible symbol of failure. Hanoi's expectation that the American democracy would not be able to sustain a long and bloody conflict in a faraway land turned out to be more correct than Westmoreland's strategy of attrition, which was supposed to inflict such heavy casualties on the Communists as to force them to cease their aggression. (1978, 432).

Could it have been that commanders, faced with a "no-win" situation, were disproportionately exercising formal controls and applying sanctions to the troops? There is little evidence for this view when the period 1966–71 is compared with the entire period of observation. The shift in deployment pattern was not as severe as noted in other times. Specifically,

1. Court expulsions through the courts reached maximum in 1947 and 1976, not during Vietnam.

2. Punitive bad paper discharges peaked in 1947.

3. All bad paper (taken together) peaked in 1950.

4. All service branches were more harsh after 1975 (as measured by the relative use of punitive discharges) than at any time during Vietnam.

What made the deployment pattern of 1967–71 unique was that it was composed disproportionately of administrative bad paper and increasingly harsh expulsive court action taken against a shrinking number of *very serious* offenders.

I conclude that this was largely a symbolic purging of the ranks. The historically rising social origins of enlistees meant, among other things, that less criminality per se, i.e., crimes against the person and property, was processed through court channels. Also, Project 100,000 personnel were apparently filtering normally into the lower ranks of the enlisted skill structure. The relative flatness of the officer corps' college degree acquisition curve for the period 1967–71 also implies that civilian college graduates were entering the officer ranks at a *slower* pace than was the case before and after 1967–71. This would certainly imply that the profession of arms was clearly losing prestige among the college educated.

At the same time there was a *temporary influx* of those with college degrees into the enlisted ranks. To understand how this combination of factors may have influenced the *ethos of control* during the period it is necessary to examine the impact of military service on enlisted college graduates for clues as to the possible impact this may have had on the social control activities of the officer corps.

THE IMPACT OF THE ENLISTED COLLEGE GRADUATE ON SOCIAL CONTROL PATTERNS

An enlisted man with a college degree is atypical in that he is as educationally qualified as his officer peers of the same age but serves in a position of much lower status. Since the military has no monopoly on the underutilization of personnel in American society, however, the presence of the underutilized would not be substantively important unless there is reason to believe that therein lies a major source of discontent and unrest.

There are some theorists who suggest that this possibility is substantial, and there is partial empirical support for the case that the role of college educated soldiers on the rest of the troops in disruptive (Olson and Rae, 1971; Fink, et al., 1974). No theorists, however, have suggested the possibility of an impact of overeducated enlisted men on the officer corps. It should be remembered that the college educated are vastly under-represented with regard to actually breaking military rules. It has been suggested that their corrosive influence is indirect and operated to produce higher rates of deviance among career enlisted men by creating problems primarily by enhancing the status insecurities of Non-Coms (Moskos, 1971).

During the Vietnam War, the relative deprivation hypothesis—based on the gripes of individual soldiers he observed—was put forth by Charles Moskos. He has suggested that college educated men gripe because they are not treated with the deference they have come to expect by virtue of their middle class backgrounds. In fact, he argues, it is the *only* time in their lives that they will be so treated (Moskos, 1971). He implies that the major source of their griping stems from the officer's rank they lack. This assumes, of course, that one possible remedy to such grievances would be to place these men in the officer corps. This is probably, however, an over-optimistic interpretation for it assumes the discontent of these men is theoretically redressable *within* the military context, i.e., presumably if these men were commissioned they would be less status incongruous, and they would presumably gripe less.

In fact, there was never a time in military history when the officer ranks were completely staffed and there was no need for qualified officers. In the contemporary military there have always been shortages and increasing recruitment into the officer corps from outside, i.e., non-military academy sources, e.g., R.O.T.C. (Janowitz, 1968; Moskowitz and Roberts, 1968; Segal, 1967). Additionally, military lore is seasoned with sagas of highly visible, if not so numerous, troops who worked their way up through the ranks to receive commissions. Thus, in lore and in terms of efficient utilization of manpower, there are incentives for the military to use all qualified manpower available to fill leadership positions.

Additionally, an enlistee with a college degree has such a fact clearly specified on his military record and there is no evidence that enlisted men would conceal their educational levels. The numbers of college-educated enlisted men have also, on average, been a little more than 2% of enlisted strength and reached almost 6% of strength in 1970.

This underutilization of enlisted men is willful in two respects. First, as a matter of policy, nothing prevents the military from giving commissions to en-listed men with college degrees. Indeed, the presence of officers *without* college degrees in the system would seem to indicate that the Department of Defense is reluctant to give commissions to those in the enlisted ranks, even when there are sizable fractions of the force that would qualify on the basis of education (see Table 6.4).

Second, enlisted men are not prevented from applying for commissions which their educational background would surely qualify them. This, however, requires additional time in the service—over and above the length of time specified in the enlistment contract.

It perhaps never occurred to Moskos that degreed enlisted men might prefer *not* to be part of the officer corps, i.e., to do their stint in the ranks and then to leave the system rather than enjoy the high status they would be granted in the commissioned ranks. This latter possibility would even more strongly support the argument that these men pose a threat to the system for they willingly are rejecting the rewards it has to offer.

That is to say, overeducated enlisted men may not compare themselves to their like-educated counterparts who have commissions, and thus feel deprived. Nor would they feel deprived at all if their reference groups were other, less so-cially qualified enlisted men—with respect to whom they would feel superior. They may, however, be more displeased with the operation of the military system, and more critical of it, without regard to the individuated grievances they un-doubtedly have.

This possibility was undoubtedly the concern of the researchers at a contract firm who prepared a report entitled "Determinants of the Potential for Dissi-dence in the U.S. Army" (Olsen and Rae, 1971). Nowhere in this report, however, was it suggested or implied that granting commissions to those in the enlisted ranks might sooth unrest.

The existence of disproportionate numbers of college educated enlisted men in the system might have triggered a response among *certain segments* of the officer corps who lack their qualifications. The possible threat to the legitimacy of the system may not be so much the sum of gripes but apostasy: the implicit denun-ciation of the virtues presumably associated with being an officer. In hindsight, it does not appear a wise decision to enter a protracted, unpopular war using men who have the qualifications to become officers but fail to do so. Such an interpre-tation, of course, implies that when the war is over, and the underutilized return to civilian life, a major source of stress will be removed. To this possibility I now turn.

ORGANIZATIONAL REACTION AND EDUCATIONAL HETEROGENEITY

The research question becomes: Was the surplus of Administrative over Punitive Bad Paper sensitive to movements in the degree of educational credentials accumulation of the officer corps relative to enlisted men? A sensitivity indicator is created: NRAT. Its numerator (NET) is the amount of surplus Administrative Bad Paper in the system, i.e., the administrative minus the punitive discharge rate, expressed as a percent of strength. NET is thus a rate, per unit strength, at which commanders used administrative discharges over punitive ones.

It will be recalled that this represents the degree of involvement of junior and senior officer cadres, remembering that the senior cadres sanction for the more serious offenses requiring the military courts, i.e., BCDs and DHDs. Juniors are more likely to sanction administratively (see Chapter III). The numerator of NRAT is thus a good indicator of the degree to which lower level commanders participate in the sanctioning process, as well as an indicator of the degree to which such commanders are using their discretion to expel wayward troops. Stated otherwise, a positive value for NET *requires* a disproportionate amount of management decisions made by junior officers.

The denominator (EDRAT) is the ratio of Officers' educational discrepancy (lack of a college degree) to enlisted men's possession of a college degree. EDRAT is also a rate. It shows how many non-college educated officers are in the system for each soldier with a college degree. The comparison of both rates shows the *degree* of response in NET Bad Paper to educational attainment of officers relative to enlisted men. This is shown in Chart 6.2, which displays the relative sensitivity of movements in organizational reaction to deviance to the rate at which officers accumulate college degrees relative to enlisted men.

The graph displays the responsiveness of a social control activity (NET Bad Paper) to a social attribute of the officer cadres relative to their charges (their relative-comparative rate of educational attainment).

The chart provides a visual interpretation of how responsive one type of organizational reaction (NET Bad Paper) was to the relative educational qualifications of officers to enlisted men. In light of what I have already shown concerning the stability and fluctuation of enlistee accumulation rates, i.e., enlisted degree fraction ran roughly 2% of enlisted force; the fraction increased due to the draft and during the Vietnam War, NRAT (in measuring the responsiveness of NET to the *relative* standing of officers without degrees to those in the enlisted ranks with degrees) is an indirect measure of officer marginality relative to each

CHART 6.2. NRAT: THE RESPONSIVENESS OF NET BAD PAPER TO EDUCATIONAL CREDENTIALS ACCUMULATIONS OF THE OFFICE CORPS RELATIVE TO THAT OF THE ENLISTED FORCE. DOD, 1952–78.

Series Name   Year   NRAT*
Number of Ordered Pairs 17

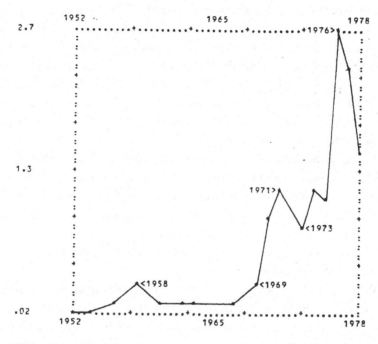

*Rounded (Fiscal years)
KEY: *Relative responsiveness is measured by the steepness of the plot. Absolute responsiveness is measured by the height of the maximum.*
Source: *Chapter endnote 6.*

other and of homogeneity with regard to enlistees. As NRAT grows larger (on the X axis) it means that more and more bad paper was given as the officer corps became more homogeneous with regard to possessing a college degree relative to increases in the rate of degree accumulation in the enlisted ranks. The plot shows:

1. The responsiveness of NET bad paper to the changing officer and enlistee degree accumulation ratio was *highly* variable.

2. Mobilization for Vietnam (1967–70) saw increased administrative bad paper while the military was accessing enlisted college graduates faster than they were being discharged.

3. When Enlisted Flight (i.e., the exodus of enlisted men with college degrees) was greatest (1971–73), the responsiveness of the rate of NET bad paper to discrepancies in the rate of officer–enlisted degree accumulation actually declined. That is, the rate had not yet peaked, and it does not appear that enlisted flight was therefore a likely source for the peaking of reaction rates.

It thus appears that, with regard to surplus bad paper, presumed comparisons between non-degreed officers and enlisted college graduates leaving the system are either not as important as expected, or the relation is masked by the ascendance of other social forces. In fact, the greatest movement in NET Bad paper occurred during 1973–76 *after* the Vietnam Era college graduates who served in the system, as enlisted men, were veterans and the military continued to bring in officers with college degrees at increasing numbers. Percent of the officer corps with college degrees (1973–76) increased from 82.1% to 92.1%: the largest increase during the period under review.

This is quite suggestive evidence that during the part of the Vietnam War which contained the most fighting (1967–71) officers and men become closest to being homogeneous at least with regard to educational credentials. This alone, however, while specifying one way in which the Vietnam War was unique, is also suggestive of the possibility that the officer–enlisted distinction takes on differing functions during war and peace, as evidenced by the different observed patterns of social control.

While NET bad paper rose during the Vietnam War when the concentration of enlistees with college degrees was highest, these men, by and large, started leaving the system in largest numbers between 1971–73—and NET began to drop. NET, however, started to rise quite notably as the All Volunteer Force was being implemented. Indeed, as the war wound down, enlisted troops with college degrees left the system, college men entered the peacetime officer corps in increasing numbers, and the system returned to "normal" with more bad paper levied against a shrinking force. To explain this pattern it is necessary to examine changes in the volume of deviance in the military along with the changes in the decisions of commanders to punish the troops.

NOTES: CHAPTER VI

Materials from this chapter have been modified and published as: "The Officer–enlisted Distinction and Patterns of Organizational Reaction to Social Deviance in the U.S. Military" 1990. *Social Forces* Vol. 68(4), 1191–1209.

1. These criteria follow from three assumptions. 1. War plays a central role in the structure, function, and operation of the military system. 2. There is a relation between deviance rates and the social qualifications of soldiers. 3. Rates of deviance are, in large degree, the

product of social differentiation. My interest in the social distinctiveness of the officer corps as a source of varying control strategies is informed by the general notion that homogeneous groups experience less deviance than heterogeneous ones. Hence modern societies more so than traditional ones; pluralistic societies more than those where there are few competitors for scarce recourses; and very complex organizations more than less complex ones. The *degree* to which the social distinctiveness of the officer corps may be important is, however, an empirical question.

2. This appears to be an outcome of the rather limited mission of the United States military, namely defense and the preparation for war. Militaries with other purposes such as nation building, internal policing and deviance control in civilian populations, or peace keeping (for example, U.N. forces) have criteria other than success at war by which their forces and commanders can be judged. Other institutions which share the military's reliance on coercion (the prisons, for example) are also often evaluated using post-institutional outcomes, such as recidivism rates as a measure of institutional effectiveness. In this case the debate that follows usually centers upon what may be seen as the central mission of the institution. The point is that institutions with more than one central mission, or purpose, are less likely to have incumbents held directly accountable for the diffuse goals of that institution. For this reason, whatever else the military may do is usually seen as secondary to winning at war. Lewy (1978) for example has argued quite rigorously that the conduct of American forces in Vietnam was well within the boundaries of international law, and that our soldiers *given the limitations of the false strategic assumptions under which they labored,* performed quite well. None the less, Vietnam produced few heroes, and it has been a full dozen years after the war ended before a public parade for Vietnam vets was held in New York City. Presumably, wars are won by effective soldiers who are led by commanders held in high public esteem. The Vietnam War, however, was fought by soldiers, on average, with higher levels of education and skill than either World War II or Korea, and with more college-educated officers and enlisted men than was the case in the earlier wars.

3. For a discussion of some aspect of the social representativeness of the American military see: Ambrose, 1973; Barber 1973; Butler, 1976; DOA, 1971, 1972; Fernandez, 1979; Fisher and Harford, 1973; Hackel, 1970; Holbrook, 1971; Janowitz, 1973a, 1973b; Janowitz and Moskos, 1974; Karpinos, 1967, 1975b; Latham, 1974; Lee and Parker, 1977; Marmion, 1971; McNall, 1973; Moskos, 1971b, 1973a; Saunders, 1974; Sinaiko, 1977; Sullivan, 1970; USARI, 1977; U.S. Senate, 1978; Vitola, 1974.

4. Department of Defense Enlisted Force Educational Distributions.

EMAX=Variation from Minimum=ENL-ENLM
PMAX=Percentage Change in EMAX
PMAX=EMAX/ENLM Times 100
ENLM=Minimum Enlisted College Grad. Percentage
ENL=Enlisted Force With College Degrees (Percent)

TABLE 6.5. ENLISTED FORCE EDUCATIONAL DISTRIBUTIONS 1952-78,
DOD. FISCAL YEARS.

Fiscal Year	EMAX*	ENL*	ENLM	PMAX*
1952	1.4	2.8	1.4	100.0
1954	1.8	3.2	1.4	128.6
1956	1.4	2.8	1.4	100.0

1958	.5	1.9	1.4	35.7
1960	.1	1.5	1.4	7.1
1962	0	1.4	1.4	0
1963	0	1.4	1.4	0
1967	.8	2.2	1.4	57.1
1969	3.5	4.9	1.4	250.0
1970	4.4	5.8	1.4	314.3
1971	3.6	5.0	1.4	257.1
1973	.5	1.9	1.4	35.7
1974	.3	1.7	1.4	21.4
1975	.2	1.6	1.4	14.3
1976	1.0	2.4	1.4	71.4
1977	1.3	2.7	1.4	92.9
1978	.7	2.1	1.4	50.0

*Rounded
Source: LTR, USAFMPC, 1982.

5. Department of Defense Officer Corps Educational Computation

OMAX=Variation From Minimum=OFF-OFFM
POFF=Percentage Change in OMAX
POFF=OMAX/OFFM Times 100
OFF=Percentage of Officers With Degrees
OFFM=Minimum Value for Officers With Degrees

TABLE 6.6. OFFICER CORPS EDUCATIONAL COMPUTATIONS 1952–78, DOD.

Fiscal Year	OMAX*	OFF*	OFFM*	POFF*
1952	0	46.6	46.6	0
1954	3.1	49.7	46.6	6.7
1956	8.9	55.5	46.6	19.1
1958	9.5	56.1	46.6	20.4
1960	10.6	57.2	46.6	22.7
1962	18.0	64.6	46.6	38.6
1963	22.8	69.4	46.6	48.9
1967	25.7	72.3	46.6	55.2

1969	26.3	72.9	46.6	56.4
1970	29.7	76.3	46.6	63.7
1971	26.8	73.4	46.6	57.5
1973	35.5	82.1	46.6	46.2
1974	40.8	87.4	46.6	87.6
1975	42.2	88.8	46.6	90.6
1976	44.6	91.2	46.6	95.7
1977	46.9	93.5	46.6	100.6
1978	47.0	93.6	46.6	100.9

Fiscal Year	PMAX**	POFF
1952	100.0	0
1954	128.6	6.7
1956	100.0	19.1
1958	35.7	20.4
1960	7.1	22.7
1962	0	38.6
1963	0	48.9
1967	57.1	55.2
1969	250.0	56.4
1970	314.3	63.7
1971	257.1	57.5
1973	35.7	76.2
1974	21.4	87.6
1975	14.3	90.6
1976	71.4	95.7
1977	92.9	100.6
1978	50.0	100.8

*Rounded (Fiscal Years)
Source: Chapter endnote 3.

6. EDRAT, NET and NRAT

TABLE 6.7. EDRAT, NET AND NRAT

Fiscal Year	EDRAT*	NET*	NRAT*
1952	2.60	.04	.02
1954	2.14	.14	.07
1956	2.16	.41	.19
1958	3.15	.90	.29
1960	3.89	.48	.12
1962	3.44	.57	.16
1963	2.98	.41	.14
1967	1.40	.21	.15
1969	.75	.25	.33
1970	.55	.54	.98
1971	.72	.89	1.23
1973	1.28	1.14	.89
1974	1.01	1.20	1.19
1975	.95	1.09	1.14
1976	.49	1.30	2.65
1977	.32	.75	2.34
1978	.41	.63	1.54

*Rounded.

Source: Chapter endnote 3.

KEY: In 1952 for every enlisted person with a college degree, 2.60 officers were without one; NET Bad Paper was .04 of strength, and the value for NRAT was .02

CHAPTER VII. ORGANIZATIONAL REACTION AND THE VOLUME OF DEVIANCE
IN THE ARMY: THE VIETNAM ERA

This chapter probes deeper into the sanctioning behavior of commanders during a critical period, i.e., 1964–72, when organizational reaction patterns were atypical. Two lines of argument are examined which identify the sources of organizational reaction as either the result of soldierly behavior *or* the social control decisions of commanders. For this task, absenteeism is conceptualized as a volitional type of deviance initiated by soldiers and other control activities (courts-martial, Article 15) as forms of organizational reaction initiated by the officer corps.

Soldiers can absent themselves as well as break other attendance rules. The volume of identified deviance in the military is thus approximated by the absenteeism rate and the rate of punishment of *all other* offenses. There is, of course, the possibility of double-counting. While I lack data on offense distributions, I am willing to assume that any double-counting as may exist remains essentially small and relatively stable. In any case, as will be shown shortly, even of one makes very generous assumptions concerning accounting practices in the military, the trends in absenteeism and organizational reaction vary substantially.

Since I know, however, that the bulk of absentees *do* face the courts, the court-martial rate minus absenteeism rates, plus "all other" offenses affords a reasonable measure of the use of discretionary authority on the part of commanders. Why this is so will be explained shortly.

My analysis proceeds in four stages:

1) Examining the "problem" of absenteeism as shown by the writings on this subject.

2) Examining the importance of the war-peace cycle on rates of absenteeism.

3) Presenting data on "all other" kinds of organizational reaction minus those responses directed at absentee soldiers.

4) Qualifying my findings as applicable only to those periods when deployment patterns had shifted. The *ethos of control* for this chapter spans the Vietnam War and its aftermath.

Specifically, the hypothesis that the volume of deviance in the system, i.e., what soldiers do, determines levels of organizational reaction, is examined along with variation in the discretionary decisions made by commanders as these involve court usage and Article 15. An Article 15 is more severe than all informal controls, yet milder than all legal controls—such as the courts or bad paper. I shall begin by examining the problem of absence.

MILITARY ABSENTEES: AWOL AND DESERTION

No other topic, other than perhaps mutiny, has captured the minds of journalists, novelists, military commanders, the general public—in wartime—and certainly the social scientists who work directly for the military, than AWOL (Absent Without Official Leave) and Desertion. For the latter, the only analog in civil society is *escapee*—drawn from prison settings—since there is no domestic equivalent.

My interest lies in the importance of absenteeism—as an event—in specifying the most elementary demand that the military makes on its members: being there for duty. This emphasis on control is explicitly referred to in the military's internal accounting scheme: when AWOL a soldier is not under military control—and loses all benefits appertaining (including his right to have such time spent count as a period of creditable service). Upon return to garrison, or upon verification to military authorities of his whereabouts, he is seen again as under military control. When AWOL, the soldier's relation to the state is unambiguous: he is a fugitive.

Desertion, contrary to popular wisdom—and legal statute[1]—is protracted (30 days or longer) AWOL (absence). Since it is extremely difficult for military courts to prove intent to *not* return to military duty, the military's chronological accounting method greatly simplifies the issue of seriousness of offense: being AWOL is very serious, being a deserter is extremely serious.

The majority of courts-martial are for AWOL cases (Radine, 1977; 209) and, as such, are federal convictions which follow a soldier for the rest of his life (Radine, 211). Being absent is thus, in military eyes, a grave offense: it is more seriously punished than possessing an undesirable trait, attitude, or incapacity that, at worst, could result in a General or Undesirable Discharge, and most minor acts of criminality as well as most military and civil offenses in general.

Being AWOL is also seen as a rule violation which is remediable. AWOLs are punished with what might be called "intent to reform" and compose the largest population in military correctional facilities ostensibly charged with the correction of personnel who are seen as disciplinary problems. AWOL is an archetypical military offense in that it lacks a civilian counterpart, consumes probably a disproportionate amount of military legal resources, and is a routine concern of commanders at all levels.[2]

AWOL is also the least ambiguously defined military offense. Daily strength-force accounting in the military system requires a headcount as part of the daily routine of military life. There is more flexibility than is true for the roll call in prison settings, as the context of the worksite is more variable and it may take hours, instead of minutes, before controls are put into effect to account for tardy troops. But lateness is noted fairly quickly as each soldier has an established duty station to which he must report at the start of the duty day.

The differences in this regard are perhaps narrowing however, as formal worksite controls tend to enhance the legal imperative behind the soldier role to be, in fact, present and modern accounting methods and reporting systems have undoubtedly shortened the time necessary for lateness. Although degrees of lateness are negotiable, in part, by the definition of the situation held by the commander and the circumstances surrounding the act, absences of greater than twenty four hours are recorded as AWOLs.

AWOL is thus the least complex of deviant acts in military settings: it involves chronological accounting and a social interpretation on the part of those in control of soldiers, within a span of time that has a lower limit of twenty four hours, after which the event is pre-defined as a matter of doctrine. Before this time frame it can be transformed into *Failure to Repair*—an Article 15 offense.

SETTING THE STAGE: PERCEPTION

The problem of AWOL is conceptualized in military circles in terms that William Ryan (1972; 17) would call exceptionalistic:

> The exceptionalist viewpoint is reflected in arrangements that are private, voluntary, remedial, special, local and exclusive. Such arrangements imply that problems occur to specially defined categories of persons in an unpredictable manner. The problems are unusual, even unique, they are exceptions to the rule, they are seen as a result of individual defect, accident, or unfortunate circumstances and must be remediated by means that are particular and, as it were, tailored to the individual case.

Being AWOL is a problem that a soldier *has*. The bulk of research conducted in the past decades years on this problem informs us more of disciplinary fads surrounding the preferences of the researchers than suggests the political nature of the phenomenon. The bulk of studies conducted have vainly attempted to distinguish the AWOL from the non-AWOL. A glance at the more important pieces of military social science are illustrative of the innocence, on the part of the researchers, of the *status*-related nature of the event: The typical AWOL is, for all wars examined in this research, and all peace periods as well, an adolescent enlistee. The transformation of a juvenile delinquency issue into a serious command concern informs us more of the power of military institutions, and their researchers, to influence contemporary thinking about young men—and the implied seriousness of their shortcomings—than perhaps has been thought possible.

In addition, the American military has, perhaps unintentionally, exported these notions and research strategies to foreign soil—where they are thriving quite well among armies that can afford applied social science research funds (see Boddaert, 1970 for an example of Dutch research on the characteristics of AWOLs or any similar foreign language citation since World War II).

AWOL and desertion represent the failure of older boys to accept the constraints of the soldier role. These phenomena are political in that it is in the decided interest of the organization that this population does not become too large. Organizational controls are applied to literally bring wandering soldiers back to the fold. What ensues is a contest between soldier and the state over commanders' rights to contain their charges. In military settings, of course, the likelihood is that the state will prevail. Indeed, wayward troops are punished regularly, and the authority to do so is rarely questioned.

The phenomena are not *exclusively* political, however, as there is a normative component as well: a boundary defining capability. I suspect that the military has a decided interest in assuring that *some* form of rule breaking is singled out for punishment.

In addition, since most AWOLs return to duty after being sanctioned, a short-term confinement strategy is practiced with regard to absentees. This weakens the possibility that elimination of the behavior can be a reasonable policy goal. In fact, as I shall show, the military tolerates different amounts of absenteeism at different times.

It is an axiom of this research that to the degree that social institutions are seen to differ from one another, one such way of making such differences clear is to generate an institutionally specific stream of offenders through which collective attention can be focused.

Any specific institutional claim to distinction, requires, by necessity, the manufacture of a distinctive type of outsider by which its claim to uniqueness can be known. Caste societies literally create outcasts; religious orders: heretics; capitalist societies: particular brands of thieves and confidence men; socialist orders: enemies of the people. Educational systems create drop-outs; free-market societies create the unemployed, and the military creates AWOLs and Deserters.

Such deviants constitute an apparently necessary population which serves as a reference point by which the conforming characteristics of insiders are known. It is my belief that the size of these populations serves as a particularly accurate unobtrusive measure (Webb, et al., 1963) of institutional crises within the system. Central to my research interest is the degree to which the officer–enlisted distinction serves as a credible vehicle for social control. Organizational reaction to deviance is precipitated when this social arrangement loses its legitimacy. More on this possibility shortly.

DEFINING THE PROBLEM: INDIVIDUAL DEFICIENCIES

What follows is a rough sketch of selected social science and other writings which have addressed the problem of the AWOL soldier. It is selective in that the pieces chosen roughly represent what I see to be the most important works. It is exhaustive in that it was drawn from the published works of social scientists for which a document or abstract was available in English and which were written since World War II and the end of the Vietrnam Era.

Manson and Grayson (1946) noted the prevalence of neuropsychiatric symptoms (psychiatry's early contribution); Clark's (1948) study sought behavioral correlates—perhaps indicative of psychology's concerns in that era; the fifties presented a fair mix of flawed personality studies, and the sixties saw the quest for deviant motivations for going AWOL. Tausk's study is perhaps illustrative: in 1969, his 1917 paper was translated. It is entitled, "On The Psychology of The War Deserter." Thus indicating, perhaps, increased interest on the part of some members of the social science community of some possibly debilitating effects of the Vietnam War on troop motivation.

Hartnagel's prisoner sample (n=244) revealed insufficient socialization (1974), and the work of sociologist Shils revealed poor integration into society with weak primary group ties to units (1974). The work of Boyd and Jones (1973) surfaced flaws in the demographic nature of the troops (namely youth and lack of education) during a time when entrance requirements were less restrictive. One of the more recent works on Vietnam Era Deserters concluded (Bell and Houston, 1976, 44):

Some soldiers are statistically more likely to desert than others; reasons for desertion are multiple and personally compelling; rates increase in wartime, and desertion is hard to predict.

This piece of "in-house" research lists the most comprehensive bibliography of research reports conducted by defense department social researchers, and others, on AWOL and Desertion since World War II (53 items). The bulk of the in-house studies, i.e., those conducted under military auspices, are concerned with predicting, or controlling (deterring or reforming) problem personnel, including a few articles on attempts to properly screen military personnel and a spattering of correlation studies designed to isolate the deficiencies of absentee soldiers, and a piece or two which locate the ubiquitous remedy of all military troubles in the fine tuning of the leadership skills of those in control.

THE QUEST FOR PROFILES

The writings of social scientists unattached to the military which have appeared in scholarly journals of the period (1946–77) have been predominately written by those skilled in psychiatric or psychological techniques which have been applied to captive military samples of AWOLs in quest of deviant personalities, syndromes, character flaws and the like which presumably contain *the essence* of the transgressor of military norms. Noticeably absent from these researches is a citation which might suggest or imply that fleeing from the military system is, in part, provoked, facilitated by, or the consequence of conflict therein, i.e., in the conditions of life faced by young enlistees.

Although the Vietnam War has surfaced some concern on the part of commanders that desertion might be a political reaction to that war—when political is narrowly defined as being synonymous with dissent over the goals of the State Department—this possibility was officially laid to rest with a presidential Clemency Program finding that dissidents were a small minority of Vietnam Era Deserters and, presumably the sources of the problem reside comfortably on the shoulders of the victims: diagnosable by available command tools, i.e., proper leadership and troop screening and selection (DoAPCP, 1975, 21). The virtual consensus on the part of the military and civilian research communities to view AWOL and desertion as astructural concerns is, fortunately, not total.

Two obscure (unpublished dissertations) and one relatively unknown (to the general social science community) source suggest other factors at work. Namely: the work of Henry and Borgatta (1953), showing officers are more likely than enlisted men to entertain attitudes toward pardoning enlisted deserters. Thus differential attitudes among officers and men toward protracted absentee troops suggests the possibility of a latent acknowledgement of second thoughts on the part of individual officers over how their actions influence enlisted men.

Krise's 1958 work is suggestive that role conflict best explains military offenders' (as opposed to soldiers who committed civil-like crimes) reluctance to reform (hence allusions to discrepancies in military *role*). Finally, Edmonson's study of Revolutionary War Deserters (1971)—while not concerned with any of the twentieth century wars—found:

> From 20 to 25% of the soldiers deserted for reasons such as physical hardship and lack of pay, to homesickness and failed attempts to collect additional bounties offered to new recruits.

These studies attempt to locate the reasons for fleeing the military in terms which transcend the idiosyncrasies of individual soldiers. They are important attempts to suggest that soldiering may call forth allegiances to other than the chain of command, institutional rules, and the claims of the social pathologists (Mills, 1943).

To be absent is to choose to align one's self with a set of values that are more compelling than obligations to the military system. A likely source of such tight bonds is the family. In fact, Nisbet (1973) has noted that the tension between the military and the kinship system—in terms of competing allegiances—has marked the development of Western Civilization.

The AWOL soldier, then, embodies this historical conflict as he is acting to place a higher value on physical presence to his real or imagined comrades (family, friends, primary groups) outside the confines of the garrison than to those within.

I speculate that the above suggests that the AWOL soldier is thus making a positive choice in terms of his prime allegiances: a rebellious statement without an articulated political agenda. To be away from military control is to be invariably bonded to a civilian primary group. AWOL soldiers—like fugitives from prison—immediately seek the support and comfort of those dear to them. It is for this reason that military police invariably attempt to track down absentees by sending scouts to the soldiers reported home, and why they have an impossible task when soldiers overseas leave their military obligations at the gate of the post or base.

I am also convinced that the likelihood of strong ties rapidly emerging between troops and their civilian significant others is related to the amount of physical risk in the system. This is because the presence of such risk is much more variable than the social-psychological proclivities of the troops which, if social-psychologists are to be believed—notwithstanding those who write for the military—are grounded in the *basic personalities* of individuals, and thus relatively stable—having emerged and grown over their lifetimes.

Additionally, since soldiers—like everyone else—can be expected to undoubtedly have fond feeling for intimate civilian others, the research question becomes: Under which circumstances should such feelings *erupt* to break the bonds of the soldier role?

I suggest that the attraction to civilian based primary groups is greatly facilitated by the repulsion of the Army brought about by the presence of physical risk. We should expect to witness a decline in absenteeism when physical risks are lessened: that is, the push of physical risk is greater than the pull of primary group civilian responsibilities.

From the research cited, one must be extremely cautious of assuming that the motives of absentees necessarily change in any manner other than to suggest that enlistees exhibit varying degrees of willingness to stay in uniform. Voting with one's feet represents an extreme lack of accommodation to the military role. But it does suggest a lower limit on the control structure beyond which the system fails to coerce. At the upper limit of such a control span is, of course, death and injury: physical risk.

There is, additionally, a problem concerning print-media depictions of military absenteeism, especially desertion. Print media accounts of desertion reached maximum at roughly "early" or "mid" war periods—during the Vietnam War—when, presumably, civilians begin to question the nation's military adventures. The critics invariably *understate* their case vis-à-vis control proclivities of those in command, and *overstate* the presumed "deviant tendencies" of the troops.

That is, there is usually a spate of "decay," "demoralization," and "erosion of effectiveness" pieces directed at the "failures" of leadership, or the presumed vices of the troops—drug use in Vietnam being a case of the latter. Such writing, often by journalists—and sometimes by more sober and reflective professional officers with an eye to reform (see Bradford and Brown, 1974)—however, is a rather weak explanation of the *social control* patterns in the military.

To cite just one example, in 1968 there were eight editorials or articles in *The New York Times* concerning "desertion"; in 1969, 25 pieces appeared; and 9 were written in 1970. None appeared thereafter. Actual desertion rate maxima, as I will shortly show, were reached in 1971 for the Army, 1972 for the Air Force, 1975 for the Marines, and 1977 for the Navy. Such writings are perhaps better seen as an indicator of "war weariness" than as accurate measures of military reality. More troops clearly deserted from the military *after* the bulk of the fighting than during it. Whatever prompted increased reportage and commentary on the subject of military desertion, it was clearly not increased incidence of the behavior.

Following this line of thinking, it should not be altogether surprising to find that, after a war, the attention directed at the *apparatus of social control* becomes even less. A quick glance at the writings in the "lessons of" genre and tradition of military writing, other than to mention "morale" and the obligatory citations to "leadership" indeed overlooks the officer corps in its entirety (Summers, 1982).

Most enlistees, of course, experience a middle course: they do not go AWOL or desert; nor are they physical or social casualties. Extreme movements of either intolerance on the part of enlistees to remain in uniform, or an escalation of physical risk, suggest the possibility that the two extremes may, in fact, be related: controls may be applied precisely to insure that the ranks of those who find military service intolerable remains small in proportion to the presence of physical risk.

BRANCH VARIATION IN DESERTION RATES

Table 7.1 examines desertion activity in the Army in perspective with activities in the other branches (1965–1980). Maximum and minimum values are shown to give some sense of the variation in protracted absence.

TABLE 7.1. DESERTION RATES, ALL BRANCHES, MINIMA AND MAXIMA

Branch	Minimum	Maximum
Marines	16.1 (1966)	105.0 (1975)
Army	6.7 (1966)	73.5 (1971)
Navy	6.7 (1965)	31.6 (1977)
Air Force	.4 (1965)	2.8 (1972)

Source: See chapter endnote 3.

There is quite a noticeable difference in desertion rates between the branches. The ground forces clearly experience the greatest rates—with the Marines clearly in the lead (105 per thousand strength) followed by the Army (73.5 per thousand). Sea force maxima and minima run about one half of the Army figures and the Air Force stands in a class by itself: with its maximum rate (2.8 per thousand) being less than half of the Navy's minimum. While all branches were experiencing minimum rates in the early part of the Vietnam War, maxima for the Army and Air Force occurred near the end of the war whereas Marine and Naval forces saw their greatest losses in the post-war period. Marines and sailors are apparently less willing to stay in their branches during peacetime than in the case for those in the Air Force or the Army.

Desertion is extended absence—it is an extreme case of AWOL—the major difference is that the deserter has chosen to be away permanently. The two offenses differ substantively in terms of punishments received, and presumably in terms of the commitments of the offenders to the military. AWOLs return to the fold and are punished or expelled. Deserters are punished *and* expelled. AWOL rates,[4] as would be expected, follow desertion rates[5] quite closely. This is illustrated by the Army (in Chart 7.1).

CHART 7.1. U.S. ARMY, DESERTION AND AWOL RATES. FISCAL YEARS 1965–1980.

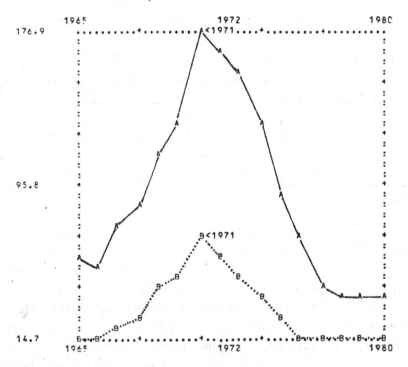

	X-AXIS X	Y-AXIS Y	
Pair	Series	Series	Symbol
1	Year	ARWOL	A ‹AWOL
2	Year	ARDES	B ‹Desertion
Number of Ordered Pairs		16	

KEY: *In 1971, Army AWOL Rates per 1,000 strength stood at 176.9.*
Source: *Chapter endnote 5*

It should be noted that the Army pattern of closely matching contours of both AWOL and Desertion curves is observed for all branches, as the correlation coefficient (R) between AWOL and Desertion for each branch is: Air Force (.984), Navy (.969), Marines (.962) and Army (.958).

The closeness of the association between AWOL and Desertion rates is suggestive that protracted absence is a logical extension of whatever social forces precipitate short term excursions from the soldier role—only more so as the case may be: AWOL and Desertion are the same type of offense.

To be absent effectively neutralizes the claims of the military to control its charges: hence the extreme dangerousness of such actions to organizations based on coercion. Voting with one's feet is not far, symbolically, from treason: an outright dis-allegiance to national authority, or more correctly, an allegiance to an authority that transcends the soldier role and its claims.

The military thus generates a stream of organizational émigrés that, it appears, it has a decided interest in reforming or punishing for past temporal transgressions. This population of absentees may serve as a source of internal cohesion and order in the ranks. Attention is directed to a highly visible group of public order offenders and various sanctions are imposed.

THE EXTENT AND MEANING OF ABSENTEEISM

Taken together, AWOL and Desertion are offenses which involve the least discretion on the part of commanders: they are the least ambiguous examples of deviant acts. They are also the single most common type of regularly occurring form of rule violation as well as the most frequently occurring serious offense type. I shall use the sum of AWOL and Desertion rates as an indicator of behavioral deviance which is most typically military as well as an indicator of the collective unwillingness of enlistees to perform their soldierly roles in the U.S. Army. Such rates thus approximate pure deviance in the military system, they address the research question: "What were the frequencies of uniquely military rule violations that require the least amount of interpretation on the part of the officer cadres?" Chart 7.2 presents all absenteeism for the U.S. Army, 1965–1979.

It must be noted that I am necessarily distorting the magnitude of absenteeism in the U.S. Army by combining incidence rates. While some simultaneity is present, i.e., some troops are AWOL and some are deserters at the same time, the actual event rate is not precisely known. AWOL incidences (see Note 4) *understate* the true event rate, while desertion incidences (see Note 5) do so to a lesser degree.

For a worst case analysis with regard to the degree to which the rates are valid indicators of the amount of soldier-initiated, unambiguous deviance in the Army, let us momentarily assume that there were no desertions, *per se*: that desertion rates as depicted, represent all possible sources of accounting error which correct for all *overstatement* of offence rates.

CHART 7.2. COMBINED AWOL AND DESERTION RATES: U.S. ARMY, 1965–1979.

X-AXIS	*Y-AXIS*
Series Name	*Year OUT*
Number of Ordered Pairs	*15*

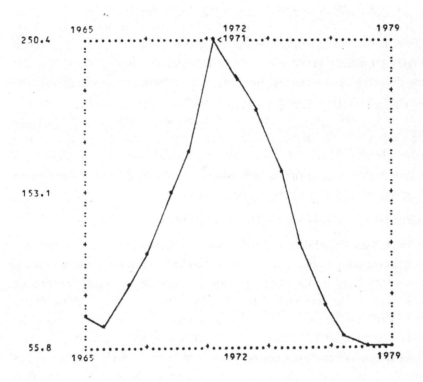

KEY: *AWOL and Desertion incidences in the U.S. Army totaled 250.4 per 1,000 strength in 1971.*
Source: Chapter endnote 3

This is a most generous assumption as the rates tend to be understatements, and Desertions do in fact occur and are punished severely. In any event, even if I subtract all desertion incidences and count only AWOLs as true soldier initiated deviance, the rates are quite substantial and cannot be dismissed. In fact, for the period under review, the desertion rate was about 1/3 of the AWOL rate (see Note 3), on average, or about 1 protracted absence for every two shorter term absences.

My major argument, however, is directed at the *rapid* expansion and contractions of both deviance rates which occurred in quite a striking manner. Thee clearly was a *deviance wave* composed of absentees during the Vietnam War.

The overall shape of the plot clearly follows the war cycle. When one recalls the strength plot for the Army—and that a buildup of forces is proportional to the amount of physical risk in the system—enlistees clearly became less willing to remain in uniform as physical risk escalated. The rapid rise and fall of absenteeism rates, however, is clearly inconsistent with most typical social science explanations offered for absenteeism for the simple reason that the demographic and social-psychological attributes of the enlisted force change slowly over time.

In addition, the scale of the absenteeism phenomena is substantial. The data make suspect an interpretation that improper socialization, disrespect for authority, or any other supposed deficiency of the troops could be a realistic explanation for such rapid movement in deviance rates, as it is extremely improbable that such pathological imbalances could have come and gone in so short a period of time.

SOLDIER-INITIATED DEVIANCE RATES

Absenteeism rates have a number of attributes which distinguish them from other forms of deviance in military settings: the response they elicit from the officer corps is unambiguous. Doubtless a few cases of absenteeism are due to accounting error, but this form of rule breaking is the least likely to be refutable as it is the most demonstrable of violations. In addition to being a victimless offense (Schur, 1969) it is also the type of rule breaking that is least likely to have an ideological component.

This latter attribute represents a potential for these types of offense to support the legitimacy of the military control system since the legal agenda in such cases is focused almost entirely on whether or not a given soldier in fact *did* or *did not* go AWOL (or desert). This kind of dispositional dispute leaves intact the authority to make such decisions.

That is to say, for absenteeism, the courts are less likely to impute motive (Lofland, 1969) to a wayward soldier, but rather to concern themselves with the factuality of the rule breaking. When this is the agenda, it is likely that legitimate authority will be enhanced.

There are, of course, natural limits on the amount of deviance that can be tolerated within social institutions. Excessive amounts of disruption can result in social disorganization. Since this is a real possibility in the military—as in other institutions—controls are not limited to enforcing acts of law, i.e., use of the courts.

THE SECOND TIER OF CONTROL

The military system, in addition to the three court-martial types (General, Special and Summary) discussed in Chapter II—which constitute *legal* controls—has a second form of control which may be termed quasi-legal or, as is the common military usage, non-judicial punishment or Article 15. The numerical reference is to Article 15 of the Uniform Code of Military Justice (UCMJ) which:

> ...authorizes any commanding officer, no matter how small his unit, to impose punishment on the men in his command and without having to prove his case before a court-martial (Rivkin, 1970, 225).

The punishment imposed under Article 15 has certain legal implications (it carries force of law enforcement provisions, and limited appeal rights) but, unlike strictly legal sanctions, it is not as permanent a disposition (it does not appear on a man's record after he leaves the military system—but is recorded internally in military personnel dockets). For my purposes it shall be considered a limited form of institutional control. The salient characteristics of Article 15 sanctions are provided below as a succinct summary. All citations are from Radine, 1970, 186-87.

> Nonjudicial punishment as specified by Article 15 is not adjudged in the way one would normally think of as a trial. Rather, analogous to being cited for violation of the traffic code (getting a traffic ticket), the accused soldier may decide not to contest his case and accept the provisions of Article 15 and receive punishment without his guilt having been established in court. A soldier's use of the term *Article 15* is similar to a civilian's use of the term *ticket*. A soldier might say, I got three Article 15s this year, just as a civilian might say, I got three tickets this year. There are provisions for a limited appeal of Article 15s.

> To provide some idea of the extensive use by commanders of Article 15s, legal clerks have commented (in interviews) that the usual rate of Article 15s in a permanent party company (comprising around 200 to 300 men) is approximately ten or twenty a month. Too many Article 15s, however, might suggest that a commander cannot control his men with leadership techniques and is resorting to harsher forms of punishment.

> The limits to punishment under Article 15 vary and are dependent on whether the accused is an officer (a rare case) or where the act is committed (for example, on a vessel). An Article 15 could result in restrictions to post, reduction in grade, forfeiture of pay, and correctional custody. For example, thirty days is the maximum prison term if the Article 15 is given by a field grade officer (Major or above); by a company grade officer (Captain), correctional custody may be seven days.

> Article 15s, of course, can be given only for infractions of the UCMJ, but, as we will see, almost any resistance to military authority can be construed to be an offense against the UCMJ. Furthermore, they are only used

for minor offenses. The main value of Article 15s for commanders is as a form of punishment to maintain discipline.

In summary:

> The Article 15 is an enormously useful technique of social control: it is almost entirely in the province of the commanding officer, and there is little chance of that the soldier will use his limited appeal rights. Some reasons that the task force (i.e., *The Task Force on the Administration of Military Justice*—RJS) heard for the fact that most soldiers do not appeal their Article 15 punishments were that it would be a useless gesture or, worse that it would result in some form of retaliation from their commanders. If the punishment of an Article 15 happened to be confinement or restriction, there would be little incentive to appeal because the appeal procedure is so slow that the soldier would have served his time before the appeal was processed. If a soldier were likely to appeal, he probably would have turned down the Article 15 in the first place and asked for an actual trial, that is, a court-martial. (Note: Radine points out that if a soldier refuses to take an Article 15, the case is tried at a court-martial, and he knowingly risks a more severe punishment. (1970, 186)).

Commanders' actions under Article 15 thus *identify* wayward soldiers in the personnel system in a very broad manner which can be intensified or dismissed in the eyes of the subsequent commanders who have occasion to scan personnel records. Each commander has the clear discretionary option of using the Article 15 or some other means (i.e., counseling, verbal dressing down or warnings) in handling soldiers seen to be remiss in their duties. The choice to use punishment under Article 15 is forthrightly a decision to label certain kinds of rule breakers.

Unlike statute violations which share some degree of consensus among officers and troops as being fairly serious, i.e., formally written rules and law violations, and for which a court-martial action may be considered, there are no rigidly defined Article 15 offenses: an Article 15 can be given by a commanding officer when he arrives at the conclusion that "something must be done" to control a given soldier. This is not to suggest that Article 15s are administered randomly, but rather that they reflect the discretionary judgment of commanding officers to use punishment when they believe other means of control have either failed or will not result in the desired change in soldierly conduct; this being a prerogative of command.

At the system level, the rate at which Article 15s are given reflects commanders' collective judgments as to the efficacy of informal controls in the military. Put another way, the officer corps, by selecting Article 15 as a means of control *simultaneously* creates a need for the acknowledgment of the disciplinary component of command which is measured by the selfsame activity it is supposed to suppress:

troop indiscipline. Perceived wayward behavior thus calls forth some command response—one option of which is non-judicial punishment.

There is, for this reason, a natural limit on the number of Article 15s that can be given: sufficient enough to reflect commanders' perceptions of adequate discipline at a point in time, but not in excess of that amount that would imply—to other officers—that a given commander lacks the requisite leadership ability to control his charges.

Article 15 rates represent the lowest level of the *formal* control hierarchy: punitive actions are taken and documents are generated. Chart 7.3 depicts cross-branch Article 15 activity for the period (fiscal 1965-80).

CROSS BRANCH CONTROL PATTERNS: ARTICLE 15

Article 15 profiles are quite branch specific. The Air Force experienced the lowest rates: its officers chose Article 15 punishment such that 29 to 56 troops per thousand were formally sanctioned during the period. This represents roughly a doubling of the rate from a low of 29 (1966) to the peak in 1980 (56.6). The rate climbed sharply in 1972 (from 36.3 to 50.3), remained fairly stable until 1975 when it dipped and increased to its peak in 1980. For the Air Force, non-judicial punishment was a late-war and peace period phenomenon.

Naval and Army officers reacted quite differently in terms of severity and frequency of sanctioning. Naval officers became decreasingly reliant on non-judicial sanctions during 1968–70, their use stabilized in 1971–72, and then roughly doubled during 1973–74 (from 99.6 in 1972 to 202.9 in 1974). For the Navy, non-judicial sanctions were a late-war and post war phenomena. When one examines the rate maxima and minima, a Sailor was roughly three to four times more likely to face Article 15 discipline than an Airman.

Army officers placed increasing reliance on non-judicial punishment fairly early in the Vietnam War. The rates began higher than in any of the other branches (186.4 in 1965), dipped the next two years (1966, 67), and steadily rose to a maximum of 223.3 in 1973 with a wavy pattern thereafter. For the Army, increased Article 15 sanctioning essentially followed the span of the Vietnam War. For the entire period, Army non-judicial sanctioning ranged from 156 to 223 events per thousand active duty personnel.

At any given time, however, roughly fifteen to twenty percent of the Army was being called before the officer cadres for sanctioning. This compares with roughly nine to twenty percent for the Navy. The Army, however, reached the roughly 20 percent figure in 1969 (196.6) and essentially remained at that level thereafter. The Navy hit a 20 percent peak (202.9) in 1974.

CHART 7.3. ARTICLE 15 RATES PER 1,000 STRENGTH, FISCAL YEARS
1965-80, BY SERVICE BRANCH.

X-AXIS		Y-AXIS	
X		Y	
Pair	Series	Series	Symbol
1	Year	ARTAF	A ‹Air Force
2	Year	ARTNV	B ‹Navy
3	Year	ARTMC	C ‹Marines
4	Year	ARTAR	D ‹Army
Number of Ordered Pairs			16

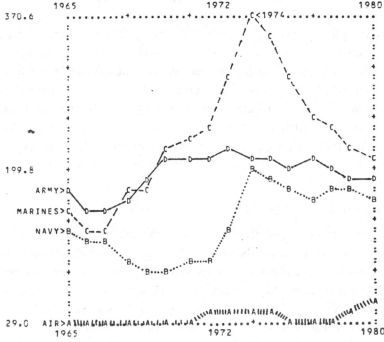

KEY: In 1974, The Marine Corps Article 15 Rate was 370.6 per 1,000 Active Duty Marines.
Source: Chapter endnote 3.

Soldiers were always more likely than Sailors to be called before the brass
for the entire period. They were more than twice as likely during the middle and
later parts of the war (1969–72) when Army Article 15 rates doubled those of the
Navy. Parity was roughly achieved in 1974 in the postwar period (Army = 219,
Navy = 202 per thousand), which was a peak for the Navy and about normal for
the Army.

During the Vietnam War and thereafter, the willingness of commanders to
use Article 15 sanctions was clearly embedded in the branch-context wherein
they controlled their charges. The Air Force used less Article 15s than did the

other branches. Naval officers sanctioned more frequently than air commanders, but less than Army officers. Navy rates were higher after 1970 and, after peaking in 1974, were closer to the rates prevailing in the Army—which were fairly high throughout the period. The Marine Corps profile was both severe and sustained.

In the early stages of the Vietnam War (1965–67) Article 15 rates in the Marine Corps were lower than the Army, but fairly high in comparison with the Air Force, and in the same range as those in the Navy. The upward climb began in 1968 (186.9 per thousand) and peaked in 1974 (370.6). The downward movement was just as rapid with the 1980 value (214.8) close to 1968 levels (186.9).

Marine commanders were active agents of control. The doubling of Marine Corps rates from 1968 to 1974 was typical of the pattern in the other branches but the magnitude range was extreme—from roughly 18% to 38% of the Marine troops being brought before their commanders for Article 15 sanctioning. In fiscal 1974—after the Vietnam War ended—a wayward Marine (370.6), Sailor (202.9) and Soldier (219.3) were roughly seven, four and four times, respectively, more likely to face an Article 15 from their commanders than a like-situated Airman (51.4). Article 15 sanctioning on the part of Marine commanders was a post-war phenomenon. Table 7.2 presents a summary of Article 15 activities of commanders in the various branches.

OFFICER-INITIATED INTERPRETIVE CONTROLS

The two tiers of organizational reaction in the military system (Courts-marital and Article 15) represent the *universe of legal sanctions* available to commanders for use against their charges. Court imposed controls represent sanctions applied for the violation of military statutes. Article 15s represent the control of broad classes of troublemakers who are less than criminal but who, nevertheless, represent that fact that something had to be done to instill discipline. Something less severe than a formal court proceeding, yet more severe than informal controls.

TABLE 7.2. ARTICLE 15 (COMMANDERS' DISCRETIONARY SANCTIONING) PATTERNS, ALL BRANCHES. TRENDS, 1965-80.

Minimum Activity:	All Branches:	1965–67
Maximum Activity:	Marines:	Post-war
	Army:	Stable after 1970
	Navy:	Late-war, Post-war
	Air Force:	Late-war, Post-war

COMPARISON OF POST-WAR SANCTIONING RATES RELATIVE TO THE AIR FORCE

(AIR FORCE = 1)

Air Force:	1
Army:	4
Navy:	4
Marines:	7

CHART 7.4. U.S. ARMY CONTROL RATES (COURTS-MARTIAL PLUS
ARTICLE 15S). FISCAL 1965–1979.

Source: Chapter endnote 3.

	X-AXIS	Y-AXIS
Series Name	*Year*	*TROL*
Number of Ordered Pairs		15

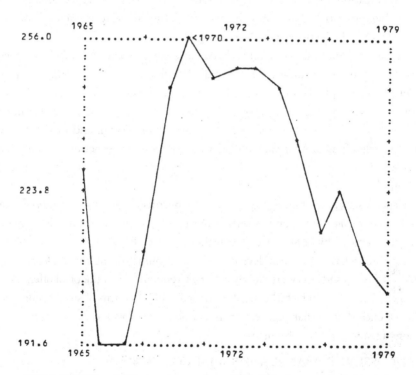

KEY: *In 1970, 256 per 1,000 strength received some form of official sanction in the U.S. Army.*

Officer-initiated interpretive controls are diffuse and can be applied to a rather large universe of acts. AWOL and Desertion are, on the other hand, quite specific offenses. Chart 7.4 plots the sum of all legal controls in the U.S. Army. It includes *all* forms of organizational reaction corresponding to rule breaking.

It is important to note that final *dispositions*, i.e., containment, expulsion, bad paper discharge, and the like are not examined here. Nor are informal, medical, or psychiatric forms of control. Chart 7.4 thus represents the formal response to infractions punishable under the U.C.M.J.

The rate of application of *all* formal controls in the Army clearly follows the presence of physical risk in the system. Formal controls rose most rapidly between 1967 and 1970, and declined thereafter. Formal reaction also follows the volume of deviance in the system—at least when absenteeism rates are used as an indicator of soldier-initiated deviance. Absenteeism also rose sharply between 1966 and 1971 and declined thereafter.

Are rates of organizational reaction simply pure responses to deviance therein, or are functions other than punishment being served? To find out, I will now examine the rate differences in purely soldier initiated deviant acts and all forms of organizational reaction. Chart 7.5 examines the NET difference between all unambiguous forms of deviant behavior and all the diffuse forms of legal control used by the officer corps in the U.S. Army.

Chart 7.5 plots the difference between soldier initiated acts of deviance (AWOLs plus Desertions) and commander initiated responses (all legal controls: Courts-martial plus Article 15s). The former represents a narrow band of behavior, the latter a rather wide range of response to *every other* kind of rule breaking possible in the military system. I assume that since AWOL and Desertion are punishable offenses, that each offender did, in fact, face sanctioning. Some deserters, of course, remain uncaught, but their numbers are small as a percent of strength.[6]

There is an unmistakable diminution of controls used against soldiers for offenses *other than* AWOL and Desertion until 1971, and an unmistakable increase of such actions by commanders thereafter. This adds valuable information to the overall relation between deviance and sanctioning during the Vietnam War. AWOL and Desertions were clearly coming to compose the bulk of all offenses as the war escalated. In fact, the negative value for 1971 in terms of surplus controls is evidence that in that year less than half of all controls were composed of actions against *other than* absentees.

DISCUSSION: DEVIANCE AND SOCIAL CONTROL

While it is clear that commanders' reactions to other than AWOL offenses increased as absences declined after 1971, is it possible that soldiers' *potential for deviance* increased as well? Klockars has noted:

> The matter of "potential for deviance," by which I mean people's estimations of the probability that one type of deviance implies the capacity

---

154

for other types, merits systematic criminological investigation (Klockars, 1981).

My data cannot answer this question directly, but I can offer the following conjecture.

CHART 7.5. SURPLUS CONTROL IN THE U.S. ARMY: (COURTS-MARTIAL AND ARTICLE 15S) MINUS (AWOL AND DESERTION RATES) PER 1,000 STRENGTH. FISCAL 1965–79.

Source: chapter endnote 3.

	X-AXIS	Y-AXIS
Series Name	Year	SURP
Number of Ordered Pairs		15

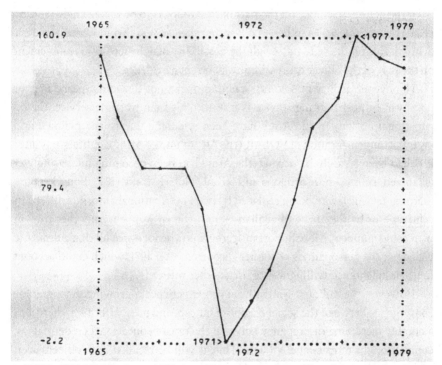

KEY:In 1977, 160.9 troops per 1,000 strength received some form of formal sanction other than for AWOL or Desertion.

I have no way of knowing if soldiers who remained in the Army after 1971, and who might have gone AWOL earlier—under the strain of physical risk—were choosing to break other military rules. That is, I cannot specify the "potential for deviance" possessed by absentees.

In the absence of physical risk, however, it is certainly clear that the Army was experiencing substantial control activity directed at offenses other than absenteeism. Perhaps the officer corps was becoming attentive to enforcing rules they otherwise would choose to ignore.

While aggregate data cannot clearly refute the former possibility, i.e., that soldiers who may not break one type of military rule in war would do so during peace, they do lend tentative support for the latter (heightened officer corps response). It is unlikely that soldiers who would chose to remain uniform, i.e., to not go AWOL or Desert, would prefer to break other rules when the social cost of AWOL/Desertion (after all the fighting is over) to them is greatly *reduced*. Quite simply, punishment for leaving the soldier role in peacetime requires more normative work on the part of commanders for a convincing case to be made *when a war is not being waged* than when one is.

If the collective choice on the part of the troops is to be increasingly deviant, i.e., to break other rules in lieu of absenting themselves, I would need some evidence of this tendency to outweigh the possibility of enhanced rule enforcement on the part of the officer cadres. I know of no such evidence.

The overall quality of soldiers was improving, not declining; peacetime, or post-war, or post fighting service is less arduous than wartime service; the occupational options in the Army have been widening due to the planned and eventual implementation of VOLAR (the All-Volunteer Army); military pay after 1971 had been steadily increasing; the Army had been becoming increasingly civilianized, i.e., the more arduous and trivial soldierly tasks (K.P., housekeeping, morning reveille) were being replaced by more occupational (Moskos, 1977b) incentives—or by the hiring of civilians—and women were entering the Army in increasing numbers. More importantly, there is no evidence at all that a dramatic change in the personalities of soldiers occurred, after 1971, which could account for their heightened willingness to break other rules.

However, the military system began to experience a growing demographic convergence between the social origins of officers and men. After 1971, there was a notably increasing discrepancy between the rate of educational credentials accumulation for officers and soldiers. This, it will be recalled, saw officers accumulating college degrees at an accelerated pace while enlistees with same were leaving the system while disproportionate numbers of enlistees with college experience were entering the system. This, I suggest, in the absence of physical risk, *generated pressure to amplify the officer–enlisted distinction as a means of instilling order.*

Additionally, as the fighting decreased, AWOL and Desertion rates declined at the same time as they were becoming less threatening to the Army. Concurrent with this decline there was a notable increase in controls which required much more *interpretive work* on the part of the officer corps, i.e., Article 15s and Courts-martial. Simply put, it appears that a void was created when physical risk declined—and this void was filled using interpretive controls. There were simply *more ways of becoming deviant* after 1971—or so it would appear.

The *surplus* of officer-initiated interpretive controls over soldier initiated un-ambiguous acts of deviance was clearly inversely related to physical risk in the system. In addition, control rates, after 1971, clearly increased disproportionately to the decline in the central form of deviant behavior (AWOL and Desertion). Whatever called forth increased organizational reaction after 1971, it was clearly not unwillingness to serve on the part of enlistees. Officer initiated organization-al reaction was clearly increasing while soldier initiated forms of deviance were declining. Indeed, if absenteeism is a measure of "willingness to serve," soldierly willingness increased after 1971.

My data suggest that as physical risk diminished in the U.S. Army, the likeli-hood that a typical soldier would run afoul of military rules increased quite rap-idly, although such soldiers were less prone to absent themselves. This is totally consistent with the findings on Bad Paper discharge for the entire military system.

SUMMARY

In the Army, the most populous branch of the military with the most stable, and relatively high Article 15 rates, surplus control became minimal in 1971 and grew rapidly thereafter. While the Army is not the entire DoD, the relative stabil-ity of its Article 15 rates, coupled with the declining contribution of AWOL and Desertion to the overall use of controls after 1971, offers a striking case for a clear polarization of control activity. Physical risk during mobilization for war can explain increases in AWOL and Desertion, but not the upward movement of *dis-cretionary* controls in its absence after the bulk of the fighting was over. Officers in the Army were unmistakably increasingly using Article 15 for "other offenses" that were being discovered[7] as AWOL and Desertion rates plummeted.

Chapter VI demonstrated the atypically of the period 1966–71 in the DoD with regard to the observed educational homogeneity of officers and the troops. This corresponded quite well with the buildup in strength for mobilization (see Table 6.1)—and therefore the increased presence of physical risk. Social origin explanations appear to account for at least some of the observed sanctioning be-havior of commanders with regard to administrative bad paper discharges and harsh *expulsions*.

The peace-war cycle, however, appears to play a more important role in ex-plaining the decision of commanders to punish soldiers. It appears that during war a disproportionate amount of control activity is directed against *unambiguous* forms of deviance such as AWOL and Desertion. When physical risk declined after 1971, sanctions for highly interpretive forms of deviance, i.e., all "other" possibilities exclusive of absenteeism, increased dramatically.

Looking at the overall DoD origins patterns in addition to the patterns of deviance and control in the Army it is quite possible that mobilization for the Vietnam War produced a *symbolic* purging and *exclusion* pattern, i.e., the bad paper and harsh courts-martial movements; mixed amounts of controls directed at unambiguous offenders (absentees); and after 1971—with risk removed from the system—heightened use of commanders discretionary Article 15 authority. War thus appears to act as a constraint on the social control activities of commanders in the presence of physical risk. The observed use of sanctions against more interpretive offenses clearly rises in the absence of such risk.

NOTES: CHAPTER VII

1. Bell and Houston (1975, 55) provide the following definition of desertion:

   If an absence extends beyond 29 consecutive days, a soldier is dropped from the unit's roles as a *deserter*. Although most men administratively qualified as deserters meet the 30 day requirement, a man can also be dropped from the rolls as a deserter if his unauthorized absence is less than 30 days and he meets any of the following seven requirements: 1) has access to classified material which "could result in grave or serious damage to the United States;" 2) seeks political asylum in, voluntarily resides in, or is being detained by a foreign county; 3) absents himself from his unit without authority while under charges for previous unauthorized absences; 4) enters the armed forces of another country; 5) leaves his unit while it is deployed overseas; 6) escapes from confinement; 7) leaves under circumstances which lead his commander to believe that he does not intend to return. There is also a legal definition: a man is a deserter if he has been convicted of desertion by a court-martial.

2. Civilians also face the possibility of confronting agents of social control when their absence can be interpreted as an example of their failure to meet officially defined responsibilities consistent with status positions. For example, husbands who desert, absenteeism on the job, and truants. With regard to the latter, some sociologists have noted the presence of what are called "status offenses" among adolescents: offenses for which an adult would normally not be prosecuted.

   The analytical utility of this concept in military settings is only partial. This is primarily because soldiers who absent themselves face agents of control without regard to their age *and*, as soldiers, they are violating a clear *role expectation* that they, in fact, be present to perform their role. Soldiers are closer to professionals in this regard than they are to adolescents. While the typical absentee *is*, more likely than not, an adolescent, the source of the threat to the organization does not lie in his youthfulness which anticipates the typical amount of license and lack of restrictions granted adults. At least, I should think, any more than a doctor's being charged with "malpractice" reflects his status rather than his role. In both cases, the status is a necessary condition for the role expectation to be credible. But it is not a sufficient condition. The role of adolescent is less rigidly defined than is that of the soldier. More importantly, most civilian "status offenses" are punished under restitutive laws: a job is lost; alimony is paid; authorities are notified. Civilian absence is less of a threat to the social order than military absence in most cases.

3. Symbols, Sources and Computations for this chapter.

SYMBOLS: The following symbols refer to indicators appropriate as measures of organizational reaction discussed in this chapter.

YEAR: Fiscal year.

ARBOD: Strength of the Army. The number of personnel on active duty. SOURCE: Letter, DoAAJ, 1982.

A15AR: Article 15 rates per 1,000 troop strength. SOURCE: as above.

CMTAR: Courts-martial rate (all types) per 1,000 active duty Army strength. SOURCE: Chapter II.

ARDES: Army desertion rates per 1,000 strength. See also notes 4 and 5 concerning how desertion and AWOL are defined.

ARWOL: AWOL rates per 1,000 strength. See "ARDES" comments above. SOURCE: as above.

SURP: All controls (Article 15 rates plus court-martial rates) minus AWOL and Desertion rates, per 1,000 strength. See text for methodological notes on computation and meaning of this indicator.

TROL: All controls (Article 15 plus court-martial rates) per 1,000 strength.

OUT: The sum of AWOL and Desertion rates, per 1,000 strength. See text for limitations in the construction and meaning of this indicator.

The following were used in plots for this chapter:

Year	ARBOD ARWOL*	ARDES*	A15AR*	CMTAR*	SURP*
1965	1016832 60.1	15.7	186.4	42.7	153.3
1966	1096803 57.2	14.7	156.4	35.2	119.7
1967	1430009 78.0	21.4	158.4	34.9	93.9
1968	1512176 89.7	29.1	174.3	38.1	93.6
1969	1528707 112.3	42.4	196.9	49.9	92.1
1970	1473191 132.0	52.3	216.0	40.0	71.7
1971	1279857 176.9	73.5	212.5	35.7	-2.2
1972	993587 166.4	62.0	218.6	31.8	22.0
1973	852098 159.2	52.1	223.3	26.8	38.8

1974	799301 129.9	41.1	219.3	27.5	75.8
1975	790741 95.4	26.0	214.0	20.6	113.2
1976	783748 70.3	17.7	204.0	13.4	129.4
1977	779181 47.0	16.7	214.1	10.5	160.9
1978	770708 40.4	15.4	200.3	10.0	154.5
1979	758748 38.0	18.1	193.0	9.9	146.8

Year	TROL*	OUT*
1965	229.1	78.5
1966	191.6	71.9
1967	193.3	99.4
1968	212.4	118.8
1969	246.8	154.7
1970	256.0	184.3
1971	248.2	250.4
1972	250.4	228.4
1973	250.1	211.3
1974	246.8	171.0
1975	234.6	121.4
1976	217.4	88.0
1977	224.6	63.7
1978	210.3	55.8
1979	202.9	56.1

*Rounded

4. AWOL statistics are kept in the form of rates per 1,000 men in the force. They are thus incidences rather than numbers of individual absences. (see Bell and Houston, 1976, 42)

5. Desertion statistics are also incidences, as per above. Both AWOL and Desertion statistics somewhat underestimate the true "event rate" in that the figures do not carry over from year to year—when a man's absence crosses the fiscal year he is not counted again. On the other hand, multiple offenses are possible—which overstate the true "event rate." Research that has been done suggests that a man deserts only once in a given

year, for the most part (86% to 93% of all persons who deserted during FY 1972–74 did so only once) (see Bell and Houston, as above).

6. The highest rate of desertion in the Army was 73.5 per 1,000 strength in 1971. If 50% of these soldiers were never apprehended, i.e., 36.75 per 1,000 strength, this would represent less than 15% of the "control event rate," i.e., 248 per thousand official responses to deviance of some kind for the same year. Thus, even if protracted absentees were escaping capture during 1971, over one fifth of strength was still receiving some kind of sanction for rule breaking.

7. I use "discovered" in the sense used by Conrad (Peter Conrad: *The Medicalization of Deviance in American Culture*, in Rubington and Weinberg (Eds.), 1981, 75-83), i.e., I place emphasis on the *social factors* that set the context for the emergence of a new diagnostic category. Commanders were clearly more willing to use Article 15 sanctions after 1971, than before 1971. In that the *ethos of control* is measured by such shifts in the conditions under which control is applied, the conditions had clearly changed after 1971.

CHAPTER VIII. SOCIAL DEVIANCE IN MILITARY INSTITUTIONS: SUMMARY
AND IMPLICATIONS

> Bulls, too, were enlisted in the service of war, and the experiment was made of
> launching savage boars against the enemy. Some even tried an advance guard of
> doughty lions. Lions with armed trainers and harsh masters to discipline them
> and keep them on the lead. But these experiments failed. The savage brutes,
> enflamed by promiscuous carnage, spread indiscriminate confusion among the
> cavaliers, as they tossed the terrifying manes upon their heads this way and that
> ... The bulls tossed their own employers and trampled them underfoot ...The
> infuriated boars with their stout tusks slashed their allies ... Even such beasts
> as their masters had once thought tame enough at home were seen to boil over
> in the stir of action--wounds, yells, stampedes, panic and turmoil; and none of
> them would obey the recall.
> — Lucretius: *On The Nature of The Universe.* (Latham, 1965, 211-212.)

Commanders have always experienced some difficulty with the control
of their charges. Nevertheless, social control patterns and techniques underlie
the most striking characteristic of military settings: order and purposefulness.
However, to frame a sociological inquiry such that the causes of control activities
can be gleaned from knowledge of the characteristics of disruptors is decidedly
misplaced.

I have tried to show that the management of shifting types and numbers of
deviants in the military can be fruitfully understood in light of the kinds of organizational strategies which have evolved in the face of pressing contingencies.
Emerging patters of control constitute an *ethos* on the part of the officer corps.
Less than planned, but more than crescive, such decisions to punish wayward

soldiers represent accommodations to sources of strain within a complex institutional order.

This research has focused exclusively on the outcomes of varied deviance management decisions on the part of the officer corps. What follows is necessarily a tentative exploration of social control *requirements* as they have emerged over time.

THE COURTS

Overall court-martial rates indicate the willingness of commanders to sanction soldiers by legal means. Any relative movement in the composition of the rate thus indicates a sanction preference and helps specify the severity with which commanders discipline the troops.

FINDINGS

When court-martial rates were increasing rapidly (1946–1948) in all branches, Naval commanders were increasingly preferring harsh sanctions; other commanders were not.

When court-martial rates were increasing moderately (1951–1953) in the military, Marine and Army commanders were becoming relatively harsh; Air and Naval commanders were not.

This first set of findings explores the homogeneity of the sanctioning climate in the military at a time when commanders were increasingly using the courts in the aftermath of World War II. However, during periods of notable—but not extreme—increases in court activity (as was the case during the Korean War) Air and Naval commanders did not sanction as severely as those in the ground forces.

One possible interpretation which would have to be confirmed by future research is that more traditional organizations may be least able to adjust to rapid change. In the case of the Navy, such changes were precipitated by demobilization which had the consequence of an increased reliance on harsh formal controls. I suggest this was done to impart meaning to the daily routines of organizational life which, apparently, create more stress in the Navy than is the case in the other branches.

Shipboard service, after a major victory in war, may have damped the collective sense of morale in the Navy, and perhaps influenced commanders to increasingly rely on rule enforcement and punishment.

The major limitation of my study is that I lack adequate social-psychological data on how commanders perceive the meaning of punishment, or the influence of stress and other contingencies on the management decisions to punish the troops. I can only document the shift in development patterns and speculate as to why this occurred.

Festinger et al., for example, have demonstrated a loss of social meaning and demoralization in an isolated religious group after the prophesied end of the world failed to materialize (1955). If one views the Navy as the most physically isolated of service branches, perhaps the generational imperative to return to civil life after a popular war was felt most strongly in the Navy, and that this in turn generated a change in attitude toward violators on the part of Naval commanders.

This line of thinking would place Naval commanders in the position of having to be especially firm and harsh in rule enforcement to communicate a sense of being in control of activities which may have been seen as less than worthy of full hearted support. This could be tested and explored more deeply by identifying three groups of sailors that differ only in the presumed impact of peace on the behavior of enlisted personnel and then carefully examining the organizational responses to such behavior on the part of commanders.

I would suggest comparing rates of deviance and organizational reaction in naval gun crews, among female nurses, and among land based administrative Naval personnel during and after the war. Presumably, the medical mission of the nurses would be least influenced by the termination of hostilities, the gun crews would presumably be most anomic, and the land based sailors would place somewhere in the middle of a hypothetical morale gradient.

The range of variation in war-peace deviance rates would then be compared with the range of variation in reaction rates. If, as I suspect, commanders were reacting to the outbreak of peace by disproportionately relying on legal controls, guncrew reaction rates would be smaller than those observed among nurses and clerks. If this does not turn out to be the case, perhaps demoralized guncrew-man, in fact, are more prone to violate military rules. If my conjecture is validated, however, it will take a powerful argument indeed to demonstrate that wayward nurses and clerks pose a more serious threat to the Navy than those who apparently should feel anomic by the change in social circumstances.

The second issue concerns *relative* sanctioning: when commanders prefer one type of sanction over another under circumstances where *less* overall sanctioning is taking place. For example, after 1964, there was a clear shift to relatively harsh sanctioning as milder rates (Summary Cms) declined. That is, after 1964, courts-martial were used more sparingly but were disproportionately severe when they were used.

Combining both sets of findings, the American military becomes increasingly punitive during extreme periods of overall court activity *and* during times of stability and regular decline. Commanders were not especially harsh on the troops during moderate periods of court activity and during rapid declines. These constraints set the parameters of the *ethos*, with the rate of severe sanctioning serving as both a ceiling and a floor. Thus, since the Summary (or milder form) of court-martial is the more volatile it can absorb large numbers of soldiers, up to a point: that point being when the higher echelons become increasingly involved in the punishment process.

On the other hand, the general declines in overall court activity suggests a floor, or tipping point, beyond which declines in formal controls result in escalating harshness on the part of commanders. There seems to be a managerial inverse to the "breaking point" hypothesis that dominated much of social science research during World War II, and the later wars as well. The search for the point in which a soldier will "break" is summarized by Lang:

> World War II psychiatric rates among American troops may have also been inflated by the widely held conviction that there was, indeed, an objective "breaking point" beyond which a man could not go on. Moreover as a man approached the point of eligibility for rotation, various symptoms of stress began to manifest themselves, regardless of the absolute number of days in combat or flying missions he actually had to his credit. In Korea medical officers and troops identified a short termers syndrome. Nervousness increased as the contractual period of service reached its end, as it did also among U.S. troops in Vietnam. (1972, 79).

I would direct attention to the possibility that in a climate characterized as one in which minimal use of the courts is the norm, commanders apparently feel the need to identify extreme examples of rule breaking behavior. This tipping point occurred in 1964—the beginning of the Vietnam War—in all service branches.

DISCUSSION:

Coercive institutions in the United States, notably the prisons (Wright, 1973), the Army (Radine, 1977), and to a lesser degree, the schools (Mayer, 1963) have become less historically reliant on outright punishment and more dependent on internal controls which are seen to be the product of socialization, or as responses to external rewards such as incentives.

There is, however, a *third source of control* in complex organizations which involves the degree to which the level of technical culture is incorporated into the group dynamics of organizational tasks. Radine calls this "co-optive rational control" (1977). The most important manifestation of such control, since World War II, is systems design and simulation.

The principle is this: social control is more effective when it is embedded in the totality of a situation than in a specific individual (Radine, 1977, 134). The theoretical underpinning of such a possibility was stated by Maury D. Feld who, while assessing the historical development of modern, i.e., since 1700, military forces noted:

> Only a systemic method of instruction can create a reliable system of control (1977, 17).

The systems approach imposes mechanical functional requirements in a warning system, or weapons system—or for that matter an automated factory—upon a team oriented task structure. Machines and men interact in the accomplishment of a project which is evaluated as a group cooperative activity. Radine notes:

> In a situation with a high division of labor and a well defined communication network, any individual who is resisting can be easily located and replaced. The systems approach does not tolerate resistance (1977, 130).

The implications of such arrangement are made quite clear.

> Thus the structuring of a situation through the use of technologically developed equipment and realistic team training can produce a degree of conformity and effectiveness of a far greater level of magnitude than that which may be elicited by leadership techniques alone. It is very difficult for the individual to sense the degree to which this form of domination can control his behavior. Perhaps this is what Sartre and other existentialists were foretelling when they wrote that "the situation" drastically, but imperceptibly, limits freedom (1977, 142).

If this is the case, branch variation in court usage, in part, should be explainable by examining the levels of technical culture available in each branch.

CROSS-BRANCH COMPARISONS

Cross-branch court-martial rates tended to be strongly associated with each other suggesting a general control climate in the military system. This relationship was, however, more notable in the traditional branches (Army, Navy, Marines) which were more similar to each other with regard to their commanders' use of courts-martial than they were similar to the Air Force.

With regard to the frequency of court-martial over the entire period of observation, the Marines had the highest court-martial rates, on average, followed by the Army, the Navy and the Air Force.

I have not directly measured the level of technology available in each of the branches, but the rates of court usage clearly declined as one moves from the Marines to the land-bound Army, to the ship-bound Navy, and finally to the highly-technical Air Force. Commanders use formal control less as the level of technology in the branches rises. This can be stated as a proposition for future research:

> The use of formal controls is inversely related to the number of man-machine
> interfaces in the system.

Members of highly integrated man-machine systems are less expendable and
are likely to face controls inherent in the structure of their work. Conversely:

> The deviant ranks will be disproportionately drawn from those branches with fewer
> man-machine interfaces.

I have observed from my own experience in the Air Force (1969–73), for example, that exemptions from detail work, i.e., housekeeping tasks assigned to
lower ranking enlisted men, as well as "Officer of the Day" assignments given to
low ranking officers to man company headquarters overnight, were not allocated
randomly. They followed, rather, the basic manpower priorities of the base mission. Flight line personnel and headquarters staffers were conspicuously absent
from the duty rosters. These types of personnel were simply much too valuable
to the organization to be used as candidates for extra, or nighttime, duties since
they would miss work for the period of time it took to accomplish the auxiliary
tasks.

It is, of course, *an assumption* that the application of social controls will follow
the same organizational logic that allocates less critical personnel to additional
duties. Further research will have to clarify this possibility.

One possibility for the change in commanders' court responses to deviance
may lie in the changing expectations of the officer-role with regard to how officers are expected to participate in the punishment process. The eventual virtual
disappearance of the use of the Summary Court in the Air Force, for example,
increasingly excludes junior officers from such participation. In light of the negative public opinion surrounding the Vietnam War, data on the control activities of more socially supported commanders, as may be the case in the Israeli Air
Force, for example, would be useful to examine. Is it the level of technology or the
degree of social support for military activity that influences managerial decisions
to sanction the troops?

The Durkheimian insight and the work of contemporary researchers in search
of an axiomatic relationship between criminal behavior, punishment rituals and
social integration within large groups has been concisely stated by Richard Berk
et.al., in their attempt to explore these possibilities in California prisons. It is
called "The constancy of punishment hypothesis."

> Over relatively long periods and in the absence of social upheavals, the
> number of people punished should represent a constant fraction of the
> population (1981, 805).

My research suggests that the hypothesis must be modified to account for differing levels of technical culture as sources of social control in the military. This could be testable in future research by using the following guidelines:

1. Conceptualize a gradient of available technical culture.

2. Use the Air Force and the Marines as two extremes for a baseline measure.

3. Plot movements in organizational reaction rates to deviance in the Air Force and Marines. Compare these with the movement in the other branches.

To the degree that level of technical culture influences organizational reaction rates, the hypothesis is confirmed or refuted. More importantly, it would be extremely fruitful to attempt to isolate the *mechanisms* through which increasing levels of technical culture serve as functional substitutes for formal controls. There is a Judaeo-Christian adage that "Idle hands are the Devil's workshop." Indeed, it could probably be argued that much of the athletic rigor of military training—in addition to building stamina and good health—likely keeps soldiers too busy, or tired, or both, to get into serious trouble.

In addition, the levels of alcohol use in the military (Bryant, 1974a; Cahalan and Cisin, 1975b; Cahalan et al., 1974; USGPO, 1971, 1974) are also likely to keep many problems within manageable and predictable proportions. There is no evidence that either critics or revolutionaries are known to congregate in servicemen's bars or on the athletic field.

Moreover, it is my impression that technological sources of social control require a much higher degree of active cognitive participation on the part of the troops than did the historical ration of grog issued to sailors. There is little research on how this may heighten the stress on the officer corps who, it logically follows, must demonstrate even higher levels of *expertise* to assume leadership positions.

While commanders may need more expertise to run a modern military force, the general educational level of the troops is also rising. Structure alone may prove insufficient to insure control. Feld's dictum must therefore be modified as follows: Only a *believable* system of instruction can insure a reliable method of control. High levels of technical culture are no guarantee of winning the hearts and minds of the troops, nor that conformity will necessarily follow. In the absence of credible forms of indoctrination, of course, it is quite possible that the officer corps will increasingly rely on the more interpretive forms of social control.

THE STRUCTURE OF BAD PAPER

There were three major trends in the structure of bad paper, these concern the *overall* bad paper discharge rate (BPD); *administrative* paper (UDS); and *punitive* paper (BCDs + DHDs).

1) The Bad Paper Discharge (BPD) rate has fluctuated widely, but had three peaks.

2) There has been a long tern *decline* in the use of punitive bad paper.

3) Administrative bad paper usage has been *increasing* regularly.

DISCUSSION

The evidence thus far presented questions a number of assumptions made by legalists that the law can be understood as a *sui generis* reality independent of the social context wherein it is applied. Perhaps the level of such generalizations is too lofty for precise interpretation. In any event, at least in military settings, some of the generalizations are questionable and some require more exact specification. I shall consider three such cases drawn from Black (1976).

1) "Law varies inversely with other social control." (1976, 6).

2) "Law varies directly with stratification." (1976, 13).

3) "Law varies directly with rank." (1976, 17).

My data force a qualification of Black's generalizations. First, Bad Paper Discharges and court-martial are two distinct forms of formal control. They differ substantially in terms of their relation to the *boundaries* of the military system.

Bad paper rates are clearly sensitive to the presence of war or peace. Court-martial activity, on the other hand, was clearly declining since roughly 1950. When legal controls *other than the courts* were used i.e., administrative paper, there was no clear inverse relationship observed between court usage and commanders' use of non-court expulsions—as the movement of NET Bad Paper so clearly documents.

For the entire period of observation it is quite clear that bad paper and court activity are not full functional substitutes. Thus, it is possible that court activity may vary indeed with "other social control," but not uniformly with the BPD rate.

Second, the stratification system (Abrahamson, 1973) has remained intact and constant in military settings during the period under review. In fact, the number of ranks available to the military has remained historically stable. Also, the officer–enlisted distinction is quite old, and *defines* caste-like differences between the ranks. There is little mobility across this barrier. Highly variable legal control patterns cannot be explained by a constant level of stratification in the military.

My data furthermore suggest, contrary to Black, that the volume of sanctioning is only somewhat related to rank. That is, while higher ranking commanders use the General Court-martial and the lower echelons use the Summary Court-martial, they do so at different rates and at different times.

Drawing from other than socio-legal perspectives, it is also clear that *some* conceptualizations have little utility in military settings. For example, ecological *differences* in military settings are more notable than their similarities since the military is a world presence. It is doubtful that the military system is a natural area of any kind.

This does not, of course, deny that there are striking similarities in *certain* military settings. For example, it is quite likely that boot camps, combat areas and training schools are more similar than they are different with regard to the organizational techniques required to manage stress and accomplish the required tasks. It becomes an empirical question as to whether, and to what degree, such homogeneity may be generalized to the military system as an institution.

On the other hand, subcultural theories are too narrowly drawn to encompass the military system since their premise is that individuals frame their interactive choices in terms of group support for a particular set of norms. If a "military subculture" made the troops increasingly law abiding—and less prone to appear before the courts—their commanders were innocent of this favorable adaptive strategy as the movement of Bad Paper Discharge waves clearly shows.

There is no definitive research on the lifespan of subcultures. Oscar Lewis, however, has suggested that subcultural accommodations and adjustments span the generations and are passed on from one to the next (1970, 69–73). It is doubtful that subcultures of wayward troops (or their commanders, for that matter) could have emerged and vanished as rapidly so as to explain plausibly both the cyclical movement of bad paper, *and* the steady decline in the use of the courts.

Future researchers may wish to follow, and qualify, this line of thinking using a smaller unit of analysis. Ideally it would be possible to locate empirically the optimally sized group wherein subcultural arguments make the most sense. For example, if bad paper and court activity were known by theatre and branch, it may in fact turn out that under certain conditions, say in combat areas, in the Army, commanders actually do choose between bad paper and using the courts. This would open the possibility that the volume of deviance in certain parts of the system may, in fact, exhibit a quota-like character.

Such trade-offs, of course, would be concealed at the system level for two historical reasons: 1. Global military presence is increasing: there are more ways for a soldier to be posted in non-combat settings; and 2. With the passage of time more soldiers increasingly serve in support roles. Nonetheless, it is crucially important to isolate those settings where trade-offs in sanctioning options might occur.

Such research would be a major step in both specifying the contribution of combat environments to the deviance identification process as well as empirically resolving a major dilemma in subcultural theory, namely: do deviants participate in a subculture before or after they commit acts of deviance?

A freshly trained army sent to combat, by definition, can have no prior experi- ence with the phenomenon of battle. This is as close as we will come, perhaps, to the adult condition of tabula rasa. Experienced soldiers, on the other hand, may be expected to develop modes of adjustment to the environment.

By comparing initial protracted deviance rates in combat zones, the best case could be made for the usefulness of subcultural arguments. In that subcultural adaptations are responses to the social environment, combat zones represent perhaps the most extreme kinds of accommodation. Are deviance rates observed related in any way to the level of technology in the different branches?

One could then compare deviance rates in constant technology settings across the peace-war cycle to isolate the "pure" or combat generated component of so- cial deviance and compare it with other rates of organizational reaction. This then becomes a benchmark. How important is branch of service? When do other than accommodative explanations become plausible? At what point do the data suggest that subcultural arguments are less persuasive than institutional ones?

More research should also be directed at the positive or integrative aspects of subcultures and their relation to social control activities. For example, being a "jet jockey" i.e., having flying missions in the Air Force, is clearly instrumental for an officer's promotion to the higher echelons (Segal, 1967); just as a combat command is likewise useful in the ground forces (Janowitz, 1961).

Do such experiences "set the tone" for junior commanders' perceptions of proper discipline regarding the troops? Virtually all of the higher ranks in the Air Force *could have* entered the Vietnam War with sorties to their credit, but propor- tionally fewer of the top Marine brass could have seen action in Korea. Does an almost assured high level of participation in the technical culture of the Air Force result in a shared universe of discourse regarding social control?

Military settings also provide the potential for resolving a crucial dilemma in the societal reaction, or labeling perspective, namely: do commanders *react* to the deviant behavior of their charges, or do they identify wayward soldiers without regard to "what was done" by them? The acid test of the labeling paradigm re- quires a contemporary analogue to witchcraft.

That is, the labeling perspective is most compelling, ideally, when the cat- egories of deviance used are very closely related to the strongly held values of dominant groups. Unfortunately, in the most convincing cases, such elites have long since passed from the scene, or are located in cultures quite different from our own.

Students in my deviance classes, for example, are easily struck by the con- temporary incongruity of witch trials, laws against women holding property or voting, and other examples of behaviors which are atypical in our society but perfectly normal in others (see Edgerton, 1976 for a fuller description and numerous examples). That, however, is precisely the weakness of contemporary attempts *to apply* the perspective. What is given in terms of novelty and clarity is question-able in terms of contemporary relevance:

> According to Walter Gove, a person is labeled as a deviant primarily as a consequence of societal characteristics—particularly, the power or resources of the individual, the social distance between the labeler and the labelee, the tolerance level of the community, and the visibility of the individual's deviant behavior. The attribute which has by far received the most attention in the literature is the resources and power of the indi-vidual, and it is argued that persons with few resources and little power are the ones most likely to have a deviant label imposed upon them (Cited in McCaghy, 1985, 83).

Critics of this position argue otherwise:

> Unfortunately for the labeling theorists, the weight of evidence is not consistent with their supposition. This is most apparent from research on judicial dispositions of adult criminals and juvenile delinquents. In test-ing the labeling approach, researchers have explored whether the severity of the sentence is better explained by legal variables, such as past offence record and seriousness of the current offense, or by extralegal variables such as race, sex, and socioeconomic status. Aside from a few exceptions, the consistent conclusion is that the extralegal variables have little effect on sentencing policy. In short, sentences are based primarily in what the person has done, nor upon who he or she is. (Cited in McCaghy, 1985, 83).

This apparent dilemma could be partially resolved if a careful study of the evolution of *an entire universe of deviance categories* were undertaken. This is possible due to an institutional imperative and bureaucratic peculiarity of the military: *all* command decisions that involve the classification of soldiers are ultimately documented (see Little, 1968b).

In the Air Force, there is a yearly serial document called the Uniform Air-man Record (UAR). It is accurate to-the-man. It contains the entire universe of administrative classifications that affect daily strength accounting. All gains and losses to the Air Force, for *all reasons* including discharge, death, retirement, im-prisonment, enlistment, AWOL etc. are available for scrutiny. A careful and cau-tious analysis of these documents, over the years, would provide empirical evi-dence concerning the *temporal order* of deviance dispositions (see Zerubavel, 1981).

More importantly, the number of possible deviant categories is known: new categories emerge and old categories vanish. For example, in 1976, under the discharge classification code "HLF" 183 airmen (182 men and one woman) were given bad paper discharges for unfitness due to Drug Abuse (UAR 1976). In 1980, this category was no longer used. In 1976, under discharge classification "HMG" 66 airmen and no women were given bad paper discharges for unsuitability due their failure in an Alcohol Abuse Treatment and Rehabilitation program. In 1980, 82 men and one woman were so judged by their commanders (UAR, 1980). In 1966, of course, such programs did not exist.

Such documents as the UAR—or the Uniform Officer Record (UOR) available for officers—afford an opportunity to test theories of deviance in contemporary settings. These documents, at least would provide a good starting point for such research.

Additionally, all of this information is part of the public record, and all of it is "unclassified." Given the military preoccupation with strength accounting, such materials are probably at least as reliable as those conducted by academic researchers, if not more so. Furthermore, all of the data are entirely unobtrusive and not likely to be biased as to the political orientation of the researchers, nor is it likely that problems of questionnaire construction, or respondent validity will emerge since both the UAR and the UOR record *dispositions*, not attitudes, impressions, or items subject to distortion through the research process.

Last, and perhaps most importantly, it is the contention of conflict theorists that those at the top of organizations, both *see* and *use* such structures for purposes quite different from those afforded underlings. Robert Presthus contends:

> The aversion to conflict in big organizations rests in part upon the perspective of its leaders who see the organization as a disciplined, cohesive system for achieving a common goal. They regard it as a rational instrument that binds together the interests of its members in a kind of all-for-one, one-for-all ethic. The other face of organization with its informal power centers and its function of satisfying individual needs for status and self-realization is neglected. Organizations are not defined this way by those who direct them. As Coser says: "The decision makers are engaged in maintaining and, if possible, in strengthening the organizational structures through and in which they exercise power and influence. Whatever conflicts occur within these structures will appear to them to be dysfunctional." (1964, 584).

To what degree is this the case in the modern military? With regard to patters of organizational reaction, do the attitudes of the elite general officers contribute to, or retard, patters of sanctioning against the troops? I do not know. However, to the degree that the opinions of the elite are important—and I have no data at all bearing on this issue—they would strengthen my argument for an ethos of control.

There is a danger, however, in relying too heavily on such data even if they were collected. If, in fact, it were shown that the elites had a unified attitude toward punishing the troops, it would have to also be shown that such consensus could change *quite rapidly* as the cast of my data on reaction rates quite clearly evidence. It is unlikely that a unified attitude could produce such a striking difference in the application of controls.

If, on the other hand, it were demonstrated that oscillations in organizational reaction rates varied directly with the degree of consensus on punishments observed among the officer elites—as would satisfy certain deviance researchers—this would violate an organizational imperative that the high command be decisive and unified. The point is that if the elite officer cadres, i.e., the decision makers or "The Military Elite" as C. Wright Mills (1956) would have it, are characterized by a high degree of consensus over the appropriate ways to punish the troops, it is unlikely that such consensus could produce a factor-of-10 variation on the BPD rate—in both directions—in the space of a few short years.

Furthermore, if the elites are characterized by dissensus over exactly how the troops should be punished, this could not explain the 30 year decline in court patterns. The solution to this dilemma is that the *ethos of control* is a property of the collective officer corps, not the elite cadres, nor the young lieutenants in isolation, nor the middle or field grades of officers. At times, however, deviance management decisions emerging from *each sector* are more important than others.

This research is a step in specifying exactly *when* this was the case. Further research may examine organizational reaction rates over a greater period of time to see if patterns in any of the wars under review are typical of the twentieth century and if they hold for militaries in both developed and developing countries. To what degree are such patterns explained by the role of the officer corps in their respective armies?

The argument also holds promise for the study of deviance in those societies in which the state is highly involved in the management and coordination of high technology organizational pursuits. For example, does the contemporary "managerial ethos" in Japan produce rates of organizational reaction similar to those in the American Air Force? If so, does this partially explain the blossoming of white collar crime in that society? If not, are there uniquely military determinants (and limitations) of organizational reaction rates that may not be applicable to civil settings?

CONTAINMENT AND EXPULSION OF DEVIANTS

When the line is drawn to expel a soldier from the system, the military reaches the absolute limit of its control: soldiers so classified are barred permanently from the ranks. I have tried to show how frequently such lines were drawn and the magnitudes involved. Are courts-martial essentially a way of instilling internal order which requires a substantial number of offenders to remain captives of the organization while serving out their punishments?

There are two relevant issues here for students of social deviance. Both concern the nature of "outsiderness": does the group punish and contain, or rather, punish and banish its deviants?

The data on containment and expulsion indicate that:

1) Courts-martial are clearly for internal consumption. At the height of expulsiveness (1947) over 95% of those court-martialed remained with the system.

2) Court expulsions have dropped dramatically since 1947.

3) Commanders clearly did not use a balanced strategy of containment and expulsion with regard to offenders facing court-martial. The military does *not* expel the overwhelming majority of those, by its definition, who have committed a fairly serious offense in that a court-martial is an indicator of such gravity.

4) Court expulsion rates did follow a pattern with regard to the early stages of mobilization for each of the three wars. In the early years of a war expulsive affinities weakened to their minima and strengthened thereafter—well into the post war aftermaths. Commanders' preferences for expulsion were most dramatic following World War II, essentially negligible after Korea, and notable after Vietnam.

Since 1950, however, commanders have been becoming less reliant on the use of legal sanctions as a means of control. Could it be that commanders have chosen to "purge the ranks" of wayward soldiers by other means? Has less frequent use of the courts resulted in more, or less expulsions from the system?

The overall preference for—or at worst parity between—administrative over the court-imposed bad paper discharges on the part of military commanders, reveals that most deviants expelled from the ranks tend to be those who have *not* committed the most serious offenses.

In the American military, it is quite clear that commanders are becoming more concerned with expelling those troops who fail to present the appropriate *persona*, than they are with expelling those who perform more grievous kinds of deviant acts—at least when patterns of expulsion and containment are closely examined. In this area, critics of labeling theory will be quite disappointed. What a soldier "does" i.e., break *serious* rules, on average, is more likely to afford him a chance at remediation than how he appears.

So, delinquency research and courthouse studies conducted in civil settings aside, I tentatively conclude that the modern military is much more concerned with impression management than legalists would care to admit. In fact, it is precisely in those areas that do *not* involve statute rule breaking i.e., administrative bad paper and Article 15 non-judicial sanctioning, where the officer corps is most active, and where it is becoming increasing involved.

DISCUSSION: SOCIAL CHANGE AND THE MILITARY

The bulk of expulsions in the military occur primarily for normative, not punitive reasons. That is, the percentage of troop strength thrown out for expressly punitive reasons, e.g., recipients of DHDs and BCDs, is small compared with those expelled with administrative bad paper discharges.

Moreover, expulsion waves i.e., the rapid increase of bad paper discharge rates, have been largely influenced by whether or not a war was being conducted (when the rates were lower) and when most of the fighting was over (when the rates were higher). That is, an exogenous factor was operating which appears to change the frequency of sanctioning via bad paper.

Such clear cut and oscillating patterns are quite troubling from many theoretical angles of vision for a number of reasons: all of which concern the dynamic of social change.

From a purely symbolic interactionist stance the amount of processural work necessary to negotiate meaning with regard to sanctions must have been massive, if not monumental, when one examines any of the bad paper waves. When one recalls that substantial amounts of sanctioning occur within a system that turnsover roughly one fourth of its manpower in any given year, it would seem that normative order would be extremely taxed, at best, and possibly chaotic, at worst.

From a purely conflict or radical perspective, the presumed divergence of interests on the part of soldiers and commanders (or the oppression of the former by the latter, if you will) necessary to produce such movements in sanctioning rates would surely be expected to generate considerable tension, at worst, or possibly rend asunder the very grounds upon which command is based. This would certainly be the theoretical possibility if on looked at the *rate* of change during a reaction wave.

For this reason, I feel comfortable assuming that the rates of bad paper discharge are responses *of the officer corps* to problems of internal order. Whether they are more or less than this awaits further data. That we do not know, in fact, what the civilian consequences of military stigma actually are precludes any conjecture as to their effectiveness. It is quite clear, on the other hand, that the decisions to use the bad paper discharge are quite volatile.

Worse still, for those who insist that control in military settings is analogous to the traditional conflicts between elites and the powerless, is that most veterans—clearly 92% in the worst case analysis—serve "honorably" and pass into the stream of civil society unstigmatized, if not unscathed by their military stint.

That is, if they survive. In fact, most veterans tend to view their military service in a favorable light.

Americans, it seems, do not expect their armies to be without the hazards associated with soldiering. I suggest that the structure of these contingencies and risks, in military settings, go a long way in explaining the types of controls applied and their movement over time.

One could easily argue that the common perception of the role of the military in "straightening out" young men; of allowing them to "settle down"; of giving them the requisite discipline to conform to the demands of an industrial labor force, and other purported "character building" consequences are predicated on the *exposure* of troops to physical and social risks. However, even as important a sociologist as Morris Janowitz has been able to be more uncritical in this regard than is usually the case.

Janowitz, reporting on the social effects of military service (in an article by the same name) (1971b; 164) reports:

> The evidence gathered here indicates that on average a period of military service is mildly beneficial to many individuals in terms of education, occupational chances and social attitudes, with the degree of benefit falling short of the more optimistic claims.

While it is true that, *on average*, a soldier in any of the wars examined was not killed or maimed; did not receive a court-martial; and did not receive a bad paper discharge; nor receive an Article 15; nor serve time in military prisons, a substantial, and growing, number of soldiers did, in fact, experience some of these possibilities.

While military service does indeed expose large numbers of troops to the routines of organizational life, in the Air Force—using the 1980 UAR—there were over 80 *involuntary* ways that such service for enlisted men was terminated at substantial cost to the individual. To assess the net impact of service in the military, on average, to such populations subject to military control it is imperative that data on these social casualties of the institution be gathered and analyzed. I suspect the hidden costs of "character building" are quite substantial and a sociological understanding of the institution is incomplete without such information.

Furthermore, any study of the status attainment of veterans in their host societies which ignores the level of control such soldiers had to overcome at the hands of their commanders, will invariably understate the true social cost of measured achievements. Sampled veterans are survivors in two senses: they have overcome the physical risks of war, *and* organizational attempts to label their service "less than honorable."

The degree to which such "organizational survival skills" as may be possessed by the troops, may be important in the civil society is uncertain. It is also totally unknown if the post-service careers of recent commanders—whom I have shown are increasingly reliant on sanctioning the troops—is different in any way from officers of an earlier generation. To the best of my knowledge no studies have assessed the post-service impact of changing control styles on the civilian careers of officers.

If, as more researchers have suggested, (Coates and Pellegrin, 1965; Kanter, 1976), the modern military is becoming more "managerial" in style, do retired officers accrue a civilian benefit for becoming more historically skilled at expelling subordinates with "problems of persona"?

SOCIAL RISK AND CONTROL

When one examines the physical and social risks of these three wars it is clear that there was a progressive *decrease* in physical risk and a progressive *increase* in social risk. For World War II, three soldiers were either killed or wounded for each bad paper discharge given. The risks were at relative parity during the Korean War; for each soldier killed or wounded one bad paper discharge was given. During the Vietnam War, for every soldier killed or wounded, roughly two Bad Paper Discharges were given. Wartime service in the U.S. military is causing less proportionate physical harm and significantly more social stigmatization of soldiers. This is clearly an institutional trend which requires a macro-sociological explanation.

I have considered a number of possible explanations for the inverse relation between physical and social risk, and have concluded that the rapid increases in the rate of Bad Paper Discharge occur within the context of a fairly stable number of rules, fairly high admissions standards for the enlisted ranks, and are being increasingly generated by a seasoned cadre of professional officers.

There is also the possibility of relative anomie: that extreme expansions and contractions of force size may generate uncertainties as to *which* rules to enforce, and some ambiguity over the degree of sanctioning required, i.e., the chaos and immediacy of mobilization and contraction may somehow influence the collective decisions of commanders to utilize Bad Paper as a sanctioning vehicle.

My unit of analysis, however, is too large to capture the possibilities of variation in the large number of sites and settings that together compose the military system. Indeed, I have not directly measured "anomie", but rather suggested that social control is not related to the rate at which the forces expand or contract. My impression, however, is that the reason military strength is not related in any way I could discern to organizational reaction rates is simply that the manner in which the military expands or contracts does not alter the *basic structure* of the control system. As Charles Perrow once mentioned in a graduate seminar:

> The corner gas station may compete quite furiously for local customers, but, however severe such competition may seem it does not in the least affect the relation of the Seven Sisters to the market for oil products.

I suggest that the shifting patterns of physical and social risk associated with military service in the enlisted ranks are related to the shifting normative basis upon which such service rests and particularly how this manifests itself in the officer cadres. My central argument assigns a disproportionate amount of influence to the officer corps because the military is a caste system *and* most of the expulsions from the ranks involve statements concerning the *persona* of soldiers.

Soldering appears to require the sacrifice of life and limb in the interest of the state. When such sacrifice is not forthcoming the institution must develop alternative methods of instilling belief in the legitimacy of the institution such that the requisite degree of conformity will be elicited. One such strategy is to rely more heavily on rule enforcement and punishment.

DISCUSSION: SOCIAL CONTROL REQUIREMENTS

In Polsky's assertion that social work concerns and moral uplift programs masquerading as social science pose a danger to the scientific study of criminology (Polsky, 1969) these tendencies are even more likely to have an influence on perceptions of the military system. Nationalistic, or anti-military, or post-war sentiments color our impressions of the conduct of armies and the sanctioning activities of their commanders.

I am concerned with such phenomena only as they apply to the *internal* functioning of the military system: the use of controls by officers against the troops. By such an approach I have sought to trace the operation of the ethos of control as it responds to the need for internal order.

Since I contend that the officer corps played a crucial role in maintaining such order, my research problem then became: How are rates of organizational reaction influenced by social forces operating within the officer corps itself?

THE OFFICER CORPS

The military system of social control *requires* the submission of enlisted men. It is my thesis that such legitimate authority as may be possessed by the officer corps is, in part, *generated* by the social distinctions between officers and men; the officer–enlisted distinction is *central* to social control in the military, and movements in the rate of social control activity indicate a change of some sort in the nature of the officer–enlisted distinction.

I hypothesized that any constellation of social arrangements which lessens the distinctiveness of officers with regard to their charges erodes the legitimacy of a system of control based on caste distinctions. I am thus in a position to address extremely fundamental issues for students of social deviance in, of course, a somewhat simplified manner given the limitations of my data. Nonetheless, it is extremely important to discover: 1) What soldiers "did" i.e., rates of deviance among the troops, 2) How commanders responded, i.e., rates of organizational reaction, and 3) How certain patterns were possibly influenced by certain characteristics of the officer corps.

TURNING POINTS IN DEPLOYMENT PATTERNS

My argument proceeded by identifying three major turning points in organizational reaction to social deviance in the military which suggest major changes in the deployment patterns used by commanders. These concern harshness, court expulsions and increases in bad paper discharges.

All three measures of organizational reaction to deviance, *taken together*, delimit a zone in time (1964–1972) where it is clear that deployment patterns had changed—at least with regard to the war-peace cycle. Relative to World War II and Korea, Vietnam Era commanders were less prone to keep deviant soldiers in the military: they were disproportionately expelling through the courts and with administrative bad paper, and they were more punitive.

To examine this quite notable period of transition I have focused on three types of explanations for the observed shift in deployment patterns:

1) That they were the result of mobilization.

2) That they could be explained by manpower characteristics resulting from changes in DOD selection criteria for admission to the armed forces.

3) That the "white collarization" of the military is important.

I have shown that the period 1967–1971 was *characterized* as the only observable time when college graduate accessions in the enlisted ranks were expanding while the rate of expansion of degreed officers was stable. These descriptive findings are illustrative *Social Origins Explanations* of organizational reaction. I speculate that social homogeneity is a threat to the officer–enlisted distinction as a means of maintaining order. Specifically, I hypothesized that as the social qualifications of officers become more similar to enlisted men, the officer–enlisted distinction becomes less legitimate. This presents a threat to claims (and demands) made by the officer corps on enlisted soldiers with regard to deference, demeanor, respect and proper behavior.

My data do not permit analysis of an order which might definitively resolve why commanders chose to shift their emphasis in sanctioning soldiers. They do, however, show that such a shift *occurred at a time when officer cadre distinctiveness relative to enlisted men was declining.* I have thus attempted to specify *when* social origins explanations may have the greatest degree of face validity with regard to their suggested role in the process of social control. The period 1967–71, also marked the convergence of two important social trends.

In the contemporary military, while participation in officership has been reaching down the class ladder, the troops, at the same time, have been becoming more socially respectable. The middle-classification of contemporary officers (a step down) has occurred conterminously with a lower-middle classification of the troops (a step upward). Thus, the *absolute* differences between the ranks of enlisted men and officers, in terms of social origins, has been narrowing by virtue that the extrema of both social origin distributions have vanished, i.e., fewer elite officers and fewer disreputable enlisted men, but the relative differences were most pronounced between 1967–1971. While a college degree gap has increasingly come to separate the officer from his charges, this was less so during 1967–71.

This temporary merging of those parts of the social spectrum from which the military draws its personnel identifies a compelling problem in social differentiation for which deviance theory has a possible solution, namely: How can two groups which are different, but which base differences in authority and prestige, in part, on caste criteria, maintain order and hierarchy.

One possibility is to clearly identify a *class of offenders* that articulates the symbolic differences between officers and men. That is, a grouping of offense types by which the dominant caste would be known by the relative absence of such types in their ranks.

The deployment pattern of 1967–71 was unique in that it *created a deviant population* which was composed disproportionately of those given administrative bad paper and increasingly harsh expulsive court actions were taken against a shrinking number of *very serious* offenders.

An officer, whatever else he may possess, has a role which requires that he be a master of military etiquette, protocol and self presentation and thus far removed from those traits commonly associated with felons at one extreme, and those which characterize the enlisted man who has received administrative bad paper—at the other. I conclude that there was largely a symbolic purging of the enlisted ranks during 1967–71. The historically rising social origins of enlistees meant, among other things, that less criminality per se, i.e., crimes against the person and property, was processed through court channels.

Although one would need actual data on offender distributions to verify this argument, my line of thinking is, however, consistent with civilian crime patterns in middle and lower class communities. In short, as the SES of the enlisted force increases crime patterns would be expected to shift.

In addition, Project, 100,000 personnel were apparently filtering normally into the lower ranks of the enlisted skill structure, and college graduates were entering the officer ranks at a *slower* pace than was the case before and after 1967– 71. This would certainly imply that the profession of arms was clearly losing prestige among the college educated.

At the same time there was a *temporary influx* of those with college degrees into the enlisted ranks. To understand how this combination of factors may have influenced the ethos of control during the period it is necessary to examine the impact of military service on enlisted college graduates for clues as to the possible influence this may have had on the social control activities of the officer corps.

The analysis at this point, however, is incomplete. The demographic trends must be embedded in a class of symbolic actors which, in the extreme, might best demonstrate the possibilities I suggest are salient. I direct my attention to a rapidly changing sector of the enlisted force: those with college degrees.

THE IMPACT OF THE ENLISTED COLLEGE GRADUATE

An enlisted man with a college degree is atypical in that he is as educationally qualified as his officer peers of the same age but serves in a position of much lower status. The existence of disproportionate numbers of college educated enlisted men in the system might have triggered a response among *certain segments* of the officer corps who lack their qualifications. In hindsight, it does not appear a wise decision to enter a protracted, unpopular war using men who have the qualifications to become officers but fail to do so.

Such an interpretation of course, implies that when the war is over, and the underutilized return to civilian life, a major source of stress will be removed. My argument thus narrows from a consideration of broad changes in the skill structure of the forces to the issue of educational heterogeneity among officers and troops.

ORGANIZATIONAL REACTION AND EDUCATIONAL HETEROGENEITY

The research question becomes: Was the surplus of Administrative over Punitive Bad Paper sensitive to movements in the degree of educational credentials accumulation of the officer corps relative to enlisted men?

There were three major findings:

1) The responsiveness of surplus bad paper to the changing officer and enlistee degree accumulation ratio was highly variable.

2) Mobilization for Vietnam (1967–1970) saw increased surplus bad paper while the military was accessing enlisted college graduates faster than they were being discharged.

3) When Enlisted Flight (i.e., the exodus of enlisted men with college degrees) was greatest (1971–73), the responsiveness of the rate of surplus bad paper to discrepancies in the rate of officer–enlisted degree accumulation actually declined. That is, the rate had not yet peaked, and it does not appear that enlisted flight was therefore a likely source of the peaking of reaction rates.

This is quite suggestive evidence that during the part of the Vietnam War which contained the most fighting (1967–71) officers and men become closest to being homogeneous at least with regard to educational credentials. This alone, however, while specifying one way in which the Vietnam War was unique, also adumbrates the possibility that the officer–enlisted distinction *takes on differing functions* during war and peace, as evidenced by the different observed patterns of social control.

While NET bad paper rose during the Vietnam War when the concentration of enlistees with college degrees was highest, these men, by and large, started leaving the system in largest numbers between 1971–73 - and NET began to drop. NET, however, started to rise quite notably as the All Volunteer Force was being implemented. Indeed, as the war would down, enlisted troops with college degrees left the system, college men entered the peace time officer corps in increasing numbers, and the system returned to "normal" with more bad paper levied against a shrinking force with notable declines in relative harshness.

These findings forced a change in the emphasis of my research question. While my data suggest that social origins explanations might be important during the shift in deployment pattern I have identified, they are *less than totally persuasive* for three reasons;

1) The movement of NET and educational credentials fluctuations may be part of a larger process I have failed to identify i.e., some characteristic of the Vietnam War which is more determinate in terms of social control processes.

2) They imply an almost mechanical link between social composition and social decision making. My observed relationship is clearly not casual, but rather a suggestive possibility.

3) My formulation, by centering on "what commanders did" i.e., react with differing amounts of NET bad paper, ignores the behavior of the soldiers. While this is consistent with my bias in the direction of favoring theories of societal reaction, it is an incomplete assessment which must be remedied.

A partial solution was offered by examining changes in the volume of deviance in the military and the changes in the decisions of commanders to punish the troops.

DEVIANCE IN THE MILITARY SYSTEM

It is an axiom of this research that to the degree that social institutions are seen to differ from one another, one such way of making such differences clear is to generate an institutionally specific stream of offenders through which collective attention can be focused.

Stated otherwise, any specific institutional claim to distinction, requires, by necessity, the manufacture of a distinctive type of outsider by which its claims to uniqueness can be known. Caste societies literally create outcasts; religious orders: heretics; capitalist societies: particular brands of thieves and confidence men; socialist orders: enemies of the people. Educational systems create dropouts; free-market societies create the unemployed, and the military creates AWOLS and Deserters.

DEFINING THE PROBLEM OF ABSENCE

There are a number of ways that the military and the social science community have conducted research on the "problem" of the AWOL soldier. Most studies attempt to identify the *deficiencies* of individuals. An alternative approach is to search for profiles of actual or potential offenders. I have presented a rough outline of the style in which such research has been conducted:

> The bulk of the in-house studies, i.e., those conducted under military auspices, are concerned with predicting, or controlling (deterring or reforming) problem personnel, including a few articles on attempts to properly screen military personnel and a spattering of correlation studies designed to isolate the deficiencies of absentee soldiers, and a piece or two which locate the ubiquitous remedy of all military troubles in the fine tuning of the leadership skills of those in control.

In addition,

> The writings of social scientists unattached to the military which have appeared in scholarly journals of the period (1946–77) have predominantly been written by those skilled in psychiatric or psychological techniques which have been applied to captive military samples of AWOLs in quest of deviant personalities, syndromes, character flaws and the like which presumably contain *the essence* of the transgressor of military norms. Noticeably absent from these researches is a citation which might suggest or imply that fleeing from the military system, is in part, provoked, facilitated by, or the consequence of conflict therein.

A student of the sociology of knowledge who is also interested in social deviance should notice that the military establishment has relied heavily on the work and models of delinquency researchers which, at worst, are terribly out-dated, and, at best, are questionable. The military is clearly not innovative at the cutting edge of social science research. A future researcher may wish to trace the movement of outmoded models and thinking from the fringes of the academic community—under the assumption that the military has not used social science luminaries since World War II—into currency in military settings.

A study of such applied research in military settings compared with the work of those who labor under banner of "police science" research would be quite an interesting undertaking. It appears that there is almost complete consensus on the part of the military and civilian research communities to view AWOL and de-sertion as astrutural concerns. That is, removed from the activities of the officer cadres, the conditions of life by enlistees; and the sources of stress in the military system. In short, AWOL and desertion are behaviors that must be controlled, an-ticipated, diagnosed, treated or purged. Such conceptualizations, of course, offer a rationale for more effective organizational response[1]

WHAT SOLDIERS DID: ABSENCE AS A DEVIANT ACT

During the period 1956–1980 there is quite a noticeable difference in deser-tion rates between the branches. The ground forces clearly experience the great-est rates—with the Marines clearly in the lead followed by the Army. Navy max-ima and minima run about one half of the Army figures and the Air Force stands in a class by itself: with its maximum rate being less than one half of the Navy's minimum.

Desertion is extended absence: it is an extreme case of AWOL. The major dif-ference is that the deserter has chosen to be away permanently. The two offenses differ substantially in terms of punishments received, and presumably in terms of the commitments of the offenders to the military. AWOLs return to the fold and are punished or expelled. Deserters are punished *and* expelled. The close as-sociation of AWOL and Desertion rates over time is observed in all branches. The correlation coefficient (R) between AWOL and Desertion for each branch is: Air Force (.984), Navy (.969), Marines (.962) and Army (.958).

THE EXTENT AND MEANING OF ABSENTEEISM

AWOL and desertion are offenses which involve the least discretion on the part of commanders: they are the least ambiguous examples of deviant acts. They are also the single most common type of regularly occurring form of rule viola-tion as well as the most frequently occurring serious offense type. I have used the sum of AWOL and Desertion rates as an indicator of behavioral deviance which is most typically military as well as an indicator of the collective unwillingness of enlistees to perform their soldierly roles.

Such rates thus approximate pure deviance in the military system, they address the research question:

> What were the frequencies of uniquely military rule violations that require the least amount of interpretation on the part of the officer cadres?

To limit the effects of technology and the differences attributable to branch missions, I have focused on absentee rates in the U.S. Army: the largest service branch with the most diversified pool of manpower. My major argument is directed at the *rapid* expansion and contractions of such rates which occurred in quite a striking manner. There clearly was a *deviant wave* composed of absentees during the Vietnam War.

The overall shape of the plot clearly follows the war cycle. When one recalls the strength plot for the Army—and that a buildup of forces is proportional to the amount of physical risk in the system—enlistees clearly became less willing to remain in uniform as physical risk escalated. The rapid rise and fall of absence, before and after 1971, however, is clearly inconsistent with most typical social science explanations offered for absenteeism for the simple reason that the demographic and social-psychological attributes of the enlisted force change slowly over time.

In addition, the scale of the absenteeism rates precludes the possibility that such events were isolated occurrences. The data clearly do not support an interpretation that improper socialization, disrespect for authority, or any other supposed deficiency of the troops could be a realistic explanation for such *rapid* movement in deviance rates, as it is extremely improbable that such pathological imbalances could have come and gone in so short a period of time.

WHAT COMMANDERS DID: ORGANIZATIONAL REACTION

In addition to the three court-martial types (General, Special and Summary) discussed in Chapter II—which constitute *legal* controls—commanders use a second form of control which may be termed quasi-legal or, as is the common military usage, non-judicial punishment or Article 15.

The two tiers of organizational reaction in the military system (Court-martial and Article 15) represent the *universe of legal sanctions* available to commanders for use against their charges. Court imposed controls represent sanctions applied for the violation of military statutes. Article 15s represent actions taken against broad classes of troublemakers who are less than criminal, but who, nevertheless, represent the fact that "something had to be done" to instill discipline. Something less severe than a formal court proceeding, yet more severe than informal controls.

Officer initiated formal controls are diffuse and can be applied to a rather large universe of acts. AWOL and Desertion are, on the other hand, quite specific offenses. Are rates of organizational reaction simply pure responses to deviance therein, or are functions other than punishment being served? To find out, I first examined the rate differences in purely soldier initiated deviant acts (AWOLs and Desertions) and all commander initiated responses (Courts-martial plus Article 15s—a quasi-legal control).

The former represents a narrow band of behavior, the latter a rather wide range of response to *every other* kind of rule breaking possible in the Army. I assume that since AWOL and Desertion are punishable by court-martial: each offender did, in fact, face the courts. Some deserters, of course, remain uncaught, but their numbers are small as a percent in strength.

There is an unmistakable diminution of controls used against soldiers for offenses *other than* AWOL and Desertion until 1971, and an unmistakable increase of such actions by commanders thereafter. This adds valuable information to the overall relation between deviance and sanctioning during the Vietnam War. AWOL and Desertions were clearly coming to compose the bulk of all offenses as the war escalated.

If the collective choice on the part of the troops is to be increasingly deviant, i.e., to break *other* rules in lieu of absenting themselves after 1971, I would need some evidence of this tendency to counter the possibility of enhanced rule enforcement on the part of the officer corps.

I know of no such evidence. The overall quality of soldiers was improving, not declining: peacetime, or post-war, or post-fighting service is less arduous than wartime service; the occupational options in the Army have been widening due to the planned eventual implementation of VOLAR; military pay after 1971 had been steadily increasing; the Army is becoming increasingly civilianized, i.e., the more symbolic and trivial soldierly tasks (K.P., housekeeping, morning reveille) are being replaced by more occupational incentives—or by the hiring of civilians—and women were entering the Army in increasing numbers.

More importantly, there is no evidence at all that a dramatic change in the personalities of soldiers occurred, after 1971, which could account for their heightened willingness to break other rules.

ACTION AND REACTION

In the Army, the more populous branch of the military, *surplus control*, that is: the reactions of commanders to all types of deviance minus the unambiguous absentee behavior of their charges, reached minimum in 1971 and grew rapidly thereafter. While the Army is not the entire Department of Defense, its Article 15 rates were atypical with regard to other branch patterns (they were less than the Marines, but higher than the Navy or the Air Force). The observed declining contribution of soldierly acts of absence to the pool of *all possible* kinds of acts to which the officer corps would react, after 1971, offers a striking case for a clear polarization of control activity.

Physical risk during mobilization for war can perhaps explain increases in AWOL and Desertion, but not the upward movement of discretionary controls in the absence of such risk after the bulk of the fighting was over. *Officers in the Army were unmistakably increasingly using Article 15 for "other offenses" that were being discovered as AWOL and Desertion rates sharply declined.*

The atypicality of the period 1966–1971 in the DOD with regard to the relative movement in the educational homogeneity of officers and the troops, corresponds quite well with the buildup in strength for mobilization—and therefore the increased presence of physical risk. I conclude that social origin explanations *may* account for at least some of the observed sanctioning behavior of commanders with regard to administrative bad paper discharges and harsh expulsions.

The peace-war cycle, however, appears to play a more important role in explaining the decision of commanders to punish internally for the most frequently occurring offenses (AWOL and Desertion, Article 15 infractions). During war, disproportionate amounts of control activity are directed against *unambiguous* forms of deviance such as AWOL and Desertion. When physical risk declined after 1971, sanctions for highly interpretive forms of deviance, i.e., all "other" possibilities exclusive of absenteeism, increased dramatically.

The overall DOD skill structure patterns, in addition to the patterns of deviance and control in the Army, reinforce the interpretation that mobilization for the Vietnam War produced a *symbolic* purging and *expulsion* pattern i.e., the bad paper and harsh courts-martial patterns. In addition, *mixed* amounts of control were directed at unambiguous offenders (absentees), and, after 1971—with risk removed from the system—heightened use of commanders' discretionary Article 15 authority was observed. War thus appears to act as a constraint on such decisions in the presence of physical risk.

Students of social deviance insist that the values of a group are known by the kinds of deviants the group discovers in its midst. In an extreme formulation, such personnel are *necessary* vehicles whereby the group can establish boundaries which are brought into high relief by their being violated. In this sense, following Erikson, "morality and immorality meet at the public scaffold" (Erikson, 1966).

During the Vietnam War, an unconventional, protracted military action against an agrarian society produced considerable dissention on the home front and a record amount of bad paper was given to the troops while the war was being fought. This occurred within a military that contained soldiers with the highest levels of formal education in our history.

It is not clear what values may have been seen by commanders as worthy of such sanctions being applied against the troops. It is less clear why soldierly rates of rule breaking should so neatly coincide with the cessation of battle and the material improvement of their lot—at a time when such soldiers were absenting themselves at a declining rate.

If the *ethos of control* is increasingly becoming an institutional property, as I suggest is the case, it is likely to be explained by forces beyond both the will of the commanders or the behavior of their charges. Behemoth inheres in the generation of organizational modes of accommodation which appear to increasingly have a life of their own.

NOTES: CHAPTER VIII

1. Consider the following: In 1976, The U.S. Army Research Institute for the Behavioral and Social Sciences conducted a study of "Characteristics of Unconvicted Army Deserters Participating in the Presidential Clemency Program" (Bell and Houston, USARI Research Problem Review 76–6). The study was part an Army project entitled, "Career Effectiveness in the Contemporary Army" and was sponsored by the Office of The Deputy Chief of Staff for Personnel, Department of The Army. The purpose of the study was:

   "To describe the typical Army participant in order to learn more about Army deserters during the Vietnam period, using the records of the enlisted Army participants in the Presidential Clemency Program." (From the "Brief" in the introduction.)

   The following is a report of the "Utilization of Findings" (as labeled in the Brief).

   "The finding that 25% of the participants were not in the deserter apprehension system has led to changes in the system. Data from the report were used in DoD preparations for defense against suits challenging the manner of processing men through the DoD portion of the Program. Suggestions for reducing desertion arising from this research are being considered. An abstract of this report was incorporated into the DoD After Action Report on the Program."

   I have no idea if researchers in the civilian academic community—who are not doing contract research—have subsequently had their efforts used for further justification of the social control of enlistees. Further research in this area may resolve this important issue in civil-military relations. When one examines how the "problem" of absence has been framed, however, it is not hard to speculate that "the findings of social science" could likely have been used for such purposes.

   I do not have enough information to discern if civilian research was, in fact, ever conducted to provide a rationale for social control. While it is highly unlikely that this is the case, there may be a linkage in the higher echelons that I am unaware of concerning the funding of such academic efforts. This remains an open question.

Bibliography

Note: Certain sources are available through the Defense Documentation Center (Cameron Station, Alexandria, Virginia, 22314) and catalogued in the Technical Abstracts Bulletin (TAB). If a work is available through these channels I have provided an alpha-numeric "AD" reference identifier at the end of the citation.

Abrahamson, M.
  1973 "Functionalism and The Functional Theory of Stratification." American Journal of Sociology 78(5), 1236-46.
Abrahamsson, B.
  1968 "The Ideology of an Elite: Conservatism and National Insecurity" in van Doorn, J. (Ed.) Armed Forces and Society. Mouton. The Hague and Paris, 71-83.
  1972 Military Professionalization and Political Power. Sage. Beverly Hill, California.
Adams, S.
  1953 "Status Congruity as a Variable in Small Group Performance." Social Forces 32, 16-22.
  1954 "Social Climate and Productivity in Small Military Groups." American Sociological Review 19, 421-25.
Adelaja, O.
  1976 "Patterns of Psychiatric Illness in The Nigerian Army." Military Medicine 141(5), 323-326.
A.J.S.
  1946 Human Behavior in Military Society. American Journal of Sociology (Special Issue) 51, 359-508.
Albert, W.G.
  1980 Predicting Involuntary Separation of Enlisted Personnel. USAF Human Resources Laboratory. Brooks AFB, Texas (AD-A082-995-2).

Allen, F.R.
    1957 "Influence of Technology on War" in Allen, F.R., et al. (Eds.) Technology and Social Change. Appleton-Century-Crofts. NY, 352-87.

Allerton, W.S.
    1957 "Army Psychiatry in Vietnam" in P.G. Bourne (Ed.) The Psychology and Physiology of Stress, With Reference to Special Studies of The Vietnam War. Academic Press. NY, 1-17.

Ambler, R.K. and Blair, J.
    1957 Recent Findings Concerning Attrition and Educational Level. Naval School of Aviation Medicine. Pensacola, Florida. July 16 (AD-154-620).

Ambrose, S.E.
    1973 "The Military and American Society: An Overview" in Ambrose and Barber (Eds.) The Military and American Society. The Free Press. NY, 3-18.

Andreski, S.
    1961 "Conservatism and Radicalism of the Military." *Archives Europeennes de Sociologie* 2, 53-61.
    1964 "Militarism" in Gould, J. and Kolb, W.L. (Eds.) A Dictionary of the Social Sciences. Crowell-Collier. N.Y., 429-30.
    1968 Military Organization and Society. Second Edition. Routledge and Kegan Paul. London.

Anonymous
    1946a "Informal Social Organization in the Army." *American Journal of Sociology* 51, 365-70.
    1946b "The Making of the Infantryman." *American Journal of Sociology* 51, 376-79.

Apan, G.
    1974 "Parachuting." *American Journal of Sociology* 80(1) (July), 124-52.

Araujo, O.
    1957 Sociologia de la Guerra (Sociology of War). Biblioteca de publicacciones officiales de la facultad de derecho y ciencias sociales de la universidad de Montevideo (Spanish language).

Aron, R.
    1957 "Conflict and War from the Viewpoint of Historical Sociology" in *The Nature of Conflict*. Compiled by the International Sociological Association. UNESCO. Paris, 177-203.
    1959 *On War*. Doubleday-Anchor, Garden City, NY.
    1961 "La mitraillette, le char d'assaut et l'idee." (Machine Gun, Tank and Idea). *Archives Europeennes de Sociologie* 2, 91-111 (French language).
    1974 Clausewitz's Conceptual System. *Armed Forces and Society* (1)1, 49-59.

Arthur, R.J.
    1966 "Psychiatric Disorders in Naval Personnel." *Military Medicine* 131, 354-61.

Ashworth, A.E.
    1968 "The Sociology of Trench Warfare: 1914-1918." *British Journal of Sociology* 19, 407-423.

Babin, N.E. and O'Mara, F.E.
    1980 "An Empirical Test of Moskos' Pluralism Model." Paper presented at the 75th Annual Convention of the American Sociological Association. N.Y., August.

Bachman, J.G. and Blair, J.D.
    1975 *Soldiers, Sailors and Civilians*. Institute for Social Research. Ann Arbor. MI.

Badillo, G. and Curry, D.G.
    1976 "The Social Incidence of Vietnam Casualties: Social Class or Race? *Armed Forces and Society* 2(3), 397-406.

Bahr, F.R.
    1970 The Expanding Role of The Department of Defense as an Instrument of Social Change. Ph.D. Dissertation. George Washington University. Washington, D.C.

Baier, D.E.
    1943 "The Marginally Useful Soldier." *American Journal of Mental Deficiency* 48, 52-66.

Bain, E.H.
    1973 The Socialization of ROTP Cadets at RMC: A Study of Personality, Leadership, Values and Motivational Characteristics of Stayers and Leavers. (Research Report: 73-3) Department of Military Leadership and Management. Royal Military College. Kingston, Ontario.

Baker, R.K.
    1967 A Study of Military Status and Status Deprivation in Three Latin American Armies. Center for Research in Social Systems. The American University. Washington, D.C. (AD-661-086).

Balbus, I.D.
    1973 *The Dialectics of Legal Repression: Black Rebels before the American Criminal Courts.* Transaction Books, New Brunswick, NJ.

Barabantchikov, A.V., et al.
    1967 Psikhologiia Voinskogo Kollektiva (Psychology of a Military Collective). Voenizdat, Moscow. (Russian language).

Barbeau, A.E.
    1970 The Black American Soldier in World War I. Ph.D. Dissertation. University of Pittsburgh, PA.

Barber, J.A., Jr.
    1973a "The Social Effects of Military Service" in Ambrose, S.E. and Barber, J.A., Jr. (Eds.) *The Military and American Society.* The Free Press. NY, 157-58.
    1973b "The Military Service and American Society: Relationships and Attitudes" in Ambrose, S.A. and Barber, J.A., Jr. (Eds.) *The Military and American Society.* The Free Press. NY, 299-310.

Barnett, C.
    1967 "The Education of Military Elites." *Journal of Contemporary History* 2(3), 15-35. Great Britain.

Barr, N.I. and Zunin, L.M.
    1971 "Clarification of the Psychiatrist's Dilemma While in Military Service." *American Journal of Orthopsychiatry* (41)4, 672-674.

Barth, E.A.T.
    1963 "Air Force Base-Host Community: A Study in Community Typology." *Social Forces* 41, 260-64.

Basowitz, H., et al.
    1955 *Anxiety and Stress.* McGraw Hill, NY.

Bassan, M.E.
    1947 "Some Factors Found Valuable in Maintaining Morale on a Small Combatant Ship." *Bulletin of the Menninger Clinic* 11, 33-42.

Beck B.
    1971 "The Military as a Welfare Institution" in C.C. Moskos, Jr. (Ed.) Public Opinion and The Military Establishment. Sage. Beverly Hills, CA, 137-148.

Becker, G.
    1978 *The Mad Genius Controversy: A Study in the Sociology of Deviance.* Sage. Beverly Hills, CA.

Becker, H.S.
    1964 *The Other Side.* Free Press. NY.
    1973 *Outsiders: Studies in the Sociology of Deviance.* Free Press. NY.

Beebe, G.W. and De Bakey, M.E.
    1952 *Battle Casualties: Incidence, Mortality and Logistic Considerations.* Charles C. Thomas. Springfield, IL.

Bell, D.
    1963 "The Dispossessed—1962." In Bell, D. (Ed.) *The Radical Right.* Doubleday. NY, 1-38.
    1973 "Notes on the Service Society: Five Dimensions of Post-Industrial Society." *Social Policy* 4(1), 103-10.

Bell, D.B. and Bell, B.W.
    1977 "Desertion and Anti-War Protest: Findings From The Ford Clemency Program. *Armed Forces and Society* (3)3, 433-43.

Bell, D. B. and Holz, R.
    1975 Summary of ARI Research on Military Delinquency. USARI for the Behavioral and Social Sciences. Alexandria, VA.

Bell, D. B. and Houston, T. J.
    1976 The Vietnam Era Deserter: Characteristics of Unconvicted Deserters in The Presidential Clemency Program. U.S.A.R.I. Research Problem Review 76-6: Department of the Army. Office of The Deputy Chief of Staff for Personnel. Arlington, VA.

Bell, D.B., et al.
    1974 "Predictions and Self-fulfilling Prophecies." Paper delivered at the Annual Convention of the American Psychological Association in New Orleans 30 Aug-3 Sep.

Bellino. R.
    1969 "Psychosomatic Problems of Military Retirement." *Psychosomatics* 10, 318-321.

Benad, G.
    1953 "Die Eingliederung des Einzelen in soziable Organismen" (Assimilation of the Individual into Social Organisms). *Soziale Welt* 4, 341-346. (German language).

Berger, M.
    1946 "Law and Custom in the Army." *Social Forces* 25, 82-87.

Berger, P.L. and Luckmann, T.
    1967 The Social construction of Reality. Anchor Books. Doubleday and Company. NY.

Bergmann, K. H., et al.
    1981 "Climate Models" in *Physics Today* October, Vol. 34(10), 44-51.

Berk, R.A., et al.
    1981 "A Test of the Stability of Punishment Hypothesis: The Case of California, 1851–1970." American Sociological Review 46 (Dec): 805-819.

Berkman, P.L.
  1946 "Life Aboard an Armed Guard Ship." *American Journal of Sociology* 51, 380-387.
Berkowitz, L.
  1956 "Group Norms Among Bomber Crews: Patterns of Perceived Crew Attitudes, Actual Crew Attitudes, and Crew Liking Related to Air Crew Effectiveness in Far Eastern Combat.: *Sociometry* 19, 141-53.
Berkun, M. and Meeland, T.
  1958 "Sociometric Effects of Race and of Combat Performance." *Sociometry* 21, 145-49.
Bernardeau, C., et al.
  1975 U.S. Armed Forces Minority Officer Recruitment. Human Resources Research Organization. Alexandria, VA (AD-A017-719-6SL).
Berry, N. H. and Nelson, P.D.
  1966 "The Rate of School Dropouts in the Marine Corps." *Personnel and Guidance Journal* September, 20-23.
Beusse, W.E.
  1974 The Impact of Military Service on Low Aptitude Men. Assistant Secretary of Defense for Manpower and Reserve Affairs. Department of Defense. Washington, D.C. (AD-785-383-1).
  1975 The Impact of Draft Vulnerability on Service Academy Attrition. USAF Human Resources Laboratory. Brooks AFB, Texas (AD-A017-081-1SL). Also classified under OASD (Manpower and Reserve Affairs). Washington, D.C. (OASD-MRA-MR-74-12).
  1977 Factors Related to the Incidence of Disciplinary Actions Among Enlisted Personnel. USAF Human Resources Laboratory. Brooks AFB, Texas (AD-A040-539-9SL).
Beusse, W. E., et al.
  1976 Perceptions of Equal Opportunity and Race Relations Among Military Personnel. USAF Human Resources Research Laboratory. Brooks AFB, Texas (AD-A-36-135-2SL).
Bey, D.R. and Chapman, R.E.
  1974 "Psychiatry—The Right Way, The Wrong Way and the Military Way." *Bulletin of the Menninger Clinic* 38(4), 343-354.
Bey, D.R. and Zecchinelli, V.A.
  1974 "G.I.'s Against Themselves: Factors Resulting in Explosive Violence in Vietnam." *Psychiatry* 37(3), 221-228.
Biderman, A.D.
  1959 "Effects of Communist Indoctrination Attempts: Some Comments Based on an Air Force Prisoner of War Study." *Social Problems* 6, 304-13.
  1963 *The March to Calumny: The Story of American POWs in the Korean War*. Macmillan. N.Y.
  1967 "What is Military?" in Tax, S. (Ed.) *The Draft: Handbook of Facts and Alternatives*. The University of Chicago Press. II, 122-37.
Biderman, A.D. and Sharp, L.M.
  1968 "The Convergence of Military and Civilian Occupational Structures: Evidence from Studies of Military Retired Employment." *American Journal of Sociology* 73, 381-99.
Bidwell, C.E.
  1961 "The Young Professional in the Army: A Study of Occupational Identity." *American Sociological Review* 26, 360-72.

Biegel, M.M.

    1968   Project Stray: A Study of Unauthorized Absenteeism and Desertion. Part 1: Deserter Information System (FOUO). Office of the Assistant Secretary of Defense. Manpower and Reserve Affairs (DoD). Washington, D.C.

Biersner, R. J., and Ryman, D.H.

    1973   Psychiatric Incidence Among Military Divers. Navy Medical Neuropsychiatric Research Unit. San Diego, CA (AD-A008-618-1SL).

Bigler, R.R.

    1963   Der einsame Soldat: eine soziologische Deutung der militarischen Organisation (The Lonely Soldier: A Sociological Interpretation of Military Organization). Verlag Huber, Frauenfeld. (German language).

Bishop, J. W., Jr.

    1968   "Military Law." *International Encyclopedia of the Social Sciences*. N.Y. Macmillan, 312-19.

    1974   *Justice Under Fire: A Study of Military Law*. Charterhouse. NY.

Bjorklund, E.

    1963   "Social anpassning under militartjansten" (Social Adjustment during Military Service). *Tidskrift i sjovasendet* 126, 404-17. (Swedish language).

Blache, J.A.

    1970   "The Organization as an Instrument of Violence: The Military Case." *Sociological Quarterly* 11(3), 331-50.

Black, D.

    1976   *The Behavior of Law*. Academic Press. NY.

Blackman, S, et al.

    1966   Psychological Factors in Military Deviance. Wakoff Research Center. Staten Island, NY, March (AD-629-630).

Blair, J.D.

    1975   Civil-Military Belief Systems: A Study of Attitudes Toward the Military System Among Military Men and Civilians. Ph.D. Dissertation. University of Michigan. Ann Arbor, MI.

Blair, J.D. and Backman, J.G.

    1976   "The Public View of the Military" in Goldman, N.L. and Segal, D.R. (Eds.) *The Social Psychology of Military Service*. Sage. Beverly Hills, CA, 215-36.

Bleda, P.R.

    1979   REALTRAIN Improves Soldier Attitudes Toward The Army. U.S.A.R.I. for the Behavioral and Social Sciences. Alexandria, VA (AD-A072-334-6SL).

Bletz, D.F.

    1971   "Mutual Misperceptions: The Academic and the Soldier in Contemporary America." *Parameters* (Journal of the Army War College)1, 2-13.

Bloch, H.S.

    1969   "Army Psychiatrist in the Combat Zone: 1967-1968." *American Journal of Psychiatry* 126, 291-92.

Block, K.

    1955   "The Study of War in American Society." *Sociologus* 5, 104-113.

Bloom, L.

    1949   "Militarization as a Research Field." *Sociology and Social Research* 28, 194-99.

Blum, A.A.

 1972 "Soldier or Worker?: A Reevaluation of the Selective Service System."
 Midwest Quarterly 13(January), 147-57.

Blumberg, A.S. (Ed.)

 1974 Current Perspectives on Criminology. Alfred A. Knopf. NY.

Bodart, G.

 1908 Militar-historisches Kriegs-Lexikon: 1618-1905. (Military-Historical
 Encyclopedia of Wars: 1618-1905). C.W. Stern. Vienna and Leipzig.
 (German language).

Boddaert, M.M.

 1970 Criminologisch in Verband Met de Desertie en de Misdrijven van Gemeen
 Recht Gepleegd Door Molitairen (Dutch language, "Criminological
 Inquiry on Desertion and Common Law Offenses by Servicemen") in
 Tijdschrift voor Sociale Wetenschappen, 15(2), 171-256.

Bogart, L. (Ed.)

 1969 *Social Research and the Desegregation of the U.S. Army*. Markham Publishing Co.
 Chicago, IL.

Bonger, W.A.

 1940 "De Oorlog als Sociologisch Probleem" (War as a Sociological Problem).
 Mens en Maatschappij 16, 81-93. (Dutch language)

Bons, P.M., et al.

 1970 "Changes in Leadership Style as a Function of Military Experience and
 Type of Command." *Personnel Psychology* 23(4), 551-68.

Booth, R.F. and Hoiberg, A.

 1973 "Change in Marine Recruits' Attitudes Related to Characteristics and
 Drill Instructors' Attitudes." *Psychological Reports* 33, 63-71.

Borgatta, E.F.

 1955 "Attitudinal Concomitants of Military Statuses." *Social Forces* 33, 342-47.

Borros, R.J.

 1973 Protection of the Procedural Rights of the Accused in the Military
 Judicial System. U.S. Naval Academy. Annapolis, Maryland. May 22
 (AD-769-496-IGA).

Borus, J.F.

 1973a "Reentry II. 'Making It' Back in the States." *American Journal of Psychiatry*
 130, 850-854.

 1973b "Reentry III. Facilitating Healthy Readjustment in Vietnam Veterans."
 Psychiatry 36, 428-439.

 1974 "Incidence of Maladjustment in Vietnam Returnees." *Archives of General
 Psychiatry* 30, 554-557.

 1975 The Reentry Transition of The Vietnam Veteran. *Armed Forces and Society*
 2(1), 97-114.

Borus, J.F., et al.

 1972 "Racial Perceptions in the Army: An Approach." *American journal of
 Psychiatry* 128, 1369-74.

Bourne, P.G.

 1967 "Some Observations on the Psychosocial Phenomena Seen in Basic
 Training." *Psychiatry* 30, 187-196.

 1970a "Military Psychiatry and the Vietnam Experience." *American Journal of
 Psychology* 127(Oct), 481-88.

1970b Men, Stress and Vietnam. Brown, Little and Company. Boston.

Bourne, PG, et al.

1968 "Affect Levels of Ten Special Forces Soldiers under Threat of Attack." *Psychological Reports* 52, 177-83.

Bower, E.M.

1967 "American Children and Families in Overseas Communities." *American Journal of Orthopsychiatry* 37(4), 787-96.

Bowers, R.V. (Ed.)

1962 Studies in Organizational Effectiveness: Contributions to Military Sociology from the 1949-1954 Contract Research Program of the Human Resources Research Institute, Air University. Air Force Office of Scientific Research. Office of Aerospace Research. Washington, D.C. (Mimeo).

1967 "The Military Establishment" in Lazarsfeld, P.F, et al. (Eds.) The Uses of Sociology. Basic Books. NY, 234-274.

Boyd, N.K. and Jones, H.H.

1973 An Analysis of Factors Related to Desertion among FY 1968 and FY 1969 Army Accessions. Manpower Development Division, Air Force Human Resources Laboratory. Air Force Systems Command. Alexandria, VA. January (AD-772-731-6).

Braatz, G.A., et al.

1971 "The Young Veteran as a Psychiatric Patient in Three Eras of Conflict." *Military Medicine* 136(5), 455-57.

Bradford, Z.B. and Brown, F.J.

1974 *The United States Army in Transition.* Sage. Beverly Hills, CA.

Bramson, L.

1971 "The Armed Forces Examining Station: A Sociological Perspective" in Moskos, C.C., Jr. (Ed.) *Public Opinion and the Military Establishment.* Sage. Beverly Hills, CA, 185-220.

Bramson, L. and Goethals, G.W. (Eds.)

1964 *War: Studies from Psychology, Sociology, Anthropology.* Basic Books. NY.

Brepohl, W.

1953 "Das Heerwesen-Kultur-soziologisch gesehen" (Army Life from the Viewpoint of Sociology of Culture). *Soziale Welt* 4, 317-324 (German language).

Brill, N.Q. and Beebe, G.W.

1955 A Follow-up Study of War Neuroses. Veterans Administration Medical Monograph. Washington, D.C.

Brodsky, S.L. and Egglestoon, N.E. (Eds.)

1970 *The Military Prisons: Theory, Research and Practice.* Southern Illinois University Press. Carbondale, IL.

Bromberg, W.

1943 "The Effects of the War on Crime." *American Sociological Review* 8, 685-91.

Brotz, W. and Wilson, E.K.

1946 "Characteristics of Military Society." *American Journal of Sociology* 51, 371-75.

Brown, C.S.

1951 The Social Attitudes of American Generals: 1898-1940. Ph.D. Dissertation. University of Wisconsin.

Browning, H.L., et al.

1973 "Income and Veteran Status: Variations among Mexican Americans, Blacks, and Anglos." *American Sociological Review* 38(1), 74-85.

Bryant, C.D. (Ed.)

1974 *Deviant Behavior: Occupational and Organizational Bases.* Rand McNally, Chicago.

1974a "Olive-Drab Drunks and GI Junkies: Alcohol and Narcotic Addition in the U.S. Military. In C.D. Bryant (Ed.), 1974, 129-145.

1974b "Socialization for Khaki-Collar Crime: Military Training as Criminalization Process" in C.D. Bryant (Ed.) 1974, 239-254.

Bucky, S.F., et al.

1973a Personality, Draft Status and Military Service. Naval Health Research Center. San Diego, CA (AD-A037-325-8SL).

1973b Intensity: The Description of a Realistic Measure of Drug Use. Navy Medical Neuropsychiatric Research Unit. San Diego, CA (AD-A-001-317-7ST).

Burchard, W.W.

1954 "Role Conflicts of Military Chaplains." *American Sociological Review* 19, 523-35.

Burns, C.D.

1933 "Militarism" in Encyclopedia of the Social Sciences. Vol. 10. McMillan. NY, 446-450.

Busquest, B.J.

1966a "El estado mayor como aristocracia military" (The General Staff as a Military Aristocracy). *Anales de Sociologia* 1(2), 76-79 (Spanish language).

1966b "La sociologia military" (Military Sociology). *Vevita Ejercito* 320, 25-30 (Spanish language).

1967 "Las cuatro ultimas generaciones militares" (The Last Four Military Generations). *Revista Espanola de la Opinion Publica* 7, 179-94 (Spanish language).

1967b "El military de carrera en Espana: estudio de sociologia military" (The Professional Soldier in Spain: A Study in Military Sociology). Ediciones Ariel. Barcelona. (Spanish language).

Butler, J.S.

1976 "Assessing Black Enlisted Participation in the Army." *Social Problems* 23(5), 559-66.

Caffey, B. and Capel, W.C.

1969 "Negro and War Attitudes of the Same Persons at Three Points Over a Thirty Three Year Period." *Psychological Reports* 25(2), 543-51.

Cahalan, D. and Cisin, I.H.

1973 Attitudes and Behavior of Naval Personnel Concerning Alcohol and Problem Drinking. Bureau of Social Science Research, Inc. Washington, D.C. (AD-A034-821-9SL).

1975a Analysis of Drinking Behavior and Attitudes by Races. Bureau of Naval Personnel. Washington, D.C. (AD-A013-237-3SL).

1975b Final Report on a Service-Wide Survey of Attitudes and Behavior of Naval Personnel Concerning Alcohol and Problem Drinking. Bureau of Social Science Research, Inc. Washington, D.C. (AD-A010-272-3SL).

Cahalan, D, et al.

1974 Drinking Practices and Problems in The U.S. Army. Information Concepts, Inc. Arlington, VA. (AD-763-851).

Campbell, D.T.
    1953   "Leadership and its Effects upon the Group." University Bureau of Business Research. Ohio State University: Number 83.

Campbell, D.T. and McCormack, T.H.
    1957   "Military Experience and Attitude toward Authority." *American Journal of Sociology* 62, 482-90.

Canter, F.M. and Canter, A.M.
    1957   "Authoritarian Attitudes and Adjustment in a Military Situation." *U.S. Armed Forces Medical Journal* 8, 1201-07.

Caplow, T.
    1947   "Rumors in War." *Social Forces* 25, 298-302.

Carmen, R.S.
    1971   "Expectations and Socialization Experiences Related to Drinking among U.S. Servicemen." *Quarterly Journal of Studies on Alcohol* 32 (4, Part A), 1040-47.

Carmichael, L. and Mead, L.C.
    1951   The Selection of Military Manpower. National Academy of Sciences. Publication Number: 209. Washington, D.C.

Carpenter, J.B. and Christal, R.E.
    1973   Development of a Data Base for Direct Analysis of Airmen Loss Rates. Air Force Human Resources Laboratory. Brooks AFB, Texas (AD-775-721-4).

Carroll, B.A.
    1970   "War Termination and Conflict Theory: Value Premises, Theories and Policies." *Annals of the American Academy of Political and Social Science* 392 (November), 14-29.

Chesler, D., et al.
    1955   "Effect on Morale of Infantry Team Replacement and Individual Replacement System." *Sociometry* 18, 331-41.

Christner, C.A. and Hemphill, J.K.
    1955   "Leader Behavior of B-29 Commanders and Changes in Crew Members' Attitudes toward the Crew." *Sociometry* 18, 82-87.

Chun, K.T., et al.
    1975   Military Attitudinal Surveys: An Overview. Institute for Social Research. Ann Arbor, MI.

Clark, J.H.
    1948   Some Behavioral Correlates of Army AWOL. Ph.D. Dissertation. University of Texas. Austin, TX.
    1949   "The Adjustment of Army AWOL's." *Journal of Abnormal and Social Psychology* 44, 394-401.

Clarke, I.F.
    1966   Voices Prophesying War: 1763-1984. Oxford University Press. NY.
    1967   "Forecasts of War in Fiction." *Comparative Studies in Society and History* 10, 1-25.

Clarkson, J.D. and Cochran, T.C. (Eds.)
    1941   War as a Social Institution. Columbia University Press. NY.

Clinard, W.B.
    1963   Sociology of Deviant Behavior. Holt, Rinehart and Winston. NY.

Clinard, M.B. and Quinney, R.
    1973 Criminal Behavior Systems: A Typology. Holt, Rinehart and Winston (2nd Edition). NY.

Clotfelter, J.
    1974 "Public Attitudes toward the Military since 'The Garrison State'" in Wilcox, A.R. (Ed.) Political Attitudes and Public Opinion, 91-104. John Wiley. NY.

Cloward, R.A. and Ohlin, L.E.
    1960 Delinquency and Opportunity: A Theory of Delinquent Gangs. Free Press. NY.

Clum, G.A. and Hoiberg, A.
    1970 Biographical Variables and Post-Hospitalization Adjustment of Psychiatric Patients in The Naval Service. Navy Medical Neuropsychiatric Research Unit. San Diego, CA (AD-711-171).

Coates, C.H.
    1958 "The Role of the Military Sociologist in Operations Research." *Sociological and Social Research* 42, 327-31.
    1966 "America's New Officer Corps." *Trans-action* 3(3), 22-24.

Coates, C.H. and Pellegrin, R.J.
    1965 Military Sociology: A Study of American Institutions and Military Life. Social Science Press, University Park, MD.

Cockerham, W.
    1973 "Selective Socialization: Airborne Training as Status Passage." *Journal of Political and Military Sociology* 1(2), 215-229.

Cohen, A.K.
    1966 Deviance and Control. Prentice-Hall. Englewood Cliffs, NJ.

Cohen, G.B.
    1956 "De Militaire Parade" (The Military Parade). *Mens en Maatschappij* 31, 282-88 (Dutch language).

Cohen, S.P.
    1964 "Rulers and Priests: A Study in Cultural Control." *Comparative Studies in Society and History* 6, 199-216.

Coffey, K.J.
    1975 "The Australian All-Volunteer Force." *Military Review* 55(4), 34-41 and 55(5), 78-83.

Coffin, T.
    1964 The Armed Society: Militarism in Modern America. Pelican. Baltimore, MD.

Colby, E.
    1937 "Army" in Encyclopedia of the Social Sciences. Vol. 2, 210-218. Macmillan. NY.

Coles, H.L. (Ed.)
    1962 *Total War and Cold War: Problems in Civilian Control of the Military*. Ohio State University Press. Columbus, OH.

Collins, R.
    1974 "Three Faces of Cruelty: Towards a Comparative Sociology of Violence." *Theory and Society* 1 (Winter), 415-40.

Conrad, P.
   1981   "The Medicalization of Deviance in American Culture" in Rubington and Weinberg (Eds.), 75-83.

Cook, F.J.
   1962   *The Warfare State. Mcmillan.* NY.

Cook, R.F. and Morton, A.S.
   1975   An Assessment of Drug Education-Prevention Programs in the U.S. Army. Department of The Army. USARI for the Behavioral and Social Sciences. USGPO identifier: 76002139.

Copper, M.N.
   1972   "The Occurrence of Mutiny in World War I: A Sociological View." *International Behavioral Scientist* 4(3), 1-10.

Cornejo, M.H.
   1930   La guerre au point de vue sociologique. (War from the Sociological Point of View). M. Giard, Publishers. Paris (French language).

Cortright, D.
   1975   *Soldiers in Revolt: The American Military Today.* Anchor Press. Garden City, NY.

Coser, L.
   1963   "The Dysfunctions of Military Secrecy." *Social Problems* 11, 13-22.
   1964   *The Functions of Social Conflict.* The Free Press. NY.

Coulet, W.
   1968   "Le nouveau reglement de discipline generale dans les armees" (The New Regulation with Regard to General Discipline in the Armed Forces). *Revue du Droit Public et de la Science Politique en France et a l'Etranger* 84, 1-82 (French language).

Cox, C.C.
   1970   *Class, Caste and Race.* Modern Reader Edition, Monthly Review Press. NY.

Cox, J.A. and Krumholtz, J.C.
   1958   "Racial Bias in Peer Ratings of Basic Airmen." *Sociometry* 21, 292-99

Crawford, E.T. and Biderman, A.D. (Eds.)
   1969   *Social Scientists and International Affairs: A Case for a Sociology of Social Science.* John Wiley and Sons. NY (Note: Contains the bibliography by E.T. Crawford formerly known as "The Social Sciences in International and Military Policy: An Analytic Bibliography.")

Crawford, K.S. and Thomas, E.D.
   1977   "Organizational Climate and Disciplinary Rates on Navy Ships." *Armed Forces and Society* 3(2), 165-82.

Cressey, D.R. and Sutherland, E.H.
   1978   *Criminology.* (10th Edition) J.B. Lippincott Company, NY.

Crowe, R.R. and Colback, E.M.
   1971   "A Psychiatric Experience With project 100,000." *Military Medicine* (136) 3, 271-73.

Cuber, J.F.
   1943   "The Adjustment of College Men to Military Life: Case Data." *Sociology and Social Research* 27, 267-76.

Cutright, P.
   1974   "The Civilian Earnings of White and Black Draftees and Non-Veterans." *American Sociological Review* 39(3), 317-27.

Dalfiume, R.M.

> 1966   Desegregation of The United States Armed Forces: 1939-1953. Ph.D. Dissertation. University of Missouri. Columbia, MO.

Daniels, A.K.

> 1969   "The Captive Professional: Bureaucratic Limitations in the Practice of Military Psychiatry." *Journal of Health and Human Behavior* 10, 255-65.

> 1970   "The Social Construction of Military Psychiatric Diagnoses" in Dreitzel, H. (Ed.) *Patterns of Communicative Behavior.* Macmillan, NY. 181-205.

> 1973   "The Philosophy of Combat Psychiatry" in Rubington and Weinberg (Eds.), 132-140.

Daniels, A.K. and Clausen, R.E.

> 1966   "Role Conflicts and their Ideological Resolution in Military Psychiatric Practice." *American Journal of Psychiatry* 123, 280-87.

Daniels, M.J.M.

> 1971   "Some Remarks on an Instrument for the Assessment of Cadet Behavior" in van Gils, M.R. (Ed.) *The Perceived Role of the Military.* Rotterdam University Press. Rotterdam, 211-20.

Datel, W.E. and Lifpak, S.T.

> 1969   "Expectations, Affect Change and Military Performance in the Army Recruit." *Psychological Reports* 24, 855-79.

Datel, W.E., et al.

> 1970   "Military Outcomes of Trainees Served by an Army Mental Hygiene Consultation Service." *Military Medicine* 135(2), 81-89.

Davenport, R.K.

> 1947   "The Negro in the Army: A Subject of Research." *Journal of Social Issues* 3(4), 32-39.

Davies, F. J. and Stivers, R. (Eds.)

> 1975   The Collective Definition of Deviance. J.B. Lippincott Company. NY.

Davis, A.K.

> 1948   "Bureaucratic Patterns in the Navy Officer Corps." *Social Forces* 27, 143-53.

Davis, F.J.

> 1954   "Conceptions of Official Leader Roles in the Air Force." *Social Forces* 32, 253-58.

De Gregori, T. and Pi-Sunyer, O.

> 1966   "Technology, Traditionalism and Military Establishments." *Technology and Culture* 7, 402-07.

De Imaz, J.L.

> 1964   *Los que Mandan: Las fuerzas armadas en Argentina* (Those in Command: The Armed Forces in Argentina). Universidad de Buenos Aires. Buenos Aires (Spanish language).

Delpez. L.

> 1952   "La notion sociologique de guerre." (The Sociological Conception of War). *Revue Generale du Droit International Public* 56, 5-33 (French language).

Demerath, N.J.

> 1952   "Initiating and Maintaining Research Relations in a Military Organization. *Journal of Social Issues* 8(3), 11-23.

Dentler, R.A. and Erikson, K.T.

1979 "The Group Function of Schizophrenia in the Military" in V.L. Swigert and R.A. Farrel (Eds.) *The Substance of Social Deviance*. Alfred Pub. Co., Sherman Oaks, CA, 2-24.

Department of Defense (DoD) OASD

1972 Types of Discharges Issued to Enlisted Personnel by Fiscal Year 1950-1972. Office of The Assistant Secretary of Defense (Manpower and Reserve Affairs). 31 Aug.

1978 Manpower, Reserve Affairs and Logistics. Report of The Joint-Service Administrative Discharge Study Group (1977-78). (AD-A060-521-2SL).

1979 Office of The Assistant Secretary of Information, Operations and Reports. *Selected Manpower Statistics*, May.

1982 Office of The Assistant Secretary of Defense: Manpower, Reserve Affairs and Logistics. Military Personnel and Force Management. Letter of 14 June.

Department of the Air Force (DAF)

1981 Letter, 23 December 81. Headquarters, Air Force Manpower and Personnel Center. Randolph AFB, Texas. HQ,USAFMPC.

1982 Letter, 8 July 82. Headquarters, Air Force Manpower and Personnel Center. Randolph AFB, Texas. HQ,USAFMPC.

Department of the Army

1960 Report to Honorable Wilber M. Brucker, Secretary of The Army. Committee on The Uniform Code of Military Justice, Good Order and Discipline in The Army. 18 January. (Known as "The Powell Report").

1965 Marginal Man and Military Service: A Review. Washington, D.C. January (AD-624-059).

1970 Report of the Special Civilian Committee For The Study of The United States Army Confinement System. Washington, D.C.

1971 Personnel Offensive (Phase 1) Final Draft: Supporting Data, Volume II. U.S. Army Combat Development Command. Personnel and Administrative Services Agency. (ACN-17792). 18 September.

1972 Fort Ord Final project VOLAR Evaluation. U.S. Army Training Center. Infantry and AR and D. Ford Ord, CA. August.

(USACF)

1979 Military Offenders Sent To The U.S. Army Correctional Facility: A Follow Up Study. Technical Report. Research and Evaluation Division, U.S. Army Correctional Facility. Fort Riley, Kansas. January.

(DoD, DoA, PCP)

1975 After Action-Report—Department of Defense Implementation of Presidential Proclamation 4313—President's Clemency Program. Department of the Army. Office of The Deputy Chief of Staff for Personnel. Washington, D.C. (DoD imprint, DoA Report).

(DoA)USAJ/Ltr.

1982 Headquarters, Department of the Army U.S. Army Judiciary, Clerk of Court. Letters dated 20 Jan 82, and 6 Jul 82. Office of The Adjutant General. Washington, D.C.

Department of the Navy (DN, HQJAG)/Ltr.

1982 Letter, 26 Jan 82. Headquarters, Department of the Navy. Judge Advocate General. Washington, D.C.

Desai, M.

1972 "Social Science Goes to War." *Survival* 17, 62-67.

Dixon, N.F.
>1976 *The Psychology of Military Incompetence.* Cape Publishers. London.

Dollard, J.
>1943 "Fear in Battle." *The Infantry Journal.* Washington, D.C.

Dorman, J.E.
>1976 "ROTC Cadet Attitudes: A Product of Socialization or Self-Selection?" *Journal of Political and Military Sociology* (4), 203-216.

Dornbusch, S.M.
>1955 "The Academy as an Assimilating Institution." *Social Forces* 33, 316-21.

Douglas, J.D.
>1967 *The Social Meaning of Suicide.* Princeton University Press. Princeton, NJ.
>1972 (Ed.) Research on Deviance. Random House. NY

Downs, J.F.
>1958 "Environment, Communication and Status Change Aboard an American Aircraft." *Human Organization* 17(3), 14-19.

Dressler, D.
>1946 "Men on Parole as Soldiers in World War II." *Social Science Review* 20, 537-50.

Drucker, E.H.
>1970 The Effects of the Merit Reward System on Morale in Basic Combat Training. Human Resources Research Organization. Alexandria, VA (AD-A026-599-1SL).
>1974a The Effects of Basic Combat Training on the Attitudes of the Soldier. Human Resources Research Organization. Alexandria, VA (AD-782-194-5).
>1974b A Longitudinal Study of Attitude Change and Alienation During Basic Combat Training. Human Resources Research organization. Alexandria, VA (AD-782-192-9).

Drucker, E.H. and Schwartz, S.
>1973 The Prediction of AWOL, Military Skills, and Leadership Potential. Human Resources Research Organization. Alexandria, VA (AD-758-161).

Dubuisson, A.U. and Kleiger, W.
>1964 Combat Performance of EM with Disciplinary Records. U.S. Army Personnel Research Office. Office of the Chief, Research and Development. Washington, D.C. (AD-605-280).

Duff, D.F. and Arthur, R.J.
>1967 "Between Two Worlds: Filipinos in the U.S. Navy." *American Journal of Psychiatry* 123(7) (January), 836-43.

Dunham, H.W.
>1944 "War and Mental Disorder; Some Sociological Considerations." *Social Forces* 22, 137-42.

Durkheim, E.
>1960 *The Division of Labor in Society.* Trans. By G. Simpson. The Free Press. Glencoe, IL, 103.

Dwyer, R.J.
>1953 "The Negro in the United States Army: His Changing Role and Status." *Sociology and Social Research* 38, 103-12.

Earles, J., et al.
>1974 Variables Related to Amphetamine Use. USAF Human Resources Laboratory. Brooks AFB, Texas (AD-783-236-3).

1975 Drug Use Data Base. USAF Human Resources Laboratory. Brooks AFB, Texas (AD-A017-169-4SL).

Eckerman, W.C., et al.

1975 Observations of Interrank Conflicts at the Company Level: Drug and Alcohol Abuse. Research Triangle Institute. Research Triangle Park, North Carolina (AD-A082-952-3).

Edgerton, R.B.

1976 *Deviance: A Cross Cultural Perspective.* Cummings Publishing Company. Reading, MA.

Edmonson, J.H.

1971 Desertion in The American Army During the Revolutionary War. Ph.D. Dissertation. Louisiana State University and Agricultural and Mechanical College, New Orleans, LA.

Edwards, D. and Berry, N.H.

1973a Prediction for the Character and Behavior Disorder in an Occupational Setting. Navy Medical Neuropsychiatric Research Unit. San Diego, CA. (AD-762-632).

1973b "Psychiatric Decisions: An Actuarial Study." Navy Medical Neuropsychiatric Research Unit. San Diego, CA (AD-780-975-9).

Edwards, D., et al.

1973 Clinical Decisions and Outcomes in a Navy Psychiatric Service. Navy Medical Neurophychiatric Research Unit. San Diego, CA (AD-763-980).

1974 "Psychiatric Crisis and Enlistment Motivation." *U.S. Navy Medicine* 63, 24-25. (AD-776-669-4).

Elliott, G.

1972 *The Twentieth Century Book of The Dead.* Scribner's. NY.

Erikson, K.T.

1964 "Notes on the Sociology of Deviance" in H.S. Becker (Ed.) *The Other Side.* The Free Press. NY, 9-21.

1966 *Wayward Puritans: A Study in the Sociology of Deviance.* John Wiley and Sons. NY.

Erwin, F.W.

1977 The Feasibility of the use of Autobiographical Information as a Predictor of Early Army Attrition. Army Research Institute for the Behavioral and Social Sciences. Department of Defense (imprint) Alexandria, VA: Department of The Army (report). National Technical Information Service Number: 78023113.

Etzioni, A.

1977 "Power Goals and Organizational Compliance Structure" in Leger and Stratton, 8.

Evans, R.

1969 The Military Draft as a Slave System: An Economic View. *Social Science Quarterly* 50(3), 535-43

Faris, J.H.

1975 "The Impact of Basic Combat Training." *Armed Forces and Society* 2(1), 115-27.

1977 "An Alternative Perspective to Savage and Gabriel." *Armed Forces and Society* 3(3), 457-62.

Farrell, R.A. and Swigert, V.L. (Eds.)

1975 Social Deviance. J.B. Lippincott Company, NY.

Feld, M.D.
>   1975 "Military Professionalism and the Mass Army." *Armed Forces and Society* 1(2), 191-214.
>
>   1977 *The Structure of Violence: Armed Forces as Social Systems.* Sage. Beverly Hills, CA.
>
>   1977a "Military Discipline as a Social Force" in Feld, M.D., 1977, 13-30.
>
>   1977b "Information and Authority" in Feld, M.D. 1977, 71-84.

Fernandez, R.L.
>   1979 Forecasting Enlisted Supply: Projections for 1979-1990. The Rand Corporation. Santa Monica, CA (AD-A077-190-7).

Festinger, L., et al.
>   1956 *When Prophecy Fails.* Harper Torchbooks, NY.

Finer, S.E.
>   1962 *The Man on Horseback: The Role of the Military in Politics.* Praegor. NY.
>
>   1977 "The Modern Army as a Bureaucracy" in Rose, P.I. (Ed.) *The Study of Modern Society.* Fourth Edition. Random House. NY, 342-46.

Fink, C., et al.
>   1974 A Systems Analysis of a Self-Paced, Variable-Length Course of Instruction. Annex A. "Training, Administrative and Disciplinary Problems Associated with The U.S. Army Clerk-Typist (MOS 71810/20) Course." Human Resources Research Organization. Alexandria, VA (AD-A077-984-3).

Finn, J. (Ed.)
>   1971 *Conscience and Command: Justice and Discipline in the Military.* Random House, NY.

Fisher, A.H., Jr.
>   1972a Preliminary Findings from the 1971 DoD Survey of Drug Use. Human Resources Research Organization. Alexandria, VA (AD-743-852).
>
>   1972b Analysis of Selected Drug Related Topics: Findings from Interviews at Four Armed Services Locations. Human Resources Research Organization. Alexandria, VA (AD-743-853).

Fisher, A.H., Jr., et al.
>   1972 Patterns of Drug Usage among Vietnam Veterans. Human Resources Research Organization. Alexandria, VA (AD-743-162).

Fisher, A.H., Jr. and Disario, M.
>   1974 Attitudes of Youth Towards Military Service In a Zero Draft Environment: Results of a National Survey Conducted in November, 1972. Human Resources Research Organization. Alexandria, VA (AD-781-370-2).

Fisher, A.H., Jr. and Harford, M.
>   1973 Trends in Enlistment Motivation: Results of AFEES Surveys of Enlisted Men from April 1971 to April 1972. Human Resources Research Organization. Alexandria, VA (AD-778-089-3).

Flyer, E.S.
>   1959 Factors Relating to Discharge for Unsuitability among 1956 Airman Accessions to the Air Force. USAF Personnel Research Laboratory. Lackland AFB, Texas (AD-230-758).
>
>   1972 Who Served in Vietman? Analysis of Factors Associated with Vietnam Duty among Army First Term Enlisted Personnel. Office of the Assistant Secretary of Defense for Manpower and Reserve Affairs. (DoD) Washington, D.C. January.

Forander, N.
> 1974 Morale and Discipline in the Forces. MPI B. Rapport, (June), 101 (Swedish). *Psychological Abstracts* (1975) Vol. 53. Citation Number: 2058.

Fox, L.J., et al
> 1970 Literature Review: Research on Military Offenders. U.S. Army Correctional Training Facility. Fort Riley, KS. November.

Fritzsch, R.B.
> 1972 The Quantity and Quality of Volunteers for Air Force Enlistment in the Absence of a Draft. Ph.D. Dissertation. George Washington University. Washington, D.C.

Fulton, W.S.
> 1971 Command Authority in Selected Aspects of The Court Martial Process. U.S. Army War College. Carlisle Barracks, PA. March 8 (AD-772-292-9GA).

Gage, R.W.
> 1964 "Patriotism and Military Discipline as a Function of Degree of Military Training." *Journal of Social Psychology* 64(1), 101-11.

Gale, L.G.
> 1969 Crime and Military Organization: Service Comparison of Rates of Adjudicated Crime in The Armed Forces of The United States. Ph.D. Dissertation. State University of New York at Buffalo. Buffalo, NY.

Galligan, F.B.
> 1973 The Theme of the Modernizing Military: A Sociological Reading of the Literature. Ph.D. Dissertation. Washington University, St. Louis, MO.

Gard, R.G., Jr.
> 1971 "The Military and American Society." *Foreign Affairs* 49(July), 698-710.
> 1973 "The Future of the Military Profession." *Adelphi Papers* 103 (Winter), 1-8. The International Institute for Strategic Studies. London.

Garfinkel, H.
> 1978 "Conditions of Successful Degradation Ceremonies" in Rubington and Weinberg (Eds.), 142-144.

Garnier, M.A.
> 1975 "Technology, Organizational Culture and Recruitment in the British Military Academy." *Journal of Political and Military Sociology* 3 (2) (Fall), 141-51.

Geldard, F.A. and Lee, M.C. (Eds)
> 1961 *Proceedings* 1st International Symposium on Military Psychology. National Academy of Sciences. National Research Council. Washington, D.C.

Gelly, R.
> 1973 "Psychotherapy in a Military Setting." *Psychotherapy and Psychosomatics* 21(1-6), 153-55. (Original in French language).

Getzels, J.W. and Guba, E.G.
> 1955 "Role Conflict and Personality." *Journal of Personality* 24, 365-70.

George, A.L.
> 1971 "Primary Groups, Organization and Military Performance" in R.W. Little (Ed.) *Handbook of Military Institutions*. Sage. Beverly Hills, CA. 293-318.

Giallombardo, R. (Ed.)
> 1966 *Juvenile Delinquency: A Book of Readings*. John Wiley and Sons, NY.

Gibbs, D.N.

    1957 "The National Serviceman and Military Delinquency." *Sociological Review* 5 (New Series), 255-63.

Ginzberg, E.

    1943 "The Occupational Adjustment of 1,000 Selectees." *American Sociological Review* 8, 256-63.

Ginzberg, E. and Bray, D.W.

    1953 *The Uneducated.* Columbia University Press. NY.

Ginzberg, E., et al.

    1959 *The Ineffective Soldier: Lessons for Management and Nation.* Columbia University Press. NY. 3 Volumes. Vol. 1: The Lost Divisions; Vol. 2: Breakdown and Recovery; Vol. 3: Patterns of Performance.

Gladstone, A.

    1959 "The Conception of the Enemy." *Journal of Conflict Resolution* 3, 132-37.

Glass, A.J.

    1955 "Principles of Combat Psychiatry." *Military Medicine* 117, 27-33.

    1957 "Observations upon the Epidemiology of Mental Illness in Troops during Warfare" in *Symposium on Preventive and Social Psychiatry.* Walter Reed Army Institute of Research. Washington, D.C. 185-97.

    1966 Neuropsychiatry in WWII. Vol. 1; U.S. Army. Office of the Surgeon General, Medical Department. Zone of The Interior. Washington, D.C.

    1970 "Draftees Shoulder Burden of Fighting, Dying in Vietnam." *National Journal* 2(33) (August 15), 1747-55.

Glazer, N.Y.

    1965 Which Men Match: A Pilot Study of Factors Affecting Membership in R.O.T.C. Ph.D. Dissertation. Cornell University. Ithaca, NY.

Goffard, S., et al.

    1966 A Study of Category IV Personnel in Basic Training. Human Resources Research Organization. Alexandria, VA. (AD-481-737).

Goldman, N.L.

    1973 "The Changing Role of Women in the Armed Forces." *American Journal of Sociology* 78(January), 892-911.

Gooberman, L.

    1974 *Operation Intercept: The Multiple Consequences of Public Policy.* Pergamon Press. NY.

Goodacre, D.M.

    1953 "Group Characteristics of Good and Poor Performing Combat Units." *Sociometry* 16, 168-79.

Goode, E.

    1975 "On Behalf of Labelling Theory." *Social Problems* 22(3), 570-83.

    1978 *Deviant Behavior: An Interactionist Approach.* Prentice-Hall. NJ.

Goode, W.J.

    1978 *The Celebration of Heroes: Prestige as a Social Control System.* University of California Press. Berkeley, CA.

Goodstadt, B. and Glickman, A.

    1975 The Current Status of Enlisted Attrition in the U.S. Navy and in the Marine Corps and the Search for Remedies. American Institute for Research in the Behavioral Sciences. Washington, D.C.

Gray, C.S.
  1975 "Hawks and Doves: Values and Policy." *Journal of Political and Military Sociology* 3(1), 85-94.
Gregory, S.W., Jr.
  1977 "Toward a Situated Description of Cohesion and Disintegration in the American Army." *Armed Forces and Society* 3(3), 463-73.
Grinker, R.R. and Spiegel, J.W.
  1945 *Men under Stress. Blakiston*, Philadelphia, PA.
Gross, E.
  1953 "Some Functional Consequences of Primary Controls in Formal Work Organizations." *American Sociological Review* 18, 368-73.
  1954 "Primary Functions of the Small Group." *American Journal of Sociology* 60, 24-29.
  1956 "Symbiosis and Consensus as Integrative Factors in Small Groups." *American Sociological Review* 21, 174-79.
Gross, E. and Miller, D.C.
  1961 "The Impact of Isolation on Worker Adjustment on Military Installations in the United States and Japan." *Estudios Sociologicos* 1, 70-83. (Original in Spanish language).
Grunzke, M.F., et al.
  1970 Comparative Performance of Low-Ability Airmen. USAF Human Resources Laboratory. Lackland AFB, Texas. January (AD-705-575).
Grusky, O.
  1964 "The Effects of Succession: A Comparative Study of Military and Business Organization" in Janowitz, M. (Ed.) The New Military: Changing Patterns of Organization. Russell Sage Foundation. NY, 83-111.
Guinn, N. and Truax, S.R.
  1973 Comparison of Volunteer Attitudes and Career Motivation among Officer and Airman Personnel. Air Force Human Resources Laboratory. Brooks AFB, Texas (AD-772-676-3).
Gunderson, E.K.E.
  1971 Epidemiology and Prognosis of Psychiatric Disorders in the Naval Service. Naval Medical Neuropsychiatric Research Unit. San Diego, CA (AD-734-195).
Gunderson, E.K.E., et. al.
  1968 "Military Status and Mental Illness." *Military Medicine*, 133(7), 543-49.
  1973 A Drug Involvement Scale for Classification of Drug Abusers. Navy Medical Neuropsychiatric Research Unit. San Diego, CA (AD-773-781-0).
  1976 "Health and Adjustment of Men at Sea" in Goldman, N.L. and Segal, D.R. (Eds.) *The Social Psychology of Military Service*. Sage. Beverly Hills, CA, 67-80.
Gunderson, E.K.E. and Ransom, A.J.
  1965 "Demographic Factors in the Incidence of Mental Illness." *Military Medicine* 135(5), 429-33 (AD-634-210).
Guttmacher, M.S. and Stewart, F.
  1945 "A Study of Absence Without Leave." *American Journal of Psychiatry* 102, 74-81.
Habeck, E.J.
  1969 Anomia and the Resocialization of the Military Offender. Ph.D. Dissertation. Catholic University of America, Washington, D.C.

Hackel, E.

 1970 Military Manpower and Political Purpose. London. Institute for Strategic Studies.

Hadley, E.E.

 1943 "Military Psychiatry: A Note on Social Status." *Psychiatry* 6, 203-16.

Hadley, E.E., et al.

 1942 "An Experiment in Military Selection." *Psychiatry* 5, 371-402.

Hagauer, R.W.

 1971 "Educational Levels in the Military and Civilian Populations of The U.S. From 1952 to 1970 with Projections of Educational Level to 1980." Report Prepared by The Directorate of Manpower and Utilization. Officer Management Systems. U.S. Army. May.

Hagen J. and Bertstein, I.N.

 1979 "Conflict in Context: The Sanctioning of Draft Resisters." *Social Problems* 27(1), October, 109-122.

Hall, E.T, Jr.

 1947 "Race Prejudice and Negro-White Relations in the Army." *American Journal of Sociology* 52, 401-09.

Hall, R.H.

 1972 The Formal Organization. Basic Books. NY.

Hall, R.L.

 1955 "Social Influence on the Aircraft Commander's Role." *American Sociological Review* 20, 292-98.

 1956 "Military Sociology" in Zetterberg, H.L. (Ed.) Sociology in the United States of America: A Trend Report. UNESCO. Paris. 59-62.

Halpin, A.W.

 1954 "The Leadership Behavior and Combat Performance of Airplane Commanders." *Journal of Abnormal and Social Psychology* 49, 19-22.

 1955 "The Leader Behavior and Leadership Ideology of Educational Administrators and Air-Craft Commanders." *Harvard Educational Review* 25, 18-31.

Hammond, P.Y.

 1961 *Organizing for Defense*. Princeton University Press. Princeton, NJ.

Haney, C., Banks, C. and Zimbardo. P.

 1977 "Interpersonal Dynamics in a Simulated Prison" in Leger and Stratton (Eds.), 65-92.

Harding, F.D. and Richards, J.A.

 1971 A Descriptive Analysis of The Classification, Assignment, and Separation Systems in the Armed Services. Human Resources Research Organization. Alexandria, VA (AD-730).

Harding, F.D, et al

 1975 "The 1972 DoD Survey of Illicit Drugs and Alcohol Use: A Report of Major Findings." August, 1975. Survey Research Branch and Data Analysis Center. OASD Report Number MR-76-3 (AD-A014-569-8SL).

Harris, F.G. and Little, R.W.

 1957 "Military Organization and Social Psychology" in *Symposium on Preventive and Social Psychiatry* Walter Reed Army Institute of Research. Washington, DC, 173-84.

Hart, R.J.
> 1978 The Relationship between Perceived Offense and Actual Discipline Rates in the Military. USARI for the Behavioral and Social Sciences. Alexandria, VA (AD-A077-947-0).

Hartnagel, T.F.
> 1974 "Absent Without Leave: A Study of The Military Offender" in *Journal of Political and Military Sociology*, Vol. 2, 205-220.

Hastie, W.H.
> 1942 "The Negro in the Army Today." *Annals of the American Academy of Political and Social Science* 223, 55-59.
> 1943 "Negro Officers in Two World Wars." *Journal of Negro Education* 12(Summer), 316-23.

Hauser, W.L.
> 1973 America's Army in Crisis: A Study in Civil-Military Relations. Johns Hopkins University Press. Baltimore, MD.

Hausrath, A.
> 1967 Utilization of Negro Manpower in The Army: A Statistical Study. Research Analysis Corporation. McLean, VA (AD 695-677). Inter-University Seminar on Armed Forces and Society. Archive: University of Chicago.

Havighurst, R.J. and Morgan, H.G.
> 1951 The Social History of a War-Boom Community. Longmans and Green. NY.

Hayes, F.W.
> 1969 "Military Aeromedical Evacuation and Psychiatric Patients During The Vietnam War." *American Journal of Psychiatry* 126(5), 658-66.

Heaton, W.R., Jr.
> 1977 "The Minorities and the Military in China." *Armed Forces and Society* 3(2), 325-42.

Heise, J.A.
> 1969 The Brass Factories. Public Affairs Press. Washington, D.C.

Henry, A.F. and Borgatta, E.F.
> 1953a A Report on Attitudes toward Desertion of Air Force Enlisted Personnel. Human Resources Research Institute. Maxwell AFB, Alabama. May.
> 1953b "Comparison of Attitudes of Enlisted and Commissioned Air Force Personnel." *American Sociological Review* 18, 669-71.

Henry, A.F., et al.
> 1955 "Armed Forces Unification and the Pentagon Officer." *Public Administration Review* 15, 173-80.
> 1962 "Role Conflict as a Factor in Organizational Effectiveness" in Bowers, R.V. (Ed.) Studies in Organizational Effectiveness. Air Force Office of Scientific Research, Washington, D.C., 5-27.

Hertz, A.
> 1946 "Zagadnienia socjologii wojska i wojny." (*Problems of the Sociology of the Military and War*). *Prezolad Sociologiczny* 8, 119-40 (Polish language).

Hiatt, R.S.
> 1969 A Study of Compliance Relationships and Organizational Delinquency in Military Units. Ph.D. Dissertation. Columbia University.

Hilberg, R.
> 1979 *The Destruction of the European Jews.* Harper Colophon. NY.

Hippchen, L.J.
  1970 "Employers Attitudes Toward Hiring Dishonorably Discharged Servicemen" in Brodsky, S.L. and Eddleson, N.E. (Eds.) *The Military Prison*. Illinois University Press. Carbondale, IL, 170-80.

Hirshi, T.
  1969 *Causes of Delinquency*. University of California Press. Berkeley, CA.
  1973 "Procedural Rules and the Study of Deviant Behavior." *Social Problems* 21(2), 151-72.

Hodges, H.E.
  1974 "A Sociological Analysis of Dud Behavior in the United States Army" in Bryant, C.D. (Ed.), 27-43.

Hofstetter, C.R. and Moore, D.W.
  1979 "Watching TV and Supporting the Military." *Armed Forces and Society* 5(2), 261-69.

Hohn, R.
  1963 Die Armee als Erziehungsschule der Nation: das Ende einer Idee (The Armed Forces as the School of the Nation: The End of an Idea). Verlag fur Wisssenschaft, Wirtschaft und Technik. Bad Harzburg. (German language).

Holbrook, J.R.
  1971 "Volunteer Army: Military Caste?" *Military Review* 51(Aug), 91-95.

Hollander, E.P.
  1954 "Authoritarianism and Leadership Choice in a Military Setting." *Journal of Abnormal and Social Psychology* 49, 365-70.

Holinghead, A.B.
  1946 "Adjustment to Military Life." *American Journal of Sociology* 51, 439-47.

Holloway, H.C.
  1974 "Epidemiology of Heroin Dependency among Soldiers in Vietnam." *Military medicine* 139(2), 108-113.

Holt, D.R.
  1972 Drug Abuse in The Army. U.S. Army War College. Carlisle Barracks, PA (AD-765-665-5).

Homans, G.C.
  1946 "The Small Warship." *American Sociological Review* 11, 294-300.

Hood, R. and Sparks, R.
  1970 *Key Issues in Criminology*. McGraw Hill, NY.

Hopkins, A.
  1975 "On the Sociology of Criminal Law." *Social Problems* 22(5), 608-19.

Horowitz, I.L.
  1967 "The Military Elites" in Lipset, S.M. and Solari, A. (Eds.) *Elites in Latin America*. Oxford University Press, NY, 146-89.
  1971 "The Military as a Subculture" in Said, A.A. (Ed.) *Subcultures in Development and Revolution*. Prentice Hall. Englewood Cliffs, NJ, 41-51.

Horton, M.M.
  1946 "Women in the United States Army." *American Journal of Sociology* 51, 448-50.

Horwitz, A.
   1977   "An Exchange on Marxian Theories of Deviance and Social Control--A Critique of Spitzer." *Social Problems* 24(3), 362-64.

Huffman, R.E.
   1970   "Which Soldiers Break Down?" *Bulletin of the Menninger Clinic* Vol. 34 (Nov), 343-51.

Hughes-Morgan, G.
   1977   "Disobedience to a Lawful Military Command." *Journal of the Royal United Services Institute* 122(1), 9-14.

Hunt, W.A.
   1951   "An Investigation of Naval Neuropsychiatric Screening Procedures" in Guetzkow, H. (Ed.) *Groups, Leadership and Men*. Carnegie Press. Pittsburgh, PA, 245-56.

Hunt, W.A., et al.
   1954   "The Serviceability of Military Personnel of Low Intelligence." *Journal of Clinical Psychology* 10, 286-88.

Hunter, F.
   1952   *Host Community and Air Force Base*. University of North Carolina Institute for Research in Social Science. Chapel Hill, NC.

Huntington, S.P.
   1956   "Civilian Control of the Military: A Theoretical Statement" in H. Eulau, et al. (Eds.) *Political Behavior: A Reader in Theory and Research*. The Free Press. Glencoe, IL, 380-84.
   1960   "Officership as a Profession" in S.P. Huntington, *The Soldier and the State*. The Belknap Press of Harvard University Press. Cambridge, MA, 7-18.

HuMRRO
   1958   Staff Memo: *A Critical Incident Study of Infantry, Airborne and Armored Junior Non-Commissioned Officers*. U.S. Army Leadership Human Research Unit. Presidio of Monterey, CA, 11 July (Human Resources Research Organization).
   1972   *Patterns of Drug Use among Vietnam Veterans*. Professional Paper 12-72. Alexandria, VA.

Hutchins, E.B. and Fiedler, F.E.
   1960   "Task-Oriented and Quasi-Therapeutic Role Functions of the Leader in Small Military Groups." *Sociometry* 23, 393-406.

Hutchinson, C.E.
   1957   "The Meaning of Military Sociology." *Sociology and Social Research* 41, 427-33.

Huzar, E.
   1942   "Pre-War Conscription." *South West Social Science Quarterly* 23, 112-119.

Ikle, F.C.
   1958   *The Social Impact of Bomb Destruction*. Ph.D. Dissertation. University of Oklahoma. Norman, OK.

Il'in, S.K.
   1967   *Moral'yni faktor v sovremennoi voine* (The Moral Factor in Modern Warfare). Boeh. Moscow (Russian language).

Ingelhart, P.
   1976   "Changing Values and Attitudes Toward Military Service among the American Public" in Goldman, N.L. and Segal, D.R. (Eds.) *The Social Psychology of Military Service*. Beverly Hills, CA. Sage. 255-278.

Ingraham, L.H.
 1974 "The Nam and The World: Heroin Use by U.S. Army Enlisted Men Serving in Vietnam." *Psychiatry* 37(2), 114-28.

Jacobs, J. B.
 1978 "Legal Change within the United States Armed Forces since World War II." *Armed Forces and Society* 4(3) May, 391-421.

Jacobs, J.B. and Retsky, H.G.
 1977 "Prison Guard" in Leger and Stratton (Eds.), 54-62.

Jackson, B.
 1972 *Outside the Law: A Thief's Primer*. Transaction Books. New Brunswick, NJ.

Jackson, J.A.
 1971 "Military Training and Civilian Employment" in van Gils, M.R. (Ed.) The Perceived Role of the Military. Rotterdam University Press. Rotterdam, 81-92.

Janis, I.L.
 1945 "Psychodynamic Aspects of Adjustment to Army Life." *Psychiatry* 8, 159-76.

Janowitz, M.
 1959 "Changing Patterns of Organizational Authority: The Military Establishment." *Administrative Science Quarterly* (3), 473-93.
 1966 "The Military Establishment: Organization and Disorganization" in Merton, R.K. and Nisbet, R.A. (Eds.) *Contemporary Social Problems*. Harcourt, Brace and World. NY, 515-52.
 1968 *The Professional Soldier: A Social and Political Portrait*. The Free Press. NY.
 1969 (Ed.) *The New Military*. W.W. Norton and Co., Inc. NY.
 1971a "Military Organization" in R.W. Little (Ed.) *Handbook of Military Institutions*. Sage. Beverly Hills, CA, 13-51.
 1971b "Basic Education and Youth Socialization in The Armed Forces" in R.W. Little (Eds.) *Handbook of Military Institutions*. Sage. Beverly Hills, CA, 167-210.
 1973a "Characteristics of the Military Environment" in Ambrose and Barber (Eds.), *The Military and American Society*. The Free Press. NY, 166-73.
 1973b "The U.S. Forces and the Zero Draft." The International Institute for Strategic Studies. London. Adelphi Papers, No. 94, 21-25.
 1973c "The Social Demography of the All-Volunteer Force." *Annals of the American Academy of Political and Social Science*. 406 (March), 86-93.
 1975a "The All-Volunteer Military as a 'Socio-political' Problem." *Social Problems* 22(3), 432-449.
 1975b "Stabilizing Military Systems: An Emerging Strategic Concept." *Military Review* 55(6), 3-10.
 1976 "Military Institutions and Citizenship in Western Societies" in Harries-Jenkins, G., and van Doorn, J. (Eds.) *The Military and the Problem of Legitimacy*. Sage. Beverly Hills, CA, 77-92.
 1977a "From Institutional to Occupational: The Need for Conceptual Clarity." *Armed Forces and Society* 4(1), 51-54.
 1977b *Military Institutions and the Developing Nations*. University of Chicago Press. Chicago, IL.

Janowitz, M. and Little R.W.
 1965 "Techniques of Organizational Control" in *Sociology and the Military Establishment*. (Revised Edition) Russell Sage Foundation. NY, 100-14.
 1974 *Sociology and the Military Establishment* (Third Edition). Sage. Beverly Hills, CA.

Janowitz, M. and Moskos, C.C., Jr.

    1974 "Racial Composition in the All-Volunteer Force." *Armed Forces and Society* 1(1), 109-123.

    1979 "Five Years of the All-Volunteer Force 1973-78." *Armed Forces and Society* 5(2), 179.

Janowitz, M. and van Doorn, J. (Eds.)

    1970 *On Military Ideology*. University of Rotterdam Press. Rotterdam.

Jernigan, G.W.

    1973 The Courts of Military Review: Evolution of Judicial Institutions. Ph.D. Dissertation. Louisiana State University and Agricultural and Mechanical College. New Orleans, LA.

Johnson, A.

    1942 "War" in Encyclopedia of The Social Sciences. Macmillan, NY, 331-41.

Johnson, H. and Wilson, G.C.

    1972 *Army in Anguish*. Pocket Books. NY. (Note: Reprints of a series of reports that appeared in *The Washington Post* in 1971).

Johnson, P.V. and Marcrum, R.H.

    1968 "Perceived Deficiencies in Individual Need Fulfillment of Career Army Officers." *Journal of Applied Psychology* 52, 457-61.

Jones, B.K.

    1973 "The Gravity of Administrative Discharges: A Legal and Empirical Evaluation." *Military Law Review* 59, 1-25.

Jones, F.E.

    1968 "The Socialization of the Infantry Recruit" in Blishen, et al. (Eds.) Canadian Society: Sociological Perspectives. Macmillan of Canada. Toronto, 353-65 (Third Edition).

Josephson, E.

    1952 "Irrational Leadership in Formal Organizations." *Social Forces* 31, 109-17.

Just, W.

    1970 *Military Men*. Alfred A. Knopf. NY.

Kaempffert, W.

    1941 "War and Technology." *American Journal of Sociology* 46, 431-44.

Kaldor, M.

    1977 "Military Technology and Social Structure." *Bulletin of the Atomic Scientists* 33(6), 49-53.

Kanter, A.

    1976 "The Managerial Careers of Air Force Generals. A Test of the Janowitz Convergence Hypothesis." *Journal of Political and Military Sociology* 4(1), 121-34.

    1977 "The Career Patterns of Air Force Generals." *American Journal of Political Science* 21(2), 353-80.

Kantor, J.E. and Guinn, N.

    1975 Comparison of Performance and Career Progression of High School Graduates and Non-Graduates in the Air Force. Air Force Human Resources Laboratory. Brooks AFB, Texas (AD-A022-973-2SL).

Kaplan, R.C.

    1962 "Personality Correlates of Military Career Choice. Ph.D. Dissertation. University of Texas.

Karcher, E.K., Jr.

    1962   "Role Ambiguity a Factor in Organizational Effectiveness" in Bowers, R.V. (Ed.) *Studies in Organizational Effectiveness: Contributions to Military Sociology from the 1949-1954 Contract Research Program of the Human Resources Research Institute, Air University.* Air Force Office of Scientific Research. Office of Aerospace Research. Washington, D.C., 28-85.

Karlen, D.

    1973   "Civilianization of Military Justice: Good or Bad?" *Military Law Review*, DA PAM 27-100-60, 60(Spring).

Karpinos, B.D.

    1967   "Mental Test Failures" in Tax, S. (Ed.) *The Draft: A Handbook of Facts and Alternatives.* University of Chicago Press. Chicago, IL, 35-53.

    1972   Draftees: Disqualifications for Military Service for Medical Reasons—An Analysis over Time. HuMRRO, Alexandria, VA. Inter-University Seminar on Armed Forces and Society. Archive: University of Chicago, IL (AD-A060-770-5SL).

    1975a AFQT: Historical Data. Assistant Secretary of Defense. Manpower and Reserve Affairs. Department of Defense (AD-A014), Washington, D.C.

    1975b Applicants for Enlistment: Results of Examination for Military Service (Fiscal Years 1972-73). Human Resources Research Organization. Alexandria, VA. July. Archive: Inter-University Seminar on Armed Forces and Society. University of Chicago. Chicago, IL (AD-A014-316-4SL).

Karsten, P.

    1974   "Anti-R.O.T.C.: Response to Vietnam or 'Consciousness III?'" In Lovell, J.P. and Kronenberg, P.S. (Eds.) *New Civil-Military Relations.* Transaction Books. New Brunswick, NJ, 111-127.

Katenbrink, I.G., Jr.

    1969   "Military Service and Occupational Mobility" in Little, R.W. (Ed.) *Selective Service and American Society.* Russell Sage Foundation. NY, 163-90.

Kerckhoff, A.C. (Ed.)

    1958   The Reactions of Former Air Force Lieutenants to Two Years of Civilian Life. Air Force Personnel and Training Research Center. Lackland AFB, Texas. February.

Keegan, J.

    1976   *The Face of Battle.* Viking Press. NY.

Keehn, R.J.

    1978   "Military Rank at Separation and Mortality." *Armed Forces and Society* (4)2, 283-92.

Kelley, H.A.

    1972   Effects of Military Experience on Socialization of Vietnam Era Veterans to Work Roles. Ph.D. Dissertation. University of Southern California. Los Angeles, CA.

Kiev, A. and Giffen, M.B.

    1965   "Some Observations on Airmen Who Break Down During Basic Training." *American Journal of Psychiatry* 122, 184-88.

King, E.L.

    1972a *The Death of the Army: A Pre-Mortem.* Saturday Review Press. NY.

    1972b Annual Report. Fiscal Year 1972. U.S. Army Correctional Training Facility. Fort Riley, Kansas (AD-751-231).

King, N.W. and Eddowes, E.E.
 1976 Similarities and Differences among Superior, Marginal, and Eliminated Undergraduate Pilot Training Students. Air Force Human Resources Laboratory. Brooks AFB, Texas (AD-A028).

Kipnis, D.
 1957 "Interaction Between Members of Bomber Crews as a Determinant of Sociometric Choice." *Human Relations* 10, 263-70.

Kitsuse, J.I.
 1962 "Societal Reaction to Deviant Behavior." *Social Problems* 9(3), 247-56.

Kitsuse, J.I. and Spector, M.
 1975 "Social Problems and Deviance: Some Parallel Issues." *Social Problems* 22(3), 432-49.

Kjellberg, F.
 1965 "Some Cultural Aspects of the Military Profession." *Archives Européennes de Sociologie* 6, 283-93.

Klare, M.T.
 1972 *War without End: American Planning for the Next Vietnams.* Knopf, NY (Note: Documents third world military assistance from the U.S. and expenditures for social science research directed at third world countries.)

Klingberg, F.L.
 1966 "Predicting the Termination of War: Battle Casualties and Population Losses." *Journal of Conflict Resolution* 10, 129-71.

Klockars, C.B.
 1981 "The Fence" in Rubington and Weinberg (Eds.), 446-52.

Kluckhohn, C.
 1951 "American Culture and Military Life." Report of the Working Group on Human Behavior under Conditions of Military Service. Department of Defense. Research and Development Board. Washington, D.C.: Appendix No. 106.

Kolb, D., et al.
 1973 Differences in Family Characteristics of Heroin Injectors and Inhalers. Navy Medical Neuropsychiatric Research Unit. San Diego, CA (AD-A-001-314-4ST).
 1974a Perceptions of Drug Abuse Risk in Relation to Type of Drug Used and Level of Experience. Navy Medical Psychiatric Research Unit. San Diego, CA (AD-A-0006-765-2SL).
 1974b Pre-Service Drug Abuse: Family and Social History Characteristics. Navy Medical Neuropsychiatric Research Unit. San Diego, CA (AD-A003-774-7SL).

Kolb, D. and Gunderson, E.K.E.
 1977 "Alcoholism in the United States Navy." *Armed Forces and Society* 3(2), 183-94.

Korb, L.J., (Ed.)
 1976 The System for Educating Military Officers in the U.S. International Studies Association. Pittsburgh, PA.

Kourvetaris, G.A. and Dobratz, B.
 1976 "The Present State and Development of Sociology of the Military." *Journal of Political and Military Sociology* 4(Spring), 67-105.

  1977 (Eds.) World Perspectives in the Sociology of the Military. Transaction Books. New Brunswick, NJ.

Krebs, J.M.

  1975 New Directions of Army Alcohol and Drug Abuse Control. U.S. Army War College. Carlisle Barracks, PA (AD-A021-646-5SL).

Krendel, E.S. and Gomberg, W.

  1975 Implications of Industrial Democracy for the United States Navy. Research Report for the Office of Naval Research. Washington, D.C. Identifier: N00014-67-A-0216-0029. January.

Krise, E.F.

  1958 Role Conflict and the Social Diagnosis of The Military Offender. Ph.D. Dissertation. University of Chicago, IL.

Kroupa, E.A.

  1973 "Use of Mass Media by U.S. Army Personnel." *Journal of Broadcasting* 17(3) (Summer), 309-20.

Ladds, J.E.

  1965 A Study of Air Force Personnel Problems Associated with Remote or Isolated Assignments. M.A. Thesis. Department of Business Administration and Management. University of Nebraska. Lincoln, NE

Lammers, C.J.

  1969 "Strikes and Mutinies: A Comparative Study of Organizational Conflicts between Rulers and Ruled." *Administrative Science Quarterly* 14(4), 558-72.

Landau, S.F.

  1975 "Future Time Perspective of Delinquents and Non-delinquents: The Effect of Institutionalization." *Criminal Justice and Behavior* 2(1), 22-36.

Landing, C.H.

  1973 "Judicial Review of Military Administrative Discharges." *The Yale Law Review* 83(1),34-74.

Lang, K.

  1964 "Technology and Career Management in the Military Establishment" in Janowitz, M. (Ed.) *The New Military*. Russell Sage Foundation. NY, 39-81.

  1965a "Military Sociology: A Trend Report." *Current Sociology* 13(1), 1-55.

  1965b "Military Organizations" in J.G. March (Ed.) Handbook of Organizations. Chicago, IL. Rand McNally, 838-78.

  1968 "Military" in *International Encyclopedia of the Social Sciences*. The Macmillan Co. NY, 309.

  1971 "Military Technology and Expertise: Some Chinks in the Armor" in van Gils, M.R. (Ed.) *The Perceived Role of the Military*. Rotterdam University Press. Rotterdam. Vol. 1, 119-37.

  1972 *Military Institutions and Sociology of War: A Review of the Literature with Annotated Bibliography*. Sage. Beverly Hills, CA.

  1976 "A Comment on Kanter's 'Managerial Careers of Air Force Generals'." *Journal of Political and Military Sociology* 4(1), 141-43.

  1980 "American Military Performance in Vietnam: Background and Analysis." *Journal of Political and Military Sociology*, Vol. 8 (Fall), 169-286.

Lanier, D., Jr.

  1968 Personal Demoralization and the Socialization of Military Trainees. Ph.D. Dissertation. Case Western Reserve University. Cleveland, OH.

Lanier, L.H.
   1949 "Psychological and Social Scientists in the National Military Establishment." *American Psychologist* 4, 127-47.

Larson, A.D.
   1974 "Military Professionalism and Civil Control: A Comparative Analysis of Two Interpretations." *Journal of Political and Military Sociology* 2(1), 57-72.

Lasswell, H.D.
   1941 "The Garrison State." *American Journal of Sociology* 46, 455-68.
   1962 "The Garrison State Hypothesis Today" in Huntington, S.P. (Ed.) Changing Patterns of Military Politics. Free Press. NY, 51-70.

Latham, R.
   1965 (Trans., Intro.) *Lucretius: On the Nature of the Universe.* Penguin. Middlesex, England.

Latham, W.
   1974 The Modern Volunteer Army Program: The Benning Experiment 1970-72. Department of the Army. Washington, D.C.

Laufer, R.S. and Sloan, L.
   1975 "The Vietnam Era Veteran and Deserter: The Experience of Change." Paper presented to the American Sociological Association. San Francisco, CA, August.

Lauderdale, P.
   1978 "Deviance and Moral Boundaries" in Feldman, S.D. (Ed.) *Deciphering Deviance.* Little, Brown and Company, Boston, MA, 153-68.

Lauterbach, C.G. and Vielhaber, D.P.
   1965 The Educational Climate at West Point as Reported by First and Fourth Class Cadets. U.S. Army Hospital. West Point, NY. Report Number: TR-18 (AD-622-294). March.

Lee, G.C. and Parker, G.Y.
   1977 Ending the Draft; The Story of The All Volunteer Force. Human Resources Research Organization. Alexandria, VA (AD-A044-158-4SL).

Leger, P.G., and Stratton, J.R. (Eds.)
   1977 *The Sociology of Corrections: A Book of Readings.* John Wiley and Sons, NY.

Leigh, D.E. and Berney, R.E.
   1971 "The Distribution of Hostile Casualties on Draft Eligible Males with Differing Socio-economic Characteristics." *Social Science Quarterly* 51(4), 932-40.

Leouck, F.
   1968 "Armia a biurokracja" (The Army and Bureaucracy). *Studia Sociologiczno-Polityczne* 25, 147-75. (Polish language).

Lemert, E.M.
   1943 "Social Participation and Totalitarian War." *American Sociological Review* 8, 531-36.
   1974 "Beyond Mead: The Societal Reaction to Deviance" in *Social Problems* 21(4), 457-67.

Lermack, P.
   1972 Summary and Special Courts-martial. Ph.D. Dissertation. University of Minnesota. Minneapolis, MN.

Levi, M., et al.
    1954   "Sociometric Studies of Combat Air in Survival Training." *Sociometry* 17, 304-28.

Levy, C.J.
    1971   "ARVN as Fagots: Inverted Warfare in Vietnam." *Trans-action* 8(12), 18-27.
    1974   Spoils of War. Houghton Mifflin, Boston, MA. (Note: This study, composed of extracts of narratives of soldiers, is commonly cited as evidence of "The Violent Veteran Syndrome.")

Levy, G.H.
    1972   "Draft Susceptibility and Vietnam War Attitudes: A Research Note." *Youth in Society* 4(2), 169-76.

Lewis, O.
    1970   *Anthropological Essays*. Random House, NY, 69-73.

Lewis, R.
    1947   "Officer–enlisted men's Relationships." *American Journal of Sociology* 52, 410-19.

Lewy, G.
    1978   *America in Vietnam*. Oxford University Press, 1953-61.

Lifton, R.J.
    1973   *Home from the War: Vietnam Veterans, Neither Victims nor Executioners*. Simon and Schuster, NY.

Ligthman, E.S.
    1977   "Attrition of Applicants to the Canadian Armed Forces." *Armed Forces and Society* 3(3), 407-26.

Lindesmith, A.R.
    1943   "The Need for a Sociology of Militarism." *Sociology and Social Research* 27, 191-99.

Little, R.W.
    1956   "The 'Sick' Soldier and the Medical Ward Officer." *Human Organization* 15(1), 22-24.
    1969a "Buddy Relations and Combat performance" in M. Janowitz (Ed.) *The New Military*, 195-223.
    1969b "The Dossier in Military Organization" in Wheeler, S. (Ed.) *On Record: Files and Dossiers in American Life*. Basic Books. NY, 255-74.
    1971   (Ed.) *Handbook of Military Institutions*. Sage. Beverly Hills, CA.

Littlepage, G.E.
    1974   Situational and Dispositional Influences on AWOL Decisions. Ph.D. Dissertation. Kansas State University.

Littlepage, G.E. and Fox, L.
    1972   Personnel Control Facilities: An Analysis of AWOL Offenders awaiting Disposition. U.S. Army Correctional Training Facility. Fort Riley, Kansas.

Littlepage, G.E., et al.
    1971   Leadership and Situational Factors Related to AWOL: A Research Report. U.S. Army Correctional Training Facility. Fort Riley, Kansa.

Littlepage, G.E. and Rapporport, L.
    1977   "Factors Affecting Military AWOL" in *Journal of Political and Military Sociology* Vol. 5, 117-25.

Loether, H.J.
    1960 "Propinquity and Homogeneity as Factors in the Choice of Best Buddies in the Air Force." *Pacific Sociological Review* 3, 18-22.

Lofland, J.
    1964 "Priority Inversion in an Army Reserve Company." *Berkeley Journal of Sociology* 9, 1-15.
    1969 *Deviance and Identity*. Englewood Cliffs, NJ.

Loh, W.D.
    1975 "National Loyalties and Amnesty: A Legal and Social Psychological Analysis." *Journal of Social Issues* 31(4), 141-56.

Loory, S.H.
    1973 *Defeated*. Random House. NY.

Lopez-Reyes, R. (Ed.)
    1971 *Power and Immortality: Essays on Strategy, War, Psychology and War Control*. Exposition Press. Jericho, NY.

Lovell, J.P.
    1964 "The Professional Socialization of the West Point Cadet" in Janowitz, M. (Ed.) *The New Military: Changing Patterns of Organization*. Russell Sage Foundation. NY, 119-57.
    1977 "Apolitical Warrior or Soldier-Statesman: Commentary." *Armed Forces and Society* 4(1), 119-26.

Maccoby, M.
    1961 "The Social Psychology of Deterrence." *Bulletin of the Atomic Scientists* 17, 278-81.

Mack, R.
    1954 "The Prestige System of an Air Base: Squadron Rankings and Morale." *American Sociological Review* 19, 281-87.

Main, J.M. (Ed.)
    1970 *Conscription: The Australian Debates 1901-1970*. Cassell Australia. Melbourne.

Malinowski, B.
    1941a "War—Past, Present, and Future" in Clarkson, J.D. and Cochran, T.C. (Eds.) *War as a Social Institution*. Columbia University Press. NY, 21-31.
    1941b "An Anthropological Approach to War." *American Journal of Sociology* 46, 521-50.

Mandelbaum, D.G.
    1952 *Soldier Groups and Negro Soldiers*. University of California Press. Berkeley and Los Angeles, CA.

Mans, J.H. and van de Sandt, M.A.
    1971 "A Military Academy in Transition: A Survey Investigation" in van Gils, MR. (Ed.) The Perceived Role of the Military. Rotterdam University Press. Rotterdam, 49-70.

Mahan, J.L. and Clum, G.A.
    1971 "Longitudinal Prediction of Marine Combat Effectiveness." *Journal of Social Psychology* 83(1), 45-54.

Mandelbaum, D.G.
    1954 "Psychiatry in Military Society." *Human Organization* 13(4), 19-25.

Mannheim, H.
    1941 *War and Crime*. Watts and Company, London.

Manson, M.P. and Grayson, H.M.
    1946 Why 2,276 American Soldiers were AWOL, Deserted or Misbehaved before the Enemy." *American Journal of Psychiatry* 103, 50-54.

March, J.G. (Ed.)
    1965 *Handbook of Organizations.* Rand McNally, Chicago. IL.

Margiotta, F.D.
    1974 "A Comment on Taylor and Bletz's 'A Case for Officer Graduate Education: How Much is Enough?' *Journal of Political and Military Sociology* 2(2)(Fall), 269-71.

Marlowe, D.H.
    1959 "The Basic Training Process" in Artiss, K.L. (Ed.) The Symptom as Communication in Schizophrenia. Grune and Stratton. NY, 75-98.

Marmion, H.A.
    1971 "Where Will the Officer Corps Come From?" in Marmion, H.A. (Ed.) *The Case Against a Volunteer Army.* Quadrangle Books. Chicago, IL, 49-56.

Marchall, S.L.A.
    1964 *Men Against Fire.* William Morrison and Company, NY.

Marwald, A.
    1959 "The German General Staff: Model of Military Organization." *Orbis* 3, 38-62.

Maskin, M.H.
    1946 "Something about a Soldier." *Psychiatry* 9, 187-91.

Maskin, M.H. and Altman, L.L.
    1943 "Military Psychodynamics: Psychological Factors in the Transition from Civilian to Soldier." *Psychiatry* 6, 263-69.

Masland, J.W. and Radway, L.I.
    1957 *Soldiers and Scholars: Military Education and Military Policy.* Princeton University Press. Princeton, NJ.

Mason, J.
    1947 A Study of The Negro in Military Service. Department of Defense. Archive: Inter-University Seminar on Armed Forces and Society. University of Chicago. Chicago, IL.

Mason, W.M.
    1968 Preliminary Analysis of Social Attainment of White Males in the C.P.S. Sample of the 1964 Department of Defense Surveys, with Specific Attention to the Relation between Achievement Before Service and Achievement in Military Service, and between these Two Points and Achievement After Service. Unpublished paper, Inter-university Seminar on Armed Forces and Society. Archive: University of Chicago, IL.

Matras, J.
    1973 *Populations and Societies.* Prentice Hall, Inc. Englewood Cliffs, NJ.

Matza, D.
    1969 *Becoming Deviant.* Prentice-Hall. Englewood Cliffs, NJ.

Mattick, H.
    1957 Parole to the Army: A Research Report on Felons Paroled to the Army During World War II. Paper presented at the 87th Annual Congress of Corrections. Chicago, IL.

Mauldin, B.
    1945 *Up Front: Text and Pictures by Bill Mauldin.* Henry Holt and Sons. NY.
Maurer, D.W.
    1949 *The Big Con.* Pocket Books, NY.
Mayer, A.J. and Hoult, T.E.
    1955 "Social Stratification and Combat Survival." *Social Forces* 34, 155-59.
Mayer, M.
    1963 *The Schools.* Anchor Books. Doubleday and Company. Garden City, NY.
Mayhew, B.H., et al.
    1972 "System Size and Structural Differentiation in Military Organizations: Testing a Harmonic Series Model of the Division of Labor." *American Journal of Sociology* 77(4)(January), 750-65.

Mazuri, A.A.
    1973 "The Lumpen Proletariat and the Lumpen Militariat: African Soldiers as a New Political Class." *Political Studies* XXI(7), 1-12.
Mazuri, A.A. and Rothchild, D.
    1967 "The Soldier and the State in East Africa: Some Theoretical Conclusions on the Army Mutinies of 1964." *Western Political Quarterly* 20, 82-96.
McAllister, L.N.
    1964 "The Military" in Johnson, J.J. (Ed.) *Continuity and Change in Latin America.* Stanford University Press. Stanford, CA, 136-60.
McCabe, M.S. and Board, G.
    1976 "Stress and Mental Disorders in Basic Training." *Military Medicine* 141(10), 686-88.
McCaghy, C.H.
    1985 *Deviant Behavior: Crime, Conflict and Interest. Groups.* Second Edition. Macmillan, NY.
McCallum, M.R.
    1946 "The Study of the Delinquent in the Army." *American Journal of Sociology* 51, 479-482.
McDonagh, E.G.
    1945a "Military Social Controls." *Sociology and Social Research* 29, 197-205.
    1945b "Social Adjustments to Militarism." *Sociology and Social Research* 29, 449-57.
    1945c "Military Social Distance." *Sociology and Social Research* 29, 289-96.
McGonogal, R.A.
    1974 "Civil-Military Racism in the Seventies: The Challenge of Reducing Cultural Differences Through Planned Change" in Lovell, J.P. and Kronenberg, PS. (Eds.) *New Civil-Military Relations.* Transaction Books. New Brunswick, NJ, 153-68.
McNall, S.G.
    1973 "Toward a Middle-Class Army." Paper presented to the Research Committee on Armed Forces and Society. International Sociological Association. Amsterdam. March 29-31. Archive: Inter-University Seminar on Armed Forces and Society. University of Chicago. Chicago, IL.
Mead, G.H.
    1918 "The Psychology of Punishment and Justice." *American Journal of Sociology* 23, 577-602.

Meade, R.D. and Singh, L.
  1973 "Changes in Social Distance during Warfare: A Study of the India/Pakistan War of 1971." *Journal of Social Psychology* 90(2), 325-6.

Medalia, N.Z.
  1954 "Unit Size and Leadership Perception." *Sociometry* 17, 64-67.
  1955 "Authoritarianism, Leader Acceptance, and Group Cohesion." *Journal of Abnormal and Social Psychology* 51, 207-13.

Medalia, N.Z. and Miller, D.C.
  1955 "Human Relations Leadership and the Association of Morale and Efficiency in Work Groups: A Controlled Study with Small Military Units." *Social Forces* 33, 348-52.

Melman, S.
  1970a *Pentagon Capitalism: The Political Economy of War.* McGraw Hill. NY.
  1970b *The Defense Economy: Conversion of Industries and Occupations to Civilian Needs.* Praeger Publishers. NY.
  1971 (Comp.) *The War Economy of the United States: Readings on Military, Industry and Economy.* St. Martin's Press. NY.
  1974 *The Permanent War Economy.* Simon and Schuster. NY.

Melton, A.W.
  1957 "Military Psychology in the United States of America." *American Psychologist* 12, 740-46.

Menninger, W.C.
  1948 *Psychiatry in a Troubled World.* Macmillan, NY. (Note: extensive summary of WWII psychiatric studies.)

Mercer, J.
  1965 "Labeling the Mentally Retarded." *Social Problems* 13(1)(Summer), 21-34.

Merton, R.K.
  1935 "Science and Military Technique." *Scientific Monthly* (December), 542-45.

Merton, R.K. and Kitt, A.
  1950 "Contributions to the Theory of Reference Group Behavior" in Merton, R.K. and Lazarsfeld, P.F. (Eds.) *Continuities in Social Research: Studies in the Scope and Methods of 'The American Soldier.'* The Free Press. NY, 40-105.

Merton, R.K. and Nisbet, R.A.
  1966 *Contemporary Social Problems.* (2nd Edition). Harcourt, Brace and World. NY.

Meyers, S.M. and Biderman, A.D. (Eds.)
  1968 *Mass Behavior in Battle and Captivity: The Communist Soldier in the Korean War.* University of Chicago Press. Chicago, IL.

Michael, D.N.
  1957 "Some Factors Tending to Limit the Utility of the Social Scientist in Military Systems Analysis." *Operations Research* 5, 90-96.

Milgram, S.
  1965 "Some Conditions of Obedience and Disobedience to Authority." *Human Relations* 18, 57-76.

Miller, D.C. and Medalia, N.Z.
  1955 "Leadership and Morale in Small Organizations." *Sociological Review* 3 (New Series), 93-107.

Miller, D.C., et al.

  1962 "Morale and Human Relations as Factors in Organizational Effectiveness: An Experimental Study of Data from Fifty Comparable Squadrons" in Bowers, R.V. (Ed.) *Studies in Organizational Effectiveness: Contributions to Military Sociology from the 1949-1954 Contract Research Program of the Human Resources Research Institute, Air University.* Air Force Office of Scientific Research. Office of Aerospace Research. Washington, D.C., 86-114.

Miller, J.C. and Tollison, R.

  1971 "The Implicit Tax on Reluctant Military Recruits." *Social Science Quarterly* 51 (March), 924-31.

Millet, A.R. and Trupp, A.F.

  1981 Manning the American Armed Forces: Problems and Prospects. *Mershon Center Position Papers in Policy Sciences.* Number Five, May. The Mershon Center of The Ohio State University. Columbus, OH.

Mills, C.W.

  1943 "The Professional Ideology of The Social Pathologists." *American Journal of Sociology* 49(Sep), 165-80.

  1956 The Power Elite. Oxford University Press. NY.

Miner, J.B. and Anderson, J.K.

  1958 "The Postwar Occupational Adjustment of Emotionally Disturbed Soldiers." *Journal of Applied Psychology* 42, 317-22.

Mitchell, V.F. and Porter, L.W.

  1967 "Comparative Managerial Role Perceptions in Military and Business Hierarchies." *Journal of Applied Psychology* 51, 449-52.

Moellering, J.H.

  1973 "The Army Turns Inward." *Military Review* (July), 68-83.

Moll, A.E.

  1954 "Psychosomatic Disease due to Battle Stress" in Wittkower, E.D. and Cleghorn, R.A. (Eds.) Recent Developments in Psychiatric Medicine. Lippincott. Philadelphia, PA, 436-54.

Moore, R.A.

  1967 "The Army as a Vehicle for Social Change in Pakistan." *Journal of Developing Areas* 2(1), 57-74.

Morton, L.

  1969 "War, Science, and Social Change" in Silvert, K.H. (Ed.) The Social Reality of Scientific Myth. American Universities Field Staff Conference Series, 22-57.

Mosen, W.

  1967 "Eine Militarsoziologie: technische Entwicklung und Autoritatsprobleme in modernen Armeen" (Military Sociology: Technological Development and Authority Structure in Modern Armies). Luchterhand. Neuwied and Berlin (German language).

Moskos, C.C., Jr.

  1966 "Racial Integration in the Armed Forces." *American Journal of Sociology* 72, 132-48.

  1969 "The Negro and the Draft" in Little, R.W. (Ed.) *Selective Service and American Society.* Russell Sage Foundation. NY, 139-62.

  1970 *The American Enlisted Man.* Russell Sage Foundation. NY.

  1971a "The Social Equivalent of Military Service" in *The Teacher's College Record,* Sept., Vol. 73, 1; 7-12.

1971b "Minority Groups in Military Organization" in R.W. Little, (Ed.) *Handbook of Military Organizations.* Sage Publications. Beverly Hills, CA, 271-289.

1971c "Armed Forces and American Society: Convergence or Divergence?" in Moskos, C.C., Jr. (Ed.) *Public Opinion and the Military Establishment.* Sage. Beverly Hills, CA, 271-94.

1973a "The American Dilemma in Uniform: Race in The Armed Forces." *Annals of The American Academy of Political and Social Science* 40(6) March, 94-106.

1973b "The Emergent Military: Civil, Traditional or Plural?" *Pacific Sociological Review* 16(2), 255-280.

1974 "The Concept of the Military-Industrial Complex: Radical Critique or Liberal Bogey?" *Social Problems* 21(4, Spring), 1-15.

1977a "Why Men Fight: Combat Soldiers in Vietnam" in Rose, P.I. (Ed.) *The Study of Society*, Fourth Edition, Random House. NY, 357-68.

1977b "From Institution to Occupation: Trends in Military Organization." *Armed Forces and Society* 4(1), 41-50.

Moskowitz, H. and Roberts, J.

1968 The College Graduate and National Security: Utilization of Manpower by the U.S. Armed Forces. (Bibliography). Office of the Adjutant General (Army). USGPO. Washington, DC (June).

Moyal, J.E.

1949 "Distribution of Wars in Time." *Journal of The Royal Statistical Society* 112, 446-58.

Moyer, H.E.

1972 Justice and the Military. Public Law Education Institute. Washington, DC.

Mueller, J.E.

1971 "Trends in Popular Support for the Wars in Korea and Vietnam." *Political Science Review* 65(2)(June), 358-75.

Mueller, W.R.

1945 "The Negro in the Navy." *Social Forces* 24, 110-15.

Mullan, H.

1948 "The Regular-Service Myth." *American Journal of Sociology* 53, 276-81.

Mullins, C.J., et al.

1973a Variables Related to Pre-Service Cannabis Use in a Sample of Air Force Enlistees. USAF Human Resources Laboratory. Brooks AFB, Texas (AD-776-778-3).

1973b Correlational Analysis of Drug Abuse in The Air Force. USAF Human Resources Laboratory. Brooks AFB, Texas (AD-770-017-2).

1974 Variables Related to Hallucinogen Use. USAF Human Resources Laboratory. Brook AFB, Texas (AD-A011-615-2SL).

Murdock, G.P.

1951 "The Caste Division in the Military Services" Unpublished Paper. Archive: Inter-University Seminar on Armed Forces and Society. University of Chicago. Chicago, IL.

1954 "The Military Hierarchy and 'Caste' Divisions" in Williams, R.H. (Ed.) Human Factors in Military Operations. Operations Research Office. Johns Hopkins University. Chevy Chase, MD, 371-79.

Murray, P.T., Jr.

1972 Blacks and the Draft: An Analysis of Institutional Racism. Ph.D. Dissertation. Florida State University. Tallahassee, FL.

Mylander, M.
  1974 *The Generals: Making It, Military Style.* The Dial Press. NY.

Nail, R.L., et al.
  1972a Characteristics of Hospitalized Drug Cases in The Naval Service. Navy Medical Neuropsychiatric Research Unit. San Diego, CA (AD-749-407).
  1972b A Preliminary Study of Drug Abuse among Psychiatric Inpatients. Navy Medical Psychiatric Research Unit. San Diego, CA (AD-741-723).
  1974a Family Characteristics Associated with Heroin Dependence among Navy men in Vietnam. Navy Medical Neuropsychiatric Research Unit. San Diego, CA (AD-A0007-760-2SL).
  1974b Motives for Drug Use among Light and Heavy Users. Navy Medical Neuropsychiatric Research Unit. San Diego, CA (AD-A006-764-5SL).
  1974c Black-White Differences in Social Background and Military Drug Abuse Patterns. Navy Neuropsychiatric Research Unit. San Diego, CA (AD-A-995-7SL).

National Guard Bureau
  1968 A Study of Military Attitudes among Negro Males 16 to 25 Years of Age Nationally and in Camden, NJ. Washington, D.C. (February). Archives: Inter-University Seminar on Armed Forces and Society. University of Chicago. Chicago, IL.

Nauta, R.
  1971 "Armed Forces and Ideology" in van Gils, M.R. (Ed.) *The Perceived Role of the Military.* Rotterdam University Press. Rotterdam, 379-90.

Neff, J.U.
  1950 *War and Human Progress: An Essay on the Rise of Industrial Civilization.* Harvard University Press. Cambridge, MA.

Nelson, P.D. and Berry, N.
  1965 "Change in Sociometric Status during Military Basic Training Related to Performance Two Years Later." *Journal of Psychology* 61, 251-55.
  1968 "Cohesion in Marine Recruit Platoons." *Journal of Psychology* 68, 63-71.

Ney, V.
  1966 "Military Sociology—A Select Bibliography." *Military Affairs* 30, 234-37.

Newman, B.
  n.d.   "Marginality and The Recruitment of Other Ranks into The British Army since 1962." Unpublished paper. Inter-University Seminar on Armed Forces and Society. Archive: University of Chicago. Chicago. IL.

Nisbet, R.
  1973 "War and Western Values" in *The Social Philosophers.* Thomas Y. Crowell Co. NY, 11-90.

Nordlie, P.G.
  1973 *Black and White Perceptions of The Army's Equal Opportunity and Treatment Programs.* Human Sciences Research, Inc. McLean, VA.

Nordenstreng, K. and Hara, M.
  1969 "Homosexuals in the Military." *Fordham Law Review* 37(3), 465-76.

Norman, E.H.
  1943 *Soldier and Peasant in Japan: The Origins of Conscription.* Institute of Pacific Relations. NY.

Nottingham, E.K.
1947 "Towards an Analysis of the Effects of Two World Wars on the Role and Status of Middle Class Women in the English-Speaking World." *American Sociological Review* 12, 666-75.

O.A.S.D. (EO)
1971 The Negro in the Armed Forces: A Statistical Fact Book. Office of The Assistant Secretary of Defense for Equal Opportunity. Washington, D.C. (September). Archive: Inter-University Seminar on Armed Forces and Society. University of Chicago. Chicago, IL.

OASD/M and RA
1969 Project One Hundred Thousand: Characteristics and Performance of "New Standards" Men. Office of The Assistant Secretary of Defense. Manpower and Reserve Affairs. Washington, D.C.

O'Brien, C.P., et al.
1976 Alcohol and Drug Abuse in The Vietnam Veteran. Pennsylvania University. Philadelphia, PA (AD-A041-958-0SL), NTIS (DODXA).

Olson, H.C. and Rae, R.W.
1971 Determination of the Potential for Dissent in the U.S. Army. Vol. 1. The Nature of Dissent, 73. Research Analysis Corporation. McLean, VA. March.

OML/USMA
1975 Office of Military Leadership, United States Military Academy. West Point, NY. "A Study of Organizational Leadership." (A book of readings).

Orcutt, J.D.
1975 "Deviance as a Situated Phenomenon: Variations in the Social Interpretation of Marijuana and Alcohol Use." *Social Problems* 22(3), 346-55.

Orend, R. J., et al.
1977 Selection of Qualified Army Enlistees: Analysis of Characteristics of Soldiers Separated Under TRADOC Regulation 635-1. Human Resources Research Organization. Alexandria, VA (AD-A077-986-8).

O'Sullivan, J. and Meckler, A.M. (Eds.)
1974 *The Draft and Its Enemies: A Documentary History*. University of Illinois Press. Urbana, IL.

Palmer, F.H., et al.
1969 Collected Papers Prepared Under Work Unit AAA: Factors Affecting Efficiency and Morale in Anti-Aircraft Artillery Batteries. HuMRRO. Alexandria, VA.

Paret, P.
1971 "The History of War." *Daedalus* 100(2), 376-96.

Park, R.E.
1941 "The Social Functions of War." *American Journal of Sociology* 46, 551-70.

Parsons, T.
1951 "Deviant Behavior and Mechanisms of Control" in Parsons, T. *The Social System*. Free Press. NY, 249-345.

Patten, T.H., Jr.
1960 "Social Class and the 'Old Soldier'." *Social Problems* 8, 263-71.

Payne, G.D.

    1974 Measurement of the Psychological Characteristics of the Environment of a Military Institution: A Preliminary Study. Research Report 3-74. Melbourne, Australia. Psychological Research Unit. No. 1.

Pearlman, W.A.

    1976 "Some Implications of The Clemency Discharge." *Journal of Political and Military Sociology* (4), 309-316.

Peck, M.S.

    1974 "The Role of The Military in American Society vis-à-vis Drug Abuse: Scapegoat, National Laboratory and Potential Change Agent" in Lovell, J.P. and Kronenberg, P.S. (Eds.) *New Civil-Military Relations.* Transaction Books. New Brunswick, NJ, 169-89.

Petersen, P.B. and Lippitt, G.L.

    1968 "Comparison of Behavioral Style between Entering and Graduating Students in Officer Candidate School. *Journal of Applied Psychology* 52, 66-70.

Pettera, R.L., et al.

    1969 "Psychiatric Management of Combat Reactions with Emphasis on a Reaction Unique to Vietnam." *Military Medicine* 134, 673-79.

Plag, J.A. and Goffman, J.M.

    1973 Characteristics of Naval Recruits with Histories of Drug Abuse. Navy Medical Neuropsychiatric Research Unit. San Diego, CA (AD-764-331).

Polsky, N.

    1969 *Hustlers, Beats, and Others.* Anchor. Doubleday, NY.

Porter, W.C.

    1941 "The Military Psychiatrist at Work." *American Journal of Psychiatry* 98, 317-323.

    1942 "The Functions of a Neuropsychiatrist in an Army General Hospital." *Psychiatry* 5, 321-329.

Prattis, P.L.

    1943 "The Morale of the Negro in the Armed Services of the United States." *Journal of Negro Education* 12, 355-363.

Presthus, R.

    1964 "The Social Dysfunctions of Organizations" in *The Anarchists.* I.L. Horowitz (Ed.). Dell Publishing Company. NY, 551-562.

Preston, R.A.

    1971 "Military Academies in a Changing World: Possible Consequences of the Student Protest Movement" in van Gils, M.R. (Ed.), *The Perceived Role of the Military.* Rotterdam University Press. Rotterdam, 3-17.

Quinney, R.

    1974 *Critique of Legal Order.* Little, Brown and Company, Boston, MA.

    1975 *Criminology: Analysis and Critique of Crime in America.* Little, Brown and Company. Boston, MA.

    1977 *Class, State and Crime.* David McKay Co. NY.

Radine, L.B.

    1977 *The Taming of the Troops: Social Control in the United States Army.* Greenwood Press. CT.

Radzinowicz, L. and Wolfgang, M.E.

    1977 *Crime and Justice.* Second Revised Edition. Vol. 11. Basic Books. NY.

Rains, P.
    1975 "A Retrospective Essay on the Labeling Perspective." *Social Problems* 23(1), 1-11.

Ramchandran, S. and Dwivedi, S.D.
    1969 "Social Stratification of Psychiatric Cases in a Military Hospital." *Indian Psychological Review* 6(1), 32-36.

Ramsay, D.A.
    1975 Summary of A.R.I. Research on Drug and Alcohol Abuse. USARI for the Behavioral and Social Sciences. Arlington, VA (AD-A009-730-3SL).

Rappoport, D.
    1962 "A Comparative Theory of Military and Political Types" in Huntington, S. (Ed.) *Changing Patterns of Military Politics.* The Free Press. Glencoe, IL, 71-100.

Razzell, P.E.
    1963 "Social Origins of Officers in the Indian and British Home Army, 1758-1962." *British Journal of Sociology* 14, 248-260.

Reaser, J.M., et al.
    1975 The Prevalence of Drug Abuse in The Army: A Comparison of Urinalysis and Survey Rates. HuMMRO. Alexandria, VA (AD-A012-683-9SL).

Reckless, W.
    1942 "The Impact of War on Crime, Delinquency and Prostitution." *American Journal of Sociology* 47, 378-86.

et al.
    1956 "Self Concept as an Insulator Against Delinquency." *American Sociological Review* 21 (Dec), 744-46.
    1957 "The 'Good Boy' in a High Delinquency Area." *Journal of Criminal Law, Criminology and Police Science* 48 (May-Jun), 18-26.

Reed, M.S., et al.
    1977 "Wayward Cops: The Functions of Deviance in Groups Reconsidered." *Social Problems* 24(5), 565-75.

Rimland, B. and Neumann, I.
    1966 "A Two-Year Follow-up of Marines Assigned to a Special (Correctional) Training Branch during Recruit Training. Report No. 76-3. U.S. Naval Personnel Research Activity. San Diego, CA.

Rinaldi, M.
    1973 "The Olive-Drab Rebels: Military Organizing During the Vietnam Era." *Radical America* 8(3), 17-52.

Rivkin, R.S.
    1970 *G.I. Rights and Army Justice.* Evergreen Division, Grove Press. NY.

Robins, L.N.
    1974 "The Vietnam Drug User Returns." Special Action Office for Drug Abuse Prevention. Executive Office of the President. Special Action Office Monograph Series A, No. 2. USGPO. Washington, D.C.

Robins, L.N., et al.
    1974 "How Permanent was Vietnam Drug Addition?" *American Journal of Public Health* 64 (December), 38-43.
    1975 "Narcotic Use in Southeast Asia and Afterward: An Intensive Study of 898 Vietnam Returnees." *Archives of General Psychiatry* 33(8), 955-61.

Roff, M.

    1963   The Service-Related Experience of a Sample of Juvenile Delinquents. Institute of Child Welfare. University of Minnesota. Minneapolis, MN (AD-438-025).

Rogers, J.W. and Buffalo, M.D.

    1974   "Fighting Back: Nine Modes of Adaptation to a Deviant Label." *Social Problems* 22(1), 101-18.

Rojcewicz, S.J., Jr.

    1971   "War and Suicide." *Life Threatening Behavior* 1(1), 46-54.

Rootman, I.

    1972   "Voluntary Withdrawal from a Total Adult Socializing Organization: A Model." *Sociological Education* 45(3), 258-70.

Rose, A.M.

    1946   "The Social Structure of the Army." *American Journal of Sociology* 51, 361-64.

    1947   "Army Policies towards Negro Soldiers: A Report on a Success and a Failure." *Journal of Social Issues* 3(4), 26-31

    1951   "The Social Psychology of Desertion from Combat." *American Sociological Review* 16, 614-29.

    1955   "Factors in Mental Breakdown in Combat" in Rose, A.M. (Ed.) Mental Health and Mental Disorder: A Sociological Approach. W.W. Norton. NY, 291-313.

    1956   "Psychoneurotic Breakdown among Negro Soldiers in Combat." *Phylon* 17, 61-69.

Rosenthal. I.

    1973   Some Correlates of Anomy among Vietnam War Soldiers. Ph.D. Dissertation. New York University. NY.

Ross, J.

    1975   "The Conscript Experience in Vietnam." *Australian Outlook* 29(3), 315-22.

Rothbart, M. and Johnson, J.C.M.

    1974   "Social Class and the Vietnam War: Some Descrepant Motives for Supporting or Opposing U.S. Involvement in Southeast Asia." *Pacific Sociological Review* 17(1), 46-59.

Roucek, J.S.

    1962   "The Trend in American Military Sociology and its Educational Implications." *Duquesne Review* 8(1), 26-49.

Roucek, J.S. and Lottich, K.V.

    1964   "American Military Sociology: The American Military Mind." *Social Science Education* 3(1), 91-106.

Rubington, E. and Weinberg, M.S. (Eds.)

    1973   Deviance: The Interactionist Perspective. Second Edition. Macmillan Co. NY.

    1978   Third Edition.

    1981   Fourth Edition.

Russell, H.E., et al.

    1971   "A Study of Suicidal Behavior in the Military Setting." *Military Medicine*, 136(6), 549-552.

Ryan, W.

    1976   *Blaming the Victim*. Random House. NY.

Ryman, D.H. and Gunderson, E.K.E.

    1970   Factors Affecting the Stability of Job Attitudes in Long-Term Isolated Groups. Navy Medical Neuropsychiatric Research Unit. San Diego, DA (AD-766-452-7).

Sadler, P.J.

    1962   "Technical Change and Military Social Structure" in Geldard, F.A. (Ed.) *Defense Psychology*. Pergamon Press. NY.

Saenger, G.

    1943   "The Effect of War on Our Minority Groups." *American Sociological Review* 8, 15-22.

Sajer, G.

    1971   *The Forgotten Soldier*. Harper and Row. NY.

Sallas, R.G.

    1968   The Assimilation of Male, Volunteer Recruits to the Australian Regular Army: A Study of the Process of Militarization. Vol. 1: Introduction and Background. Australian Military Forces Research Report. Number 8-68.

Sanders, C.R.

    1973   "Doper's Wonderland: Functional Drug Use by Military Personnel in Vietnam." *Journal of Drug Issues* 3,65-78.

Sanford, N., et al.

    1971   *Sanctions for Evil: Sources of Social Destructiveness*. Beacon Press. Boston, MA.

Sarkesian, S.C.

    1972   "Political Soldiers: Perspectives on Professionalism in the U.S. Military. *Midwest Journal of Political Science* 16(May), 239-58.

    1973   *The Professional Army Officer in a Changing Society*. Nelson-Hall Co. Chicago, IL.

    1980   (Ed.) *Combat Effectiveness: Cohesion, Stress and the Volunteer Military*. Vol. 9. Sage Research Progress Series on War, Revolution and Peacekeeping. Sage. Beverly Hills, CA.

Saunders, D.N.

    1969   "Poverty in the Army." *Social Science Quarterly* 43(4), 396-405.

Saunders, J.R., et al.

    1974   Correlates of Barbiturate Use. USAF Human Resources Laboratory. Brooks AFB, Texas (AD-783-846-9).

S.A.U.S.

    1976   Statistical Abstract of the United States. U.S. Department of Commerce. Social and Economic Statistics Administration. Bureau of the Census. Washington, D.C. (published yearly).

Savage, P.L. and Gabriel, R.A.

    1976   "Cohesion and Disintegration in the American Army." *Armed Forces and Society* 2(3), 340-376.

Scarpitti, F.R. and McFarlane, P.T. (Eds.)

    1975   *Deviance: Action, Reaction, Interaction*. Addison-Wesley. Reading, MA.

Scheff, T.J.

    1977   *Being Mentally Ill: a Sociological Theory*. Aldine. Chicago, IL.

Schelling, T.C.

    1963   "War Without Pain, and Other Models." *World Politics* 15, 456-87.

Schexnider, A.J.
> 1973a The Development of Nationalism: Political Socialization among Blacks in the U.S. Armed Forces. Ph.D. Dissertation. Northwestern University. Evanston, IL.
>
> 1973b "The Development of Racial Solidarity in the Armed Forces." *Journal of Black Studies* (June), 415-435.

Schneider, D.M.
> 1946 "The Culture of the Army Clerk." *Psychiatry* 9, 123-29.
>
> 1947 "The Social Dynamics of Physical Disability in Army Basic Training." *Psychiatry* 10, 323-33.

Schossler, D.
> 1971 "The Functional Significance of the Military Socialization Process for the Internal Stability of the Military Organization" in van Gils (Ed.) The Perceived Role of the Military. Rotterdam University Press. Rotterdam, 139-47.

Schuckit, M.A.
> 1972 Alcoholism and Sociopathy: Diagnostic Confusion. Navy Medical Neuropsychiatric Unit. San Diego, CA (AD-773-780-2).

Schuckit, M.A. and Cahalan, D.
> 1974 Evaluation of Alcohol Treatment Programs. Navy Medical Neuropsychiatric Unit. San Diego, CA (AD-787-685-7ST).

Schuckit, M.A. and Gunderson, E.K.E.
> 1974a "Psychiatric Incidence Rates for Navy Women: Implications for an All Volunteer Force." *Military Medicine* 13(7), 534-36, (AD-786-596-7SL).
>
> 1974b "Suicide in the Naval Service." *American Journal of Psychiatry* 131(12), 1328-31.
>
> 1874c "The Association Between Alcoholism and Job Type in the U.S. Navy." *Quarterly Journal of Alcoholism* 35(2), 577-85.
>
> 1974d Alcoholism among Navy and Marine Corps Officers. Navy Medical Neuropsychiatric Research Unit. San Diego, CA (AD-A-004-283-8SL).
>
> 1975 Alcoholism in Navy and Marine Corps Women: A First Look." *Military Medicine* 140(4), 268-71.

Schuman, H.
> 1972 "Two Sources of Antiwar Sentiment in America." *American Journal of Sociology* 78 (November), 513-36.

Schur, E.M.
> 1969 *Our Criminal Society: The Social and Legal Sources of Crime in America.* Prentice-Hall. Englewood Cliffs, NJ.
>
> 1971 *Labeling Deviant Behavior: Its Sociological Implications.* Harper and Row. NY.
>
> 1979 *Interpreting Deviance: A Sociological Introduction.* Harper and Row. NY.

Schutz, A.
> 1977 *On Phenomenology and Social Relations.* (Ed. and Intro. by Wagner, H.R.). University of Chicago Press. Chicago, IL.

Seabright, C.L.
> 1973 A Look at Some Current Drug Abuse Prevention Programs. Human Resources Research Organization. Alexandria VA (AD-776-170-3).

Seaton, R.W.
> 1964 "Deterioration of Military Work Groups Under Deprivation Stress" in Janowitz, M. (Ed.) The New Military: Changing Patterns of Organization. Russell Sage Foundation. NY, 225-48.

Seeley, L.C., et al.
  1978 Early Development of the Military Aptitude Predictor (MAP). Army Research Institute for the Behavioral and Social Sciences. Alexandria, VA (AD-A052-953-7SL).

Segal, D.R.
  1967 "Selective Promotion in Officer Cohorts." *Sociological Quarterly* 8, 199-206.
  1974 "Entrepreneurial, Bureaucratic and Professional Models of the Military" in Tilley, K.W. (Ed.) *Leadership and Management Appraisal*. English Universities Press. London, 33-40.

Segal, D.R., et al.
  1974 "Convergence, Isomorphism, and Interdependence at the Civil-Military Interface." *Journal of Political and Military Sociology* 2, 157-72.

Selvin, H.C.
  1956 The Effects of Leadership Climate on the Non-Duty Behavior of Army Trainees. Ph.D. Dissertation. Department of Sociology. Columbia University, NY.
  1960 *The Effects of Leadership*. The Free Press. NY.

Semi, A.A.
  1972 "Considerations on the Advantages of Illness in a Military Milieu" in *Rivista Sperimentale di Freniatria e Medicina Legale delle Alienazioni Mentali* 96(5), 1481-1488. (Italian language)

Shainberg, D.
  1967 "Motivations of Adolescent Military Offenders." *Adolescence* 2, 243-55.

Sharp. L.M.
  1970 "The Role of Military Service in the Careers of College Graduates" in Sharp, L.M. (Ed.) Education and Employment: The Early Careers of College Graduates. Chapter 5. Johns Hopkins University. Baltimore, MD.

Shecerov, S.
  1919 *Economic Phenomena Before and After War: a Statistical Theory of Modern War*. Dutton, NY.

Sherman, E.F.
  1973 "Military Justice Without Military Control." *The Yale Law Review*, Vol. 82, 1398-1425.

Sherrill, R.
  1970 *Military Justice is to Justice as Military Music is to Music*. Harper and Row. NY.

Shils, E.A.
  1950 "Primary Groups in the American Army" in Merton, R.K. and Lazarsfeld, P.F. (Eds.) *Continuities in Social Research: Studies in The Scope and Method of 'The American Soldier.'* The Free Press, NY, 16-39.
  1977 "A Profile of the Military Deserter." *Armed Forces and Society* 3(3), 427-432.

Shils, E.A. and Janowitz, M.
  1948 "Cohesion and Disintegration of the Wehrmacht in World War II." *Public Opinion Quarterly* 12, 280-315.

Shoemaker. W.R. et al.
  1974 Prediction of Delinquency among Army Enlisted Men: A Multivariable Analysis. Human Resources Research Organization. Alexandria, VA (AD-778-787-2).

Short, J.F. (Ed.)
  1968 *Gang Delinquency and Delinquent Subcultures*. Harper and Row. NY.

Shoultz, J.C., Jr.
  1971 Annual Report. Fiscal Year 1971. Army Correctional Training Facility. Fort Riley, Kansas (AD-736-262).

Silsy, H.D., et al.
  1975 "Drug Abuse Prevention in the Military: A Punitive/Administrative Approach." *Military Medicine* 140(7), 486-87.

Simmel, G.
  1964 "The Stranger" in *The Sociology of Georg Simmel.* Ed. and Trans. by Kurt H. Wolf. The Free Press. NY, 402-8.
  1971 *On Individuality and Social Forms.* D.L. Levine (Ed.). University of Chicago Press. Chicago, IL.

Sinaiko, H.W.
  1977 First Term Enlisted Attrition. Vol. II, Summary. Smithsonian Institution. Washington, D.C. (AD-A043-586-7ST).

Sivard, R.L.
  1975 "Let Them Eat Bullets: A Statistical Portrait of World Militarism," *Bulletin of The Atomic Scientists* 31(4), 6-10.

Smith M.
  1946 "The Differential Impact of Selective Service Inductions on Occupations in the United States." *American Sociological Review* 11, 567-72.

Smith, R.B.
  1968 Why Soldiers Fight. Ph.D. Dissertation. Columbia University. Faculty of Political Science.
  1971a "Disaffection, Delegitimation, and Consequences: Aggregate Trends for World War II, Korea and Vietnam" in C.C. Moskos, Jr. (Ed.) *Public Opinion and the Military Establishment.* Sage Publications. Beverly Hills, CA, 221-51.
  1971b "The Vietnam War and Student Militancy." *Social Science Quarterly* 52(1), 133-56.

Smokovitis, D.
  1973 Sociological Problems of the Armed Forces in Greece. Ph.D. Dissertation. Panteios Supreme School of Political Science. Athens, Greece.

Snyder D.
  1976 "Theoretical and Methodological Problems in the Analysis of Government Coercion and Collective Violence." *Journal of Political and Military Sociology* 4(2), 277-94.

Sobel, R.
  1947 "The Old Sergeant Syndrome." *Psychiatry* 10, 315-21.

Solomon, G.F., et al.
  1971 "Three Psychiatric Casualties From Vietnam." *Archives of General Psychiatry* 25(December), 522-24.

Speier, H.
  1950 "The American Soldier and the Sociology of Military Organization" in Merton, R.K. and Lazarsfeld, P.F. (Eds.) *Continuities in Social Research: Studies in the Scope and Method of 'The American Soldier.'* The Free Press. NY, 106-132.
  1952 *Social Order and the Risks of War.* Stewart. NY.

Sperber, I.
  1970 "The Sociological Dimensions of Military Co-optation in the U.S." *Sociological Inquiry* 40(1), 61-72.

Spindler, G.D.

    1948 "American Character as Revealed by the Military." *Psychiatry* 11, 275-281.

    1951 "The Doolittle Board and Co-optation in the Army." *Social Forces* 29, 305-310.

Spitzer, S.

    1975 "Toward a Marxian Theory of Deviance." *Social Problems* 22(5), 638-51.

    1977 "A Reply to Horwitz." *Social Problems* 24(3), 364-66.

Stahl. M.J., et al.

    1980 "An Empirical Examination of the Moskos Institution-Occupation Model." *Armed Forces and Society* 6(2), Winter, 257-69.

Stanton, M.D.

    1973 "The Soldiers" in Spiegal, D. and Spiegal, P.K. (Eds.) *Outsiders USA*. Rinehart Press. San Francisco, CA, 470-502.

Star, S., et al.

    1958 "Negro Infantry Platoons in White Companies" in Macoby, E.E., et al. (Eds.) *Readings in Social Psychology*. Third Edition. Holt, NY, 596-601.

Starr, P. with J. Henry and R. Bonner

    1973 *The Discarded Army: Veterans after Vietnam*. Charterhouse. NY.

Stauss, H.

    1971 "Historical Trends of Military Sociology." Paper presented at the Pacific Sociological Association Meetings (April 8-10).

Stephenson, R.M.

    1973 "Involvement in Deviance: An Example and Some Implications." *Social Problems* 21(2), 173-89.

Stephenson, R.R.

    1965 Naval Adjustment and Delinquency: A Review of the Literature with Recommendations for Future Research. Interim Report for Aug 63-Oct 64. Naval Personnel Research Activity. San Diego, CA, May (AD-620-321). Report Number: SMR-64-23.

Stern, S.A. and Martin, A.S.

    1966 "Conscientious Objection." Unpublished Paper. Archive: Inter-University Seminar on Armed Forces and Society. University of Chicago, Chicago, IL (November).

Stevenson, R.J.

    1976 Unpublished field notes taken for a course on Military Sociology. State University of New York at Stony Brook. Part of the course involved interviewing veterans on campus, some of whom had seen combat in the Vietnam War.

    1987 "Social Controls and Martial Contingencies: Organizational and Institutional Patterns in the U.S. Military." *Journal of Political and Military Sociology*, Vol. 15(2-Fall), 263-278.

    1988 "The Containment and Expulsion of Wayward Soldiers in the U.S. Military." *The Social Science Journal*, Vol. 25(2), 195-210.

    1990 "The Officer-enlisted Distinction and Patterns of Organizational Reaction to Social Deviance in the U.S. Military." *Social Forces*, Vol. 68(4), 1191-1209.

    1991 "The Physical and Social Risks of Military Service During War." *Michigan Sociological Review*, No. 5, Fall, 66-89.

Stillman, R.J., II

    1968 Integration of the Negro in the U.S. Armed Forces. Praeger, NY.

    1969 "Negroes in the Armed Forces." *Phylon* 30, 139-59.

Stivers, R.

    1975 "Social Control in the Technological Society" in Davis, F.J. and Stivers, R. (Eds.) The Collective Definition of Deviance. The Free Press. NY, 376-91.

    1958 "Official" vs 'Administrative' Criteria for Classification of Combat Breakdown Cases." *Administrative Science Quarterly* 3, 185-94.

Stoddard, E.

    1974 "The Informal 'Code' of Police Deviancy: A Group Approach to 'Blue Coat' Crime" in Bryant, C.D. (Ed.) Deviant Behavior: Occupational and Organizational Bases, 218-38.

Stouffer, S.A., et al.

    1965 *The American Soldier: Combat and Its Aftermath. Vol. II.* Adjustment During Army Life. Vol. I. Science Editions. John Wiley and Sons. NY.

Strange, R.E. and Arthur, R.J.

    1967 "Hospital Ship Psychiatry in a War Zone." *American Journal of Psychiatry* 124, 281-86.

Strange, R.E. and Brown, D.E.

    1970 "Home From the War: A Study of Psychiatric Problems in Vietnam Returnees." *American Journal of Psychiatry* 127(4), 488-92.

Sullivan, J.A.

    1970 "Qualitative Requirements of the Armed Forces" in *Studies Prepared for the President's Commission on an All-Volunteer Armed Force.* Washington, D.C. (November). USGPO.

Summers, H.G., Jr.

    1982 On Strategy: A Critical Analysis of The Vietnam War. Presidio Press. NY.

Sutton, C.D.

    1973 The Military Mission Against Off-Base Discrimination: A Study in Administrative Behavior. Ph.D. Dissertation. Indiana University. Indianapolis, IN.

Sykes, G.M.

    1967 *Crime in Society.* (2nd Edition). Random House, NY.

    1974 A Society of Captives. Princeton University Press. Princeton, NJ.

Sykes, G.M. and Matza, D.

    1978 "On Neutralizing Delinquent Self Images" in Rubington and Weinberg (Eds.) *Deviance: The Interactionist Perspective,* 432-435.

Szasz, T.S.

    1973 "Scapegoating-Military Addicts-: The Helping Hand Strikes Again." *Transaction* 9(3), 4-6.

Tanay, E.

    1976 "The 'Dear John' Syndrome during the Vietnam War." *Diseases of the Nervous System* 37(3), 165-67.

Tauber, P.

    1971 *The Sunshine Soldiers: A True Journal of Basic Training.* Ballantine Books, NY.

Tausk, V.

    1969 "On the Psychology of the War Deserter." *Psychoanalytic Quarterly* 38(3), 354-81.

Taussig, M.K.

    1974 Those Who Served. Report of the Twentieth Century Fund Task Force on Policies Toward Veterans. Twentieth Century Fund. NY.

Tax, S. (Ed.)

    1967   *The Draft: A Handbook of Facts and Alternatives.* University of Chicago Press. Chicago, IL.

Taylor, J.N. and Black, D.

    1973   Non-Prior Service College Graduate Airmen Responses to Selected Questions from the 1971 Airman Sample Survey. USAF Human Resources Laboratory. Brooks AFB, Texas. October. (AD-771-687-0GA).

Taylor, W.J. and Bletz, D.F.

    1974   "A Case for Officer Graduate Education." *Journal of Political and Military Sociology* 2(2)(Fall), 251-267.

Teachers College Record

    1971   The Quest for Equity: National Service Options. Special Issue. 73(1).

Technical Report

    1970   Military Offenders Sent to the U.S. Army Correctional Facility: A Follow Up Study. Research and Evaluation Division. Fort Riley, Kansas.

Teitler, G.

    1977   *The Genesis of the Professional Officers' Corps.* Sage. Beverly Hills, CA.

Terry, W.

    1984   *Bloods: An Oral History of the Vietnam War by Black Veterans.* Random House. NY.

Thomas, J.P.

    1971   "The Mobility of Non-Commissioned Officers" in van Gils (Ed.) *The Perceived Role of the Military.* Rotterdam University Press. Rotterdam, 149-69.

Torrance, E.P.

    1954   The Behavior of Small Groups under the Conditions of Survival." *American Journal of Sociology* 19, 751-55.

    1957   "What Happens to the Sociometric Structure of the Small Group in Emergencies and Extreme Conditions." *Group Psychotherapy* 10, 212-20.

Toth, M.A.

    1971   "The New Draft Lottery: Some Research Implications." *American Sociologist* 6(June), 38-40.

Turner, R.H.

    1947   "The Naval Disbursing Officer as a Bureaucrat." *American Sociological Review* 12, 341-348.

Turk, A.T.

    1976   "Law as a Weapon in Social Conflict." *Social Problems* 23(3), 276-91.

UAR

    1976   Uniform Airman Record. U.S. Air Force Human Resources Laboratory. Technical Service Division. Brooks AFB, Texas.

    1980   Uniform Airman Record. U.S. Air Force Human Resources Laboratory. Technical Service Division. Brooks AFB, Texas.

United States Army (USABSRL)

    1969   Characteristics of Stockade Prisoners. U.S. Army Behavioral Science Research Laboratory. Washington, D.C.

U.S.A.R.I.

    1977   "Evaluation of Army Representation." U.S. Army Research Institute for the Behavioral and Social Sciences. Alexandria, VA Technical Report TR-77-A9.

U.S. Government Printing Office
  1947 The Effects of Strategic Bombing on German Morale. U.S. Strategic Bombing Survey. Morale Division. Washington, D.C.
  1956 Veterans Benefits in the United States. U.S. President's Commission on Veterans Pensions.
  1969 *The Manual for Courts-martial, United States.* Revised Edition. Washington, D.C.
  1970 Report of the Drug Abuse Control Commission Task Force. Reprinted in *The Congressional Record.* 3 December at S19314.
  1971 Report of a Special Subcommittee of the Armed Services Committee. U.S. House of Representatives. "Inquiry into Alleged Drug Abuse in the Armed Services." 92nd Congress, 1st Session. 23 April.
  1973 Committee on Armed Services. Report by the Special Subcommittee on Disciplinary Problems in the U.S. Navy. U.S. House of Representatives. Washington, D.C., January.
  1974 Source Material on the Vietnam Era Veteran. Prepared by the Staff for use of the Committee on Veteran's Affairs. United States Senate. 93rd Congress, 2nd Session. Senate Committee Print No. 26. 12 February.
  1978 Hearing on House Resolution 1254. Before the Military Personnel Subcommittee of the Committee on Armed Services. 95th Congress, 2nd Session. 26 September.

U.S. Senate
  1950 Employment of Homosexuals and Other Sex Perverts in Government. Committee on Expenditures in the Executive Departments. Subcommittee on Investigations.
  1962 Constitutional Rights of Military Personnel. Subcommittee on Constitutional Rights of the Senate Subcommittee on the Judiciary. 87th Congress, 2nd Session.
  1966 Military Justice. Subcommittee on Constitutional Rights of the Senate Subcommittee on the Judiciary. 89th Congress, 2nd Session.
  1971 Unemployment and Overall Readjustment of Returning Veterans. Hearings before the Subcommittee on Veterans Affairs of the Committee on Labor and Public Welfare. 91st Congress, 2nd Session (25 Nov and 3 Dec 1970).
  1972 A Study of the Problems Facing Vietnam Era Veterans on Their Readjustment to Civilian Life. Committee on Veterans Affairs. Ninety-second Congress, 2nd Session. Senate Committee Print Number 7. Washington, D.C. January 31. (Note: contains Louis Harris survey findings.)
  1978 Status of the All Volunteer Force. S 201-33. June 20. Session 95-2. (Library of Congress Number: LC 78-603145.) (Known as "The Beard Study.")

Uyeki, E.S.
  1960 "Draftee Behavior in the Cold-War Army." *Social Problems* 8, 151-58.

Vallance, T.R.
  1964 "The Future of Military Psychology: Paramilitary Psychology." *American Psychologist* 19, 119-29.

Van den Haag, E.
  1975 *Punishing Criminals.* Basic Books, NY.

Van Doorn, J.
  1965 "The Officer Corps: a Fusion of Profession and Organization." *Archives Européennes de Sociologie* 6, 262-82.

1968a (Ed.) *Armed Forces and Society: Sociological Essays.* Mouton. The Hague and Paris.

1968b "Armed Forces and Society: Patterns and Trends" in van Doorn, J. (Ed.) *Armed Forces and Society.* Mouton. The Hague and Paris, 39-51.

1970 Forces and Field: Towards a Theory of the Military System. Paper presented to the Research Committee on Armed Forces and Society. Seventh World Congress of Sociology. Varna, Bulgaria. September 14-19, 1970. Archive: University of Chicago. Inter-University Seminar on Armed Forces and Society. Chicago, IL.

1975a *The Soldier and Social Change.* Sage. Beverly Hills, CA, 102-03.

1975b "The Decline of the Mass Army in the West." *Armed Forces and Society* 1(2), 147-56.

Van Heek, F.

1964 "The Sociological Aspects of War." *International Journal of Comparative Sociology* 5, 25-39.

Van Gils, M.R. (Ed)

1971 *The Perceived Role of the Military.* Rotterdam University Press. Rotterdam.

Veterans Administration Reports.

1971 Data on Vietnam Era Veterans. Reports and Statistics Service. Office of the Controller. Veterans Administration. Washington, D.C.

Vidich, A.J. and Stein, M.R.

1960 "The Dissolved Identity in Military Life." Stein, M.R. and Vidich, A.J. (Eds.) *Identity and Anxiety: Survival of the Person in Mass Society.* The Free Press. NY, 493-506.

Villemez, W.J. and Kasarda, J.D.

1976 "Veteran Status and Socio-economic Attainment." *Armed Forces and Society* 2(3), 407-20.

Vitola, B.M., et al.

1974 Quality of the All-Volunteer Force. Air Force Human Resources Laboratory. Brooks AFB, Texas (AD-781-755-4).

1977 Impact of Various Enlistment Standards on the Procurement-Training System. Air Force Human Resources Laboratory. Brooks AFB, Texas (AD-A040-752-8SL).

von Heisseler, J.H.

1965-66 "Militar und Technik: Arbeitssoziologische Studien zum Einfluss der Technisierung auf die Sozialstruktur des modernen Militars" (Military and Technology: Studies in the Sociology of Work on the Influence of Technological Complexity on the Social Structure of the Modern Military) in Picht, G. (Ed.) *Studien zur politischen und gesellschaftlichen Situation de Bundeswehr.* Echart-Verlag. Witten and Berlin. (German language), 68-158.

Von Wiese, L. and Honbingsheim, P.

1958 *Kriegssoziologie* (Sociology of War). Fischer. Stuttgart, Germany. (German language)

Vujosevic, K., et al.

1973 "Alcoholism in the Army Environment." *Socijaina Psihijatriia* 1(2-3), 187-96. (Yugoslavian).

V.V.A.W.

1972 *The Winter Soldier Investigation: An Inquiry into American War Crimes.* Beacon Press. Boston, MA. (Vietnam Veterans Against the War).

1982 *The Veteran*. Vietnam Veterans Against the War. Special Demonstration Issue, April-May, 2. National Office: P.O. Box 25592, Chicago, IL 60625.

Vold, G.B.

1973 *Theoretical Criminology*. Oxford University Press, NY.

Wachtel, S.B. and Fay, L.C.

1946 "Allocation of Grades in the Army Air Forces." *American Journal of Sociology* 51, 395-403.

Walter, P.

1958 "Military Sociology" in Roucek, J.S. (Ed.) *Contemporary Sociology*. Philosophical Library. NY, 655-72.

Walzer, M.

1970 *Essay on Disobedience, War and Citizenship*. Harvard University Press. Cambridge, MA.

Wamsley, G.L.

1969a "Decision-Making in Local Boards: A Case Study" in Little, R.W. (Ed.) *Selective Service and American Society*. Russell Sage Foundation, NY, 83-108.

1969b *Selective Service and a Changing America*. Charles E. Merrill Co. Columbus, OH.

1972 "Contrasting Institutions of Air Force Socialization: Happenstance or Bellwether?" *American Journal of Sociology* 78 (September), 389-417.

Warner, P.

1976 *The Soldier: His Daily Life Through the Ages*. Taplinger Publishing Co. NY.

Warren, R.L.

1946 "The Naval Reserve Officer: A Study in Assimilation." *American Sociological Review* 11, 202-11.

Waters, L.K.

1965 A Study of the Interpersonal Values Reported by Naval Aviation Pre-Flight Students. Naval School of Aviation Medicine. Pensacola, FL. 9 July. (AD-622-231) Report Number: NSAM-938.

Weber, M.

1964a *The Theory of Social and Economic Organization*. T. Parsons (Ed.). The Free Press. NY.

1964b "The Formal and Substantive Rationality of Economic Action." Parsons, T. (Ed.) *The Theory of Social and Economic Organization*. Free Press. NY, 184-86.

1968 "The Origins of Discipline in War" in Roth, G. and Wittch, C. (Eds.), *Economy and Society*. Vol. 3, 1150-55.

Webb, E.J., et al.

1966 *Unobtrusive Measures: Non-Reactive Research in the Social Sciences*. Rand McNally, NY.

Weeks, J.L., et al.

1974 Prediction of Drug Abuse by the Life Values Questionnaire. USAF Human Resources Research Laboratory. Brooks AFB, Texas (AS-A-000-048-9SL).

Weeks, J.L. and Mullins, C.J.

1975 Prediction of Drug Abuse by the Social Factors Questionnaire. USAF Human Resources Laboratory. Brooks AFB, Texas (AD-A017-170-2SL).

Weigert, K. M.

1974 "Stratification, Ideology and Opportunity Beliefs among Black Soldiers." *The Public Opinion Quarterly* 38(1), 57-68. (Spring).

Weil, F.E.G.

1947 "The Negro in the Armed Forces." *Social Forces* 26, 95-98.

Weinberg, S.K.
> 1945 "Problems of Adjustment in Army Units." *American Journal of Sociology* 50, 271-78.
>
> 1946 "The Combat Neuroses." *American Journal of Sociology* 51, 465-78.

Weinstein, E.A.
> 1947 "The Function of Interpresonal Relations in Neurosis of Combat." *Psychiatry* 10, 307-14.

Wellford, C.
> 1975 "Labelling Theory and Criminology: An Assessment." *Social Problems* 22(3), 332-45.

Weppner, R.D.
> 1972 "Drug Abuse Patterns of Vietnamese War Veterans Hospitalized as Narcotic Addicts." *Drug Forum* 2(2), 43-54.

Wermuth, A.L.
> 1971 The Institutional Values of the Navy. Technical Report. Westinghouse Electric Corp. Center for Advanced Studies and Analysis. Falls Church, VA.

Weybrew, B.R. and Noddin, E.M.
> 1973 "Factors Related to Drug Abuse in the Submarine Service. Naval Submarine Medical Research Laboratory. Groton, CT, 24 September. (AD-777-703-0GA).

Wheeler, S.
> 1978 "Trends and Problems in the Sociological Study of Crime" in Wickman, P. and Whitten, P. (Eds.) *Readings in Criminology*. D.C. Heath and Company. Lexington, MA, 3-10.

White, W.B.
> 1968 The Military and the Melting Pot: The American Army and Minority Groups 1865-1924. Ph.D. Dissertation. University of Wisconsin. Madison, WI.

Wiatr, J.J.
> 1964 *Socjologia wojska* (Military Sociology). Wydawnictwo Ministerstwa Obrony Narodoweij. Warsaw (Polish language).
>
> 1969 "Social Prestige of the Military: A Comparative Approach" in van Doorn, J. (Ed.) *Military Profession and Military Regimes*. Mouton. The Hague and Paris, 73-80.

Wiersum, J.
> 1973 The Technical Specialist: A Sociological Portrait of a Volunteer. Paper presented at the Conference on the End of the Mass Army. Amsterdam, Sweden. Inter-University Seminar on Armed Forces and Society. Archive: University of Chicago, Chicago, IL,

Wikler, N.J.
> 1973 Vietnam and the Veterans' Consciousness: Pre-Political Thinking among American Soldiers. Ph.D. Dissertation. University of California. Berkeley, CA.

Wilbourn, J.M. and Guinn, N.
> 1973 Feasibility of Using Special Measures in the Classification and Assignment of Lower Mental Ability Airmen. Air Force Human Resources Laboratory (AD-777). Brooks A.F.B., Texas.

Wilbourn, J.M., et al.

    1976   Trends in Training Performance: 1972-1974. USAF Human Resources Laboratory. Brooks AFB, Texas (AD-A034-842-5SL).

Wilbourn, J.W.

    1973   The Air Force Reserve as an All-volunteer Force. USAF Human Resources Laboratory. Brooks AFB, Texas (AD-773-804-0).

Wilkins, W.L.

    1961   The Identification of Character and Behavior Disorders in the Military Life. Fifth Navy Science Symposium. U.S. Office of Naval Research. Washington, D.C. (ONR-9). (AD-663-680).

Williams, C.J.

    1970a Discharges from the Military: An examination of Labelling Theory. Ph.D. Dissertation. Rutgers University. New Brunswick, NJ.

    1970b "Being Discovered: A Study of Homosexuals in the Military." *Social Problems* 18(2), 217-27.

Williams, C.J. and Weinberg, M.S.

    1970   "The Military: Its Processing of Accused Homosexuals." *American Behavioral Scientist* 14(2), 203-17.

Williams, R.H. (Ed.)

    1954   Human Factors in Military Operations: Some Applications of the Social Sciences to Operations Research. Technical Memo: ORO-T-259. Operations Research Office. Chevy Chase, MD.

Williams, S.B. and Leavitt, H.J.

    1947   "Methods of Selecting Marine Corps Officers" in Kelley, G.A. (Ed.) New Methods in Applied Psychology. University of Maryland Press, College Park, MD, 96-99.

Willis, J.

    1972   Who Died in Vietnam?: An Analysis of the Social Background of Vietnam War Casualties. Ph.D. Dissertation. Purdue University. Lafayette, IN.

Wilson, C.

    1956   *The Outsider*, Dell, NY.

Wilson, J.Q.

    1977   "Police Discretion" in *Crime and Justice*, Vol. II. L. Radzinowicz and M.E. Wolfgang (Eds.). Basic Books, NY, 129-145.

    1978   "Police Work in Two Cities" in Rubington and Weinberg (Eds.), 169-77.

Wilson, T.R., et al.

    1974   Employment Assistance to Ex-Servicemen With Other Than Honorable Discharges: A Case Study of The Department of Labor's Exemplary Rehabilitation Certificate Program. Human Resources Research Organization (PB-234). Manpower Administration. Washington, D.C.

Windle, C. and Wojcik, J.

    1967   Bibliografia socjologii wojska I wojny w Polsce po II Woznie Swiatowej (Bibliography of Military Sociology and of War in post World War II Poland). Wojskowa Akademia Polityczna. Katdra Socjologii Wojskowej. Warsaw. (Polish language).

Winslow, R.W.

    1970   *Society in Transition: A Societal Approach to Deviancy*. Free Press. NY.

Wool, H.
> 1959 "The Armed Services as a Training Institution" in Ginzberg, E. (Ed.) The Nation's Children. Vol. 2. Columbia University Press. NY, 158-85.
>
> 1966 "Military and Civilian Occupational Structures." *Monthly Labor Review* 88, 29-33.

Wright, E.O. (Ed.)
> 1973 *The Politics of Punishment: A Critical Analysis of Prisons in America.* Harper and Row. NY.

Wright, Q.
> 1924 "Changes in the Conception of War." *American Journal of International Law* 18, 775-67.
>
> 1964 *A Study of War.* Abridged by L.L. Wright, University of Chicago Press, Chicago, IL. (Original published in 1942).
>
> 1968 "The Study of War" in *International Encyclopedia of the Social Sciences.* Vol. 16. Macmillan and Free Press. NY, 453-68.

Yarbrough, R.D.
> 1963 Interpersonal Maturity and the Effective Soldier: A Comparative Study of the Interpersonal Maturity Levels of Effective and Non-Effective Army Basic Trainees. Ph.D. Dissertation. Tulane University. New Orleans, LA.

Yarmolinsky, A. (Special Editor)
> 1973 "The Military and American Society." *Annals of The American Academy of Political and Social Science* 406 (March).

Zahn, G.D.
> 1969 *The Military Chaplaincy: A Study of Role Strain in the Royal Air Force.* University of Toronto Press. Toronto.

Zeitlin, M. and Lutternamm, J.R.
> 1973 "Death in Vietnam: Class, Poverty and the Risks of War." *Politics and Society* 3(3), 313-25.

Zeleny, L.D.
> 1947 "Selection of Compatible Flying Partners." *American Journal of Sociology* 52, 424-31.

Zentner, H.
> 1951 "Morale: Certain Theoretical Implications of Data in 'The American Soldier'." *American Sociological Review* 16, 297-307.

Zerubaval, E.
> 1981 *Hidden Rhythms: Schedules and Calendars in Social Life.* University of California Press. Berkeley, CA.

Znaniecki, F.
> 1943 "The Impact of War on Personality Organization." *Sociology and Social Research* 27, 171-80.

Zuckerman, S.
> 1962 "Judgment and Control in Modern Warfare." *Foreign Affairs* 40, 196-212.

Zurcher, L.A., Jr.
> 1965 "The Sailor Aboard Ship: A Study of Role Behavior in a Total Institution." *Social Forces* 43, 389-99.
>
> 1967 "The Naval Recruit Training Center: A Study of Role Assimilation in a Total Institution." *Sociological Inquiry* 37, 85-98.

ACKNOWLEDGEMENTS

I have benefited in many ways from the encouragement and support offered over the years by many people who gave freely of their time and passed on lessons that I have tried to incorporate in this work. Most important is Professor Kurt Lang, whose enthusiasm and encyclopedic knowledge of military sociology convinced me that this field showed much promise for a student of social deviance.

Much of my exposure to the writings of social scientists on military topics took place in the thirty eight months I worked with Dr. Lang on a bibliographic research project designed to identify portions of the social science literature relevant to the study of military institutions and the sociology of war. With considerable patience he offered a kindly ear, a willingness to share his knowledge, and a scholar's pencil—which was put to many of the emerging ideas that were to result in this study. I am grateful to him for his guidance and our many discussions on the nature of "things military."

I am also grateful to Professors Hanan C. Selvin, John H. Gagnon, Lyle Hallowell and David Burner. Each has helped me to grow while sharing their expertise and enthusiasm.

The following scholars also read rough drafts of parts of the manuscript in its various stages of completion. They were most helpful and encouraging: Lewis Coser, Erich Goode, Ted Goertzel, Edward Lanning, Ned Polsky, Michael Schwartz, and Gene Weinstein.

This work could have never been accomplished without the love and concern of two special ladies in my life: my wife Rosa and my daughter Geraldine. They have been both understanding and sources of inspiration during a very protracted project which, at times, appeared to be futile. Their unquestioning belief in my capabilities was tested with the frequent sacrifice of innumerable afternoons, weekends and holidays.

The data for this study came from archival materials in the public record and I wish to thank Irvin W. Kron, Director of the Government Documents Section, University Library at Stony Brook, for his many hours of assistance in working with the microfiche equipment and inter-library loan facilities. While it is true that a good library is invaluable for locating previous studies, a large part of such a resource inheres in the personages and good will of research librarians and their staffs.

The following people in the Department of Defense and military service branches were also helpful in acquiring crucial data without which this project would never have been completed. Captain R.J. Fleeson, USN, and Colonel Michael W. Gilmartin, USA Office of the Deputy Director, Personnel and Administration Services, Office of the Assistant Secretary of Defense, Manpower Reserve Affairs and Logistics: Military Personnel and Force Planning, Washington, D.C.; James D. Kemper, Jr., Clerk of Court, Department of the Army, United States Army Judiciary, Falls Church, Virginia; Captain J.J. Gregory, USN, Deputy Assistant Judge Advocate General (Military Justice), Department of the Navy, Office of the Judge Advocate General, Alexandria, Virginia; Colonel Richard T. Yery, USAF, Chief, Military Justice Division, Office of the Judge Advocate General, Department of the Air Force, Washington, D.C.; Lt. Colonel Quentin W. Korte, USAF, Chief: Information Retrieval Branch, Director of Manpower and Personnel Data Systems, Randolph AFB, Texas; Louise D. Ellis, Education Specialist, Education Directorate, the Adjutant General's Office, Department of the Army, Washington, D.C., and Sergeant Ryan and Lt. Colonel Baker, Department of the Army, Office of the Deputy Chief of Staff for Personnel (DAPE-MPE), the Pentagon, Alexandria, Virginia.

I also wish to thank Roger Pijacki, Director, Social Science Data Lab, for his patience in introducing a reluctant student to the computer facilities in the Social and Behavioral Science Building, and more importantly for increasing my ability use the TSP and DPS formats. Norman Goodman, Chair, Department of Sociology, was helpful in making sure that I always had an office in which to work, and sometimes a course to teach as well. The staff of the Department of Sociology was of invaluable assistance. Thank you Rosemarie Sciales, Joan Fraser, Anita Eller, Carole Roland, Veronica Abjornson, Wanda Olivera, and Judy Thompson.

I wish to especially thank the editors at Algora Publishing for promptly and meticulously offering useful comments to improve the quality and clarity of my work—and refreshingly overcoming my anxiety over new technology.